BIODIVERSITY CONSERVATION AND SUSTAINABLE LIVELIHOODS IN KONDHPUNGAR VILLAGE

BIODIVERSITY CONSERVATION AND SUSTAINABLE LIVELIHOODS

IN KONDHPUNGAR VILLAGE

Kailash C. Malhotra,
Singru Hontal

Joint Publication of
IGRMS and IRDWSI

GYAN

First Published - 2014

Cataloging in Publication Data--DK
Courtesy: D.K. Agencies (P) Ltd. <docinfo@dkagencies.com>

Malhotra, K. C.
Biodiversity conservation and sustainable livelihoods in Kondhpungar village / Kailash C. Malhotra, Singru Hontal.
p. cm.
Includes index.
ISBN 9788121212304

1. Biodiversity conservation--India--Kondhpungar. 2. Sustainable development--India--Kondhpungar. 3. Rural development--India--Kondhpungar. I. Hontal, Singru, joint author. II. Title.

DDC 333.95160954162 23

Published by:
Gyan Publishing House
23, Main Ansari Road, Daryaganj,
New Delhi - 110002
Phones : 23282060, 23261060
Fax : (011) 23285914
E-mail: books@gyanbooks.com
website: gyanbooks.com

and

Indira Gandhi Rashtriya Manav Sangrahalaya
Shamla Hills, Bhopal
Phones: 0755-2661290, 2661319
Fax: 91-755-2661458
Email: directorigrms@gmail.com

Laser Typesetting: Rajender Vashist, Delhi
Printed at: G. Print Process, Delhi

For the Study and Preparation of the Book a Team of Advisors and Researchers was Constituted

Advisors

Dr. William Stanley
Dr. Sasi Prabha Stanley
Prof. K. K. Basa

Research Team

Prof. Kailash C.Malhotra
(Research Director)

Members of IRDWSI

Benudhar Sutar
Balay Kumar Sen
Prabhat Kumar Khosla
Madhab Dalapti
Mohan Hontal
Ajay Kumar Rout
Hari Tading
Dayadan Suna
Hemalata Hontal
Marshal Pradhan
Uttam Nayak
Prasant Mandal
Gideon Soren

Members of Kondhpungar Village

Singru Hontal
Sambru Hontal
Sapura Hontal
Hari Hontal
Kesu Hontal
Laxmidhar Hontal
Tikimo Hontal
Rajmani Hontal
Ratai Hontal
Kausalya Hontal

Support Team

Raghu Velankar
Ganesh Yadav
V. Sudhakar
Binod Khosla
V. Ramashree
M. Patnaik
Ranbir Singh
Sidhartha Kumar Das

Contents

Preface 13
Acknowledgements 17
Acronym 19
List of Tables 21
List of Figures 27
List of Plates 29

1. Kondhpungar Village **33**

1.1. Introduction 1.2. Village Profile 1.3. Geographical Area 1.4. People • Kondhs • Kuvi Kondh 1.5. Education 1.6. Languages Spoken 1.7. Land Holding Pattern 1.7.1. Inter-household Variation in Total Land Holdings 1.8 Sources of Livelihood • Annual Income Among the Households• Income From Livestock • Income From Forest Products • Income From Wage Labour• Distribution of Total Annual Income • Relative Contribution of Different Sources of Livelihood to Total Annual Income • Income Generation Activities Undertaken by SHG in Kondhpungar 1.9 Annual Calendar of Main Festivals in the Village • Rakhyas Puja • Spiritually Empowered Seeds 1.10. Traditional Governance System 1.11 Present Governance System• People's Organisation • Self-Help Group • Rural Health and Environmental Programme (Rhep) 1.12 Growing Partnership: People of Kondhpungar and IRDWSI 1.13. Glimpses of Kondhpungar's Journey 1988-2008.

2. Objectives, Concepts and Methods **101**

2.1. Objectives of the Study 2.2. Various Concepts Used • Biodiversity •Sustainable Use of Biodiversity• Sustainable Livelihoods 2.3 Methodology Adopted • Formation of Study Team • Capacity Building • Team Formation • Data Collection • Nomenclature •

Validation of Nomenclature • Duration of Study • Photo Documentation.

3. Biodiversity Bearing Areas in Kondhpungar **109**

3.1. Introduction 3.2. Identification of Biodiversity Bearing Areas 3.3. Description of Biodiversity Bearing Areas 3.3.1. Landscape Biodiversity Bearing Areas 3.3.1.1. Homestead Gardens • Variation in Size of Badas • Biodiversity in Individual Homestead Gardens • Biodiversity in Homestead Gardens: Salient Features and Summary • Vegetables and Other Plants Grown in Badas • Wild Plants Found in Badas • Wild Animals Sighted in Badas 3.3.1.2. Domesticated Animals • Inter-household Variation • Inter-Household Variation in Total Numbers of Animals Maintained • Preferred Domesticated Animals 3.3.1.3. Herbal Garden • Medicinal Plants Planted in the Garden • Survival Status of Planted Species • Wild Plants Species Found in Herbal Garden • Wild Animals Sighted in Herbal Garden 3.3.1.4. Farm Land • Domesticated Plant Species •Wild Plants Species Occurring in Farm Lands •Wild Animals Sighted in Farm Lands 3.3.1.5. Wet Lands •Crop Grown in Wet Lands •Wild Plants Species Occurring in Wet Lands• Wild Animals Sighted in Wet Lands 3.3.1.6. Rainfed Lands •Crops and Trees Grown in Rainfed Lands • Wild Plant Species Found in Rainfed Lands • Wild Animal Species Sighted in Rainfed Lands 3.3.1.7. Shifting Cultivation • Crops Grown in Shifting Cultivation Fields • Trees Grown in Shifting Cultivation Fields • Wild Plants Occurring in Shifting Cultivation Fields • Wild Animals Sighted in Shifting Cultivation Fields 3,3.1.8. Social Forestry Plantation• Names of the Plant Species Planted • Wild Plants Occurring in Social Forestry Patch • Wild Animals Sighted in Social Forestry Patch 3.3.1.9. Cashew Nut Plantation • Wild Plants Occurring in Cashew Nut Plantation Patch • Wild Animals Sighted in Cashew Nut Plantation Area 3.3.1.10. Eucalyptus Plantation • Wild Plant Species Occurring in Eucalyptus Plantation Area • Wild Animals Sighted in Eucalyptus Plantation Area 3.3.1.11. Silver Oak Plantation • Wild Plant Species Occurring in Silver Oak Plantation Area • Wild Animals Sighted in Silver Oak Plantation

Patch 3.3.1.12. Protected Forest • Plants Planted in the Protected Forests • Wild Plant Species Occurring in Protected Forest • Wild Animal Sighted in Protected Forest 3.3.1.13. Sacred Grove • Wild Plant Species Occurring in the Sacred Grove • Wild Animals Sighted in Sacred Grove 3.3.1.14. Road Side Plantation • Wild Plants Species Occurring on Road Side • Wild Animal Sighted on Road Side 3.3.2. Waterscape Elements Bearing Biodiversity 3.3.2.1. Tank 1 • Plants Planted on the Embankment of the Tank • Wild Plants Occurring on the Embankment of the Tank • Aquatic Fauna Found in the Tank • Wild Animals Found in and Around the Tank 3.3.2.2. Tank 2 • Aquatic Animals Found in and Around the Tank • Plants Raised on the Tank Bund • Wild Plants Occurring on the Tank Bund• Wild Animals Seen Around the Tank 3.3.2.3. Tank 3• Aquatic Animals Found in and Around the Tank • Plants Raised on the Tank Bund • Wild Plants Occurring on the Tank • Wild Animals Seen Around the Tank 3.3.2.4. Check Dam • Aquatic Animals Found in and Around the Check Dam • Aquatic and Terrestrial Plant Species • Wild Plants Occurring on the Check Dam • Wild Animals Seen Around the Check Dam 3.3.2.5. Streams • Stream 1: Kotra am Jhola • Wild Plants Occurring Along the Stream Kotra amJhola • Wild Animals Sighted Around the Stream Kotra am Jhola • Stream 2: Kudi Kanda Jhola • Wild Plants Occurring Along the Stream Kudi Kanda Jhola • Wild Animals Sighted Around Kudi Kanda Jhola • Stream 3: Boko Sakadi • Aquatic Wild Plants Found Along the Boko Sakadi Stream • Wild Plants Occurring Along the Boko Sakadi Stream • Wild Animals Sighted Around Boko Sakadi Stream.

4. A Comparative Analysis of the Distribution of Biodiversity in Various Land and Waterscape Elements **209**

4.1. A Comparative Analysis of the Occurrence of Cultivated Plant Species in Different Land and Waterscape Elements • Variation in Number of Cultivated Plants Occurring in Different Land and Waterscape Elements • Inter-area Variation in Cultivated Tree Species in 20 Biodiversity Bearing

Areas Varietal Diversity in Select Cultivated Crops • Varietal Diversity in Paddy, Ragi and Suan 4.2. A Comparative Analysis of the Occurrence of Wild Plant Species in Different Land and Waterscape Elements • Variation in Number of Wild Plant Species Occurring in Different Land and Waterscape Elements • Inter-wild Plant Species Variation in 20 Land and Waterscape Areas • Wild Mushrooms Occurring in the Village 4.3. A Comparative Analysis of the Occurrence of Wild Animal Species in Different Land and Waterscape Elements • Variation in Number of Wild Animal Species Occurring in Different Land and Waterscape Elements • Inter-wild Animal Species Variation in 20 Land and Waterscape Areas 4.4. A Comparative Analysis of the Occurrence of Aquatic and Wild Animal Species in Different Waterscape Elements

5. Biodiversity and Sustainable Livelihoods **257**

5.1. Cultivated Crops, Vegetables and Trees and their Usages • Diversity of Usages • Pattern of Consumption 5.2. Wild Plants and their Usages 5.2.1. Diversity of Usages • Food Security • Health Care Security • Energy Security •Fodder Security • Timber • Financial Security • Spiritual Security • Social Bondage • Seasonal Availability of Various Wild Plant Products • Food, Health and Energy Security • Food Security Health Care Security • Energy Security • Edible Wild Mushrooms 5.3. Wild Animals and their Usages • Type of Usages of the Wild Animals 5.4. Use of Wild Aquatic Animals

6. History of Change in Landscape and Waterscape Elements **301**

6.1. Description of Changes in Each of the • Land and Waterscape Elements •Homestead Gardens (Badas) • Herbal Garden • Farm Land • Wet Lands • Rainfed Land • Paddy Varieties • Ragi Varities • Suan Varities • Shifting Cultivation • Social Forestry Plantation • Cashew Nut Plantation • Eucalyptus Plantation • Silver-oak Plantation • Protected Forest • Sacred Grove • Tank 1 • Tank 2 • Tank 3 • Check Dam Streams • Road Side Plantation 6.2. Domesticated Animals 6.3. Changes in the Abundance of Wild Animals 6.4. Changes in the Abundance of 12 Socially Preferred

Wild Plants 6.5. Plants Important as Source of Food For Wild Animals 6.6. Assisted Natural Regeneration of Wild Mango in Kondhpungar • Case Study 6.7. Spiritually Empowered Seeds 6.8. Grain Bank.

7. Aspirations and Future Vision **327**

7.1. Significant Observations 7.2. Future Vision 7.2.1. Institutional Arrangements 7.2.2. Management of Biodiversity Bearing Areas • Homestead Garden • Herbal Garden • Farm Land • Wet Land • Rainfed Land • Shifting Cultivation • Social Forestry Plantation • Cashew Nut Plantation • Eucalyptus Plantation • Silver Oak Plantation • Protected Forest• Sacred Grove • Tanks • Check Dam • Livestock 7.3. Knowledgeable Persons in the Village.

Appendix 1. Genealogy of the Hontal Clan 1 in Kondhpungar 343

2. Names of Cultivated Crops, Vegetables and Trees grown in Kondhpungar for the Year 2007 351

3. Names of 124 Wild Plants, their Parts used with Purpose 355

4. Names of 148 Wild Plants found in Kondhpungar 364

5. Wild Animals Sighted in Kondhpungar 367

Index 371

Preface

It is well-documented that during the last three decades in many villages across the country, domesticated and wild biodiversity both have alarmingly depleted. This depletion has severely and negatively impacted the villagers; in particular the poor, tribal, *dalit*, other backward communities, etc. They face innumerable problems in accessing even the basic subsistence needs of fuel wood, fodder, small timber, food and medicines, etc. The worst affected are women who are the main gatherers of non-timber forest products.

Sensing these grim scenario,the Government of India enacted The Biological Diversity Act, 2002 and Biological Diversity Rules, 2004.

The Biological Diversity Act aims to promote conservation, sustainable use and equitable sharing of the benefits of India's biodiversity resources. For this purpose, the act promotes at all levels, good documentation of biological diversity; their uses and its associated knowledge.

One of the author's of this book, Kailash C. Malhotra, has been associated for several years in developing methodologies for documenting biodiversity. This effort was carried out under the leadership of Prof. Madhav Gadgil. Their efforts resulted in a comprehensive compendium of methodologies for preparing People's Biodiversity Registers (PBRs).

Many of us in the country decided that while the implementation of the act might take some time, we should in a humble way initiate the process of making PBRs at some select villages in the country.

For the past several years author has been working in partnership with Integrated Rural Development for the Weaker Sections of India (IRDWSI), an NGO-based in Semiliguda block of Koraput district of Odisha. It was therefore, natural that he initiated a dialogue with the IRDWSI to launch the process of preparing PBRs in Southern Odisha. Consequently, two workshops were organised in September 2002 and May 2003. Besides the staff of IRDWSI, a number of Community Based Organisations (CBOs), NGOs and academicians from Odisha and Andhra Pradesh participated in these workshops. Colleagues from International Centre for Community Forestry (ICCF) at Indian Institute of Forest Management (IIFM), Bhopal also participated in the workshops.

Mr. Singru Hontal of Kondhpungar village, the co-author of this book, participated in the workshops. He along with other people of Kondhpungar came forward and expressed a desire to prepare the PBR of their village. This was because the village in the recent past had experienced a depletion of their forest resources. Also the village had already initiated efforts in collaboration with IRDWSI and IIFM for restituting the depleted natural and domesticated biodiversity. The people realised that the only source of their livelihood was the biodiversity of their village as it has been in the past and present and will be in future. It was therefore important that the village documents the biodiversity and develops short-term and long-term management plans.

The process of documentation of the biodiversity and related aspects started from 19th September, 2006. The people of Kondhpungar under the leadership of Singru Hontal and the staff of IRDWSI under the leadership of Dr. William Stanley and Sasi Prabha finalised the logistics and strategy for initiating the study in the village. Mr. Malhotra provided the overall guidance and accepted the responsibility to coordinate their efforts.

The materials contained in this book are the result of dedicated and sincere efforts of a number of men, women and youth from Kondhpungar and IRDWSI. Several organisations, in particular, IIFM provided intellectual inputs.

The book in seven chapters gives details on the objectives of the study, various concepts and methods used, introduction to the village; Kondhpungar, the areas bearing biodiversity in the village, the nature and extent of flora and fauna found in the village; their status, historical changes in biodiversity and its contribution to sustainable livelihoods and aspirations and future vision of the people of Kondhpungar. The book among other aspects covers specially the following features of the biodiversity in the village:

(i) an account of the biodiversity bearing landscape and waterscape elements in the village;

(ii) documentation of nature and extent of domesticated and wild fauna and flora occurring in various biodiversity bearing areas;

(iii) an analysis of the various usages of the documented biodiversity;

(iv) an analysis of the contribution made by the biodiversity for livelihoods of the people;

(v) contributions made by the biodiversity towards the sustenance of the needs of the people like fuel wood, grassing, medicine, food etc;

(vi) a description of the present status of the various landscape and waterscape elements in the village;

(vii) an analysis of the physical changes that have occurred in the various landscapes and waterscape elements in the village during the last two decades;

(viii) detailed description of changes that have occurred in domestic and wild biodiversity of the village in different land and waterscape elements;

(ix) an account of the significant changes that have occurred in the governance system of the village, and

(x) an account of the linkages that the villagers of Kondhpungar have developed with civil society organisations and different government line departments.

The future vision of the people of Kondhpungar includes detail plans on the management of the biodiversity and the new institutional arrangements that are required to achieve the future vision.

The glimpses of Kondhpungar's journey described in Chapter 1, demonstrates that if people wish, significant results can be achieved even in a remote and backward village. It is remarkable that during the last two decades Kondhpungar has improved enormously in the quality of life and economic status of the people. The aspirations and future vision plans envisaged by the villagers will undoubtedly further enhance the health of the biodiversity and strengthen livelihoods of the people.

The book, it is hoped will encourage CBOs, NGOs and academics to initiate similar efforts in other parts of the country for the preparation of several more PBRs. It is hoped that this book will be of use to individuals and organisations working at micro-level, particularly in the field of management of natural resources and sustainable livelihoods.

Kailash C. Malhotra,
Singru Hontal
Semiliguda, Koraput District,
August 2012

Acknowledgements

We would like to express our deep gratitude and the appreciations to a number of individuals and organisations without whose supports, it would have been impossible to write this book.

We are highly indebted to Dr William Stanley, Dr. Sasi Prabha Stanley, Prof K.K. Misra, Director IGRMS and the former Director Prof K.K. Basa for their invaluable advice, guidance and encouragement provided to the entire research team, individually and collectively during the course of preparation of this document. They also took time off to read initial drafts of the book and provided significant inputs.

We are extremely grateful to the research team from IRDWSI: Benudhar Sutar, Balay Kumar Sen, Prabhat Kumar Khosla, Madhab Dalapti, Mohan Hontal, Ajay Kumar Rout, Hari Tading, Dayadan Suna, Hemalata Hontal, Marshal Pradhan, Uttam Nayak, Prasant Mandal, Gideon Soren and researchers from Kondhpungar village-Singru Hontal, Sambru Hontal, Sapura Hontal, Hari Hontal, Kesu Hontal, Laxmidhar Hontal, Tikimo Hontal, Rajmani Hontal, Ratai Hontal, Kausalya Hontal for their dedicated work, commitment and intellectual inputs.

A work of this nature needed various kinds of inputs. These were provided by the able support team comprising Raghunandan Velankar, Ganesh Yadav, V. Sudhakar, Binod Khosla, V. Ramashree, M. Patnaik, Ranbir Singh and Sidhartha Kumar Das. We sincerely acknowledge their valuable contributions. Thanks to Raghunandan Velankar especially for his inputs in the identification of plants and for editing.

We are highly thankful to United Nations Development Programme (UNDP), Ministry of Rural Development of Government of India (MoRD) for partial financial support the present study.

We profusely thank Prof B.K. Tiwari and Prof S.K. Barik Coordinators, Regional Centre for National Afforestation and Eco-Development Board, NEHU, Shillong and Prof. P. Bhattacharya, Coordinator, International Centre for Community Forestry at Indian Institute of Forest Management, Bhopal for their encouragement and for providing word processing facilities.

We thank Mr. Sudhir Shrivastava of IGRMS for the editorial assistance, and for processing this document for publication.

Lastly, we record our deep appreciations to Prof. K. K. Misra, Prof K.K. Basa, Mr S.B. Ota and Dr William Stanley, Director, IRDWSI for publishing this book.

August 2012 **Kailash C. Malhotra,**
Singru Hontal
Semiliguda, Koraput District

Acronym

BMC	Biodiversity Management Committees
CBO	Community Based Organisation
DFID	Department for International Development
FFW	Food for Work Programme
FPMC	Forest Protection and Management Committee
GBH	Girth at Breast Height
ICCF	International Center for Community Forestry
IG	Income Generation
IIFM	Indian Institute of Forest Management
IRDWSI	Integrated Rural Development of Weaker Sections in India
MCC	Madras Christian College
NGO	Non-Governmental Organisation
NREGA	National Rural Employment Guarantee Scheme
NTFP	Non-Timber Forest Product
OAAA	Odisha Adivasi Adhikar Abhijan
PBR	People's Biodiversity Register
PRI	Panchayati Raj Institutions
RHEP	Rural Health and Environmental Programme
SHG	Self-Help Group
SSL	Secured Sustainable Livelihood
UNDP	United Nations Development Programme
UNWFP	United Nations World Food Programme
WWF	World Wild Fund

List of Tables

1.1. Lineages and Associated Descendents 37
1.2. Distribution of Household Size 39
1.3. Land Holding (in Acres) Pattern in the Village
1.4. Distribution of size of Badas in 15 households 43
1.5. Distribution of Shifting Cultivation Land (in acres) 46
1.6. Inter-household Variations in Total Land Holdings 47
1.7. Main Sources of Livelihoods 49
1.8. Distribution of Income (in thousands) from Agriculture Among 15 Households 50
1.9. Distribution of Income (in thousands) from Livestock Among 15 Households 52
1.10. Distribution of Income (in thousands) from Forest Products Among 15 Households 55
1.11. Distribution of Income (in thousands) from Wage Labour Among 15 Households 56
1.12. Distribution of Total Annual Income (in thousands) from all Sources Among 15 Households 57
1.13. Relative Contributions of Different Sources of Livelihood to Total Annual Income 58
1.14. Annual Calendar of Main Festivals Related to Domestic and Wild Biodiversity in the Village 63
1.15. Details of People's Organisation (Loko Sangathan) 65
1.16. Details of Sonidei Mahila Mandal (SHG) 67
1.17. Rural Health and Environmental Programme (RHEP) 68
1.18. IRDWSI Facilitated the following Activities in Partnership with the People of Kondhpungar 70
1.19. Glimpses of Kondhpungar's Journey 1988-2008 76
3.1. Landscape and Waterscape Biodiversity Bearing Areas Delineated in the Village 110
3.2. Size Distribution of Badas in 15 Households 112
3.3. Inventory of Domesticated Tree Species Occurring in Homesteads 133

3.4. Distribution of Number of Tree Species in Badas 137
3.5. Names of the Five Most Preferred Plants Species in Badas 137
3.6. Names in Oriya and Kuvi of Vegetables and Other Plants grown in Badas 139
3.7. Wild Plants Found in Badas 141
3.8. Inventory of Wild Animals in Oriya Occuring in Homesteads 142
3.9. Distribution of Number of Wild Animals in Badas 145
3.10. Number of Animals Sighted in Badas 146
3.11 Number of Wild Animal Species Sighted in Individual Badas 146
3.12. Inter-household Variation in Type and Numbers of Animals maintained 148
3.13. Distribution of Domestic Animals in the Village 149
3.14. Plants Planted in the Herbal Garden 153
3.15. Wild Plants Species Found in Herbal Garden 154
3.16. Wild Animals Sighted in Herbal Garden (Names in Oriya) 155
3.17. Inventory of Domesticated Plant Species Found in Farm Lands 157
3.18. Wild Plant Species Occurring in Farm Lands 158
3.19. Wild Animals Sighted in Farm Lands 159
3.20. Wild Plants Species Occurring in Wet Lands 162
3.21. Wild Animals Sighted in Wet Lands 163
3.22. Crops and Trees Grown in Rainfed Lands (Names in Kuvi) 164
3.23. Wild Plant Species Found in Rainfed Lands 164
3.24. Wild Animals Species Sighted in Rainfed Lands. 165
3.25. Crops Grown in Shifting Cultivation Fields 166
3.26. Trees Grown in Shifting Cultivation Fields 167
3.27. Wild Plants Occurring in Shifting Cultivation Fields 168
3.28. Wild Animals Sighted in Shifting Cultivation Fields 169
3.29. Name of the Plant Species Planted 171
3.30. Wild Plants Occurring in Social Forestry Patch 172
3.31. Wild Animals Sighted in Social Forestry Patch 173
3.32. Wild Plants Occurring in Cashew Nut Plantation 175
3.33. Wild Animals Sighted in Cashew Nut Plantation Area 176
3.34. Wild Plant Species Occurring in Eucalyptus Plantation Area 178
3.35. Wild Animals Sighted in Eucalyptus Plantation Area 179

3.36. Wild Plant Species Occurring in Silver Oak Plantation Area 180
3.37. Wild Animals Sighted in Silver Oak Plantation Patch 180
3.38. Plants Planted in the Protected Forests 181
3.39. Wild Plant Species Occurring in Protected Forest 182
3.40. Wild Animals Sighted in Protected Forest 186
3.41. Wild Plant Species Occurring in the Sacred Grove 187
3.42. Number of a Select Eight Plant Species Found in the Sacred Grove 187
3.43. Wild Animals Sighted in Sacred Grove 188
3.44. Wild Plant Species Occurring on Road Side 189
3.45. Wild Animals Sighted on Road Side 190
3.48. Fishes Found in the Tank 193
3.49. Wild Animals Found in and Around the Tank 194
3.50. Aquatic Animals Found in and Around the Tank 195
3.51. Plants Raised on the Tank Bund 195
3.52. Wild Plants Occurring on the Tank Bund 195
3.53. Wild Animals Seen Around the Tank 196
3.54. Wild Aquatic Animals Found in and Around the Tank 198
3.55. Plants Raised on the Bund of the Tank 198
3.56. Wild Plants Occurring on the Tank 199
3.57. Wild Animals Seen Around the Tank 199
3.58. Aquatic Animals Found in and Around the Check Dam 200
3.59. Aquatic and Terrestrial Plant Species 201
3.60. Wild Plants Occurring on the Check Dam 202
3.61. Wild Animals Seen Around the Check Dam 202
3.62. Wild Plants Occurring along the Stream Kotra am Jhola 203
3.63. Wild Animals Sighted Around Stream Kotra am Jhola 204
3.64. Wild Animals Sighted Kudi Kanda Jhola 205
3.65. Aquatic Wild Plants Found along the Boko Sakadi Stream 206
3.66. Wild Plants Occurring along the Boko Sakadi Stream 206
3.67. Wild Animals Sighted along Boko Sakadi Stream 207
4.1. Cultivated Plant Species Occurring in Different Landscape and Waterscape Elements 212
4.2. Occurrence of Number of Cultivated Plant Species in Different Land and Waterscape Elements Arranged in Descending Order 219

4.3. Distribution of Number of Plant Species in 20 Areas 220
4.4. Inter-area Variation in Cultivated Plant Species in 20 Biodiversity Bearing Areas 220
4.5. Varietal Diversity in Select Cultivated Crops 221
4.6. Varietal Diversity in Paddy, Ragi and Suan 224
4.7. Wild plant species occurring in different landscape and waterscape elements 226
4.8. Occurrence of Number of Wild Plant Species in Different Land and Waterscape Elements Arranged in Descending Order 241
4.9. Distribution of Number of Wild Plant Species in 20 Areas 242
4.10. Inter-wild Plant Species Variation in 20 Land and Waterscape Areas 243
4.11. Wild Mushrooms Found in the Village 244
4.12. Wild Animal Species Occurring in Different Landscape and Waterscape Elements 246
4.13. Occurrence of Number of Wild Animals in Different Landscape and Waterscape elements 246
4.14. Distribution of number of wild animal species in 20 areas 251
4.15. Inter-wild Animal Species Variation in 20 Land and Waterscape Elements 252
4.16. Occurrence of Aquatic and Wild Animal Species in Different Waterscape Elements 254
5.1. Cultivated Crops, Vegetables and Trees and their Usages 259
5.2. Number of Plant Species out of 95 used for a Select Seven Purposes 266
5.3. Pattern of Use of the 95 Cultivated Plants 266
5.4. Names of the 124 Wild Plants, their Parts used with the Purpose and their Seasonal Availability 268
5.5. The 15 Wild Plant Species that are not used Currently 276
5.6. Diversity of Usages of the Wild Plants 277
5.7. Plants Consumed as Food 278
5.8. Plant Parts Consumed as Food 279
5.9. Plant Parts used as Medicine 280
5.10. Plant Parts Consumed as Medicine 282
5.11. Names of 14 Plants that Provide Fuelwood 283
5.12. Names of 14 Fodder Yielding Plants 284
5.13. Names of the Seven Trees used as Timber 284

5.14. Names of the Twelve Trees and their Parts used for Commercial Purposes 285
5.15. Number of Plant Products Available during Different Months 288
5.16. Frequency of Availability of Number of Plant Products in Number of Months 289
5.17. Number of Plant Products used as Food and Medicines and their Seasonal Availability 290
5.18. Names of the Wild Animals and their Usages 292
5.19. Frequency Distribution of Different Taxa of Wild Animals 298
5.20. Types of Usages 299
6.1. Traditional Paddy Varieties Grown in Wet Lands 305
6.2. Traditional Paddy Varieties Grown in Rainfed Lands 306
6.3. Traditional Ragi Varieties Grown in Rainfed Lands 307
6.4. Traditional Suan Varieties grown in Rainfed Lands 308
6.5. Changes in the Abundance of Wild Animals 314
6.6. Changes in the Abundance of 12 Socially Prefered Wild Plants 318
6.7. Plants Important as Source of Food for Wild Animals 323
7.1. Knowledgeable Persons in the Village 341

List of Figures

1.1 Shows the Geographical Location of Kondhpungar Village, Situated Koraput District of Odisha 35
1.2. Location of Fifteen Households in Kondhpungar 37
1.3. Distribution of Household Size 39
1.4 Distribution of Size of Badas in 15 Households 44
1.5. Distribution of Shifting Cultivation Land 46
1.6. Inter-household Variations in Total Land Holdings 47
1.7. Distribution of Income (in thousands) from Agriculture Among 15 Households 50
1.8. Distribution of Income (in thousands) from Livestock Among 15 Households 52
1.9. Distribution of Income (in thousands) from Forest Products Among 15 Households 55
1.10. Distribution of Income (in thousands) from Wage Labour Among 15 Households 56
1.11. Distribution of Total Annual Income (in thousands) from all Sources Among 15 Households 57
1.12. Relative Contributions of Different Sources of Livelihood to Total Annual Income 58
2.1. Essential Features of Sustainable Livelihood Framework as Developed by Dfid 104
3.1. Landscape and Waterscape Biodiversity Bearing Areas Delineated in the Village 110
3.2. Size Distributions of Badas in 15 Households 113
3.3. Distribution of Number of Tree Spices in Badas 137
3.4. Names of the Five Most Preferred Plants Species in Badas 138
3.5. Distribution of Number of Wild Animals in Badas 145
3.6. Numbers of Animals Sighted in Badas 146
3.7. Number of Wild Animal Species Sighted in Individual Badas 147

4.1. Occurrence of Number of Cultivated Plant Species in Different Land and Waterscape Elements arranged in Discending order. The numbers on the X-axis Correspond with the Numbers given in Column 2 of Table 4.2 219
4.2. Per cent Distribution of Plant Species in 20 Areas 220
4.3. Inter-area Variations in Cultivated Plant Species in 20 Biodiversity Bearing Areas 221
4.4. Occurrence of Number of Wild Plant Species in Different Land and Waterscape Elements Arranged in Descending Order 242
4.5. Distribution of Percentage of Wild Plant Species in 20 Areas 242
4.6. Inter-wild Plant Species Variation in 20 Land and Waterscape Elements 244
4.7. Distribution of number of wild animal species in 20 areas 252
4.8. Occurrence of Aquatic and Wild Animal Species in Different Waterscape Elements 255
5.1. Number of Plant Species out of 95 used for a Select Seven Purposes 266
5.2. Pattern of Use of the 95 Cultivated Plants 267
5.3. Diversity of usages of the wild plant products 278
5.4. Plant Parts Consumed as Food 280
5.5. Plant Parts Consumed as Medicine 283
5.6. Number of Plant Products Available during Different Months 289
5.7. Seasonal Availability of Plant Products used as Food 290
5.8. Seasonal Availability of Plant Products used as Medicine 291
5.9. Seasonal Availability of Plant Products used as Fuelwood 291
5.10. Frequency Distribution of Different Taxa of Wild Animals 298
5.11. Frequency Distribution of Type of Usages 299
6.1. Changes in the Abundance of Wild Animals 317
7.1. Future visions: A view of the Kondhpungar village, the people of the village would like to see after ten years (Planned), Biodiversity areas 335

List of Plates

1.1. A View of Kondhpungar Village. 34
1.2. Habitation Area of the Village. 36
1.3. Tubewell in the Village. 38
1.4. A Typical Household in the Village. 38
1.5. Kondh Women. 40
1.6. Cultivation of Cabbage in Farm Lands. 42
1.7. Bean cultivation recently introduced in Badas. 43
1.8. Turmeric Cultivation in Farm Lands. 44
1.9. Paddy Cultivation in Wet Land. 45
1.10. A Flock of Goats in the Village. 51
1.11. Domesticated Country Fowl. 51
1.12. Regenerating Pasiamba Protected Forest. 53
1.13. SHG Members being Trained in Broom Making. 53
1.14. SHG Members being Trained in Tamarind Processing. 54
1.15. SHG Members making Siadi Leaf Plates. 54
1.16. Village Women Stitching Siadi Leaf Plates. 54
1.17. Bali Parab—Worship of Seeds, Mixing of Sed and Distribution of Mix Seeds Among Villagers. 62
1.18. Chaitra Parab being Celebrated in Neighbouring Village Kudi. 62
1.19. A toilet being constructed in the village under RHEP 68
1.20. IRDWSI and People of Kondhpungar are Discussing Sustainable Agricultural Practices. 69
1.21. Dialogue being Initiated for Forming People's Organisation, IRDWSI Personnel taking Part in the Deliberations. 69
1.22 Glimpses of Kondhpungar's journey. 96
2.1. Land and Waterscape Map of Kondhpungar Being Drawn. 105

2.2. Mapping of Biodiversity Bearing Areas in Kondhpungar. 106
2.3. Preparation of This Book Being Discussed. 107
3.1. Banana Cultivation in Home Gardens. 113
3.2. Pomegranate Cultivation in Home Gardens. 114
3.3. Lemon Cultivation in Home Gardens. 117
3.4. Luxurient Fruiting of Jackfruit in Farm Land. 117
3.5. Mango Orchard in Home Gardens. 138
3.6. Recently Introduced Papaya Plantation in Home Gardens. 139
3.7. Domesticated Cattle in the Village. 149
3.8. Khadisiju Shrub in Herbal Gardens. 150
3.9. Begunia in Herbal Gardens. 151
3.10. Dohona in Herbal Gardens. 151
3.11. Nilgundi in Herbal Gardens. 152
3.12. Patalgarudo in Herbal Gardens. 152
3.13. A View of the Herbal Garden with Herbal Plants and Ragi Crop grown as Intercropping. 153
3.14. Gourd Cultivation in Farm Land. 156
3.15. Chilly Cultivation in Farm Land. 156
3.16. Rainfed Land Converted into Terraces with Irrigation; Crops Being Grown During Rabi Season. 160
3.17. Irrigation Facility Brought to Rainfed Land: Crops being Grown During Rabi Season. 160
3.18. Water Channel Made in Farm Land. 161
3.19. Land Development Undertaken in Rainfed Land. 161
3.28. Eucalyptus Plantation in Kudi Kanda. 177
3.29. Puligunta Hills With Natural Dense Forest. 184
3.30. Shifting Cultivation in Bariamba Hills. 184
3.31. Eucalyptus Plantation in Lelisira Hill. 185
3.32. A View of Kupakhal Hills. 185
3.33. Sacred Grove in the Village. 188
3.34. Avenue Trees Along the Village Road; Lots of Gaps are Seen. 190
3.35. Bali Banda Tank. 192
3.36. Bamini Banda Tank. 196
3.37. Fishing Being Carried Out in Diki Banda Tank. 197
3.38. Plantation on Embankment of Diki Banda Tank. 197
3.39. A View of Check Dam. 200
3.40. A View of Check Dam. 201
3.41. Water Being Diverted for Irrigation from Boko Sakadi Stream. 205
4.1. Konta Koli Plants in Puligunta. 225

4.2. Kirchi Plants in Puligunta. 237
4.3. Dumuri (baya) Plants in Kotra Ambo. 237
4.4. Siadi Leaves in Puligunta. 238
4.5. Purda Koli (Lantana) has Colonised Hills from Kupa Khal to Kudi Kanda. 238
4.6. Golaki (Livestock Treatment) Plant in Kupa Khal. 239
4.7. Ronvelli in Puligunta Forest. 239
4.8. Char Koli Found above Kotra Ambo Hill and Kupa Khal. 240
5.1. Timber Harvested from Puligunta and Pasiamba for Preparing Agricultural Implements. 286
5.2. Timber Harvested from Puligunta and Pasiamba for Preparing Agricultural Implements. 286
5.3. Wood from Puligunta and Bamboo from Farm Land Used for Making Hunting Implements. 287
5.4. Youth of Kondhpungar with Hunting Implements. 287
5.5. Chutia Chorni Snake in Pasiamba Hills. 294
5.6. Chutia Chorni Snake in Pasiamba Hills; Scorpion (Kacha kupi) trying to Kill the Snake by attacking its Tail with its Venom. The Snake may die. The Dead Snake will be eaten by the Scorpion. 295
5.7. Hare found in Plenty in Several Places in the Village. 295
5.8. Caged Tumba (Quil). 296
5.9. Habitat for Porcupine. 296
5.10. Habitat for Porcuopine. 297
5.11. Nest with Eggs of Chiapota Bird. 297
5.12. Crabs found in Plenty Wetlands and around Diki Banda. 298
7.1. Vermi-composting: Demonstration Unit Installed by IRDWSI. 337
7.2. Gunia: Native Traditional Healer. 341

1

Kondhpungar Village

1.1 Introduction

During September 2002 and May 2003, Integrated Rural Development of Weaker Sections in India (IRDWSI), an NGO-based in Semiliguda block of Koraput District, Odisha organised two workshops on the importance of documenting biodiversity and its management to reduce vulnerability and to achieve sustainable livelihoods. Villagers from Kondhpungar were also invited and they were participated in the workshops.

After the workshops, the people of Kondhpungar had a series of meetings and deliberated on this topic. They unanimously decided that they will document the biodiversity both domesticated and wild occurring in their village and prepare a short-term and long-term management plans from the perspective of sustainable livelihoods. The people of Kondhpungar approached Dr Sasi Prabha and Dr. William Stanley of IRDWSI and conveyed their wishes of preparing such a document. IRDWSI readily accepted their request and initiated the process of documenting biodiversity of Kondhpungar village.

On 20th September 2006 a joint meeting of the people of Kondhpungar and staff of IRDWSI was organised in Kondhpungar village. In the meeting, details of the objectives, methodology etc. for documenting and preparing biodiversity management plan of the village were discussed. More details about this are given in Chapter 2.

1.2 Village Profile

In this section, basic information about the Kondhpungar village has been provided. IRDWSI in collaboration with the people of this village had conducted a baseline survey in 2004 and documented a wide-range of information about the people and its natural resources. Interested readers and researchers could, on request, obtain more information from the people of Kondhpungar and/or IRDWSI.

Plate 1.1: A View of Kondhpungar Village.

1.3 Geographical Area

The village Kondhpungar is situated in the northeast of Semiliguda town about 12-km away along the NH-43 and from this main road, a motorable road connects the village. The village falls under the revenue village Pungar. Pungar comes under Kunduli *Gram Panchayat* of Semiliguda block in Koraput district, Odisha (Fig. 1.1). Bio-geographically this part of southern Odisha falls under the Eastern Ghats region. The topography of the village consists of undulating hills and flat beds along the stream originating from the hill ranges and flowing towards west.

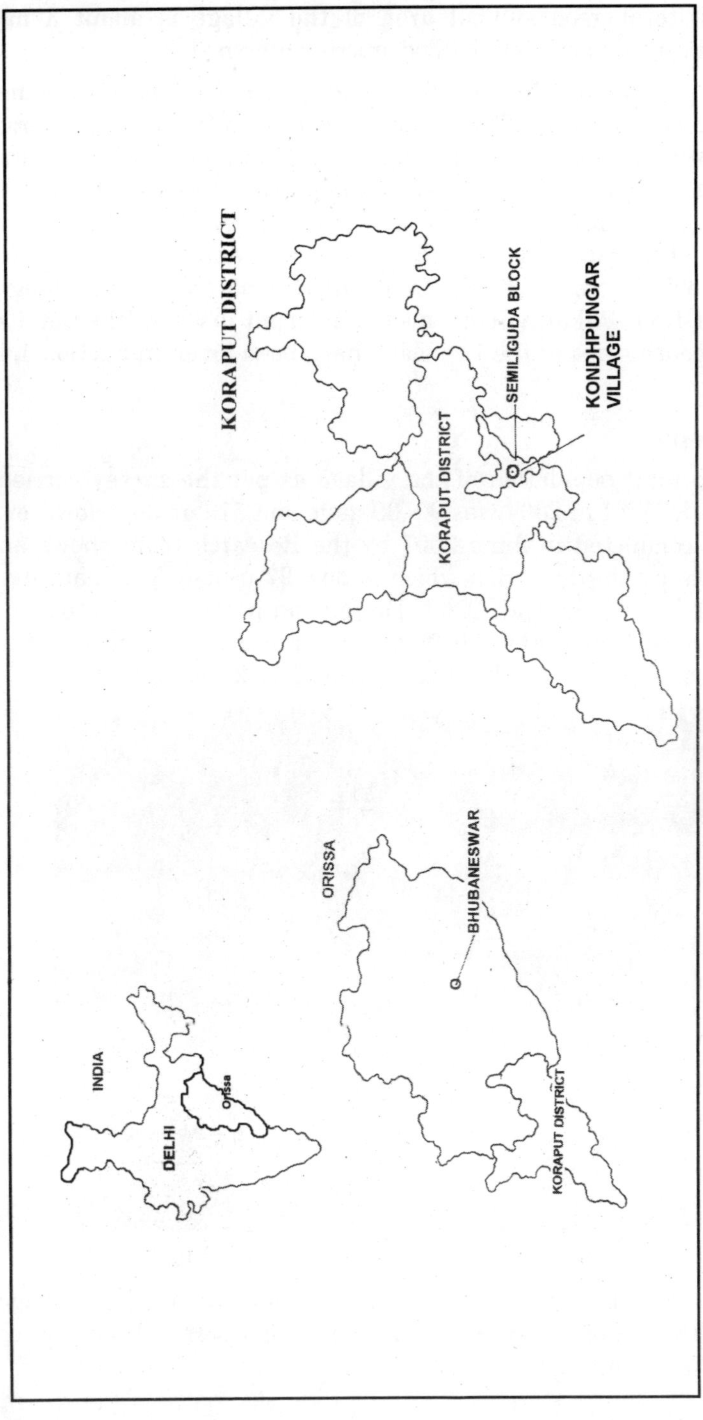

Fig. 1.1 Shows the Geographical Location of Kondhpungar Village, Situated Koraput District of Odisha (Maps not to scale).

The total geographical area of the village is about 3 m^2 constituting a very well-defined micro watershed.

As per the oral history, the Kondhs occupied this area some seven generations ago. They belong to two clans Hontal and Khora; a majority of the people belongs to the former clan. The two families of Khora clan are recent immigrants. The first family of Khora's (Dasu Khora) came to this village in 1970 from Bhitorkota village of Koraput district. He has a son who has a separate household. The second family (Malti Khora) moved into this village in 1991 from Pukali village, also in Koraput district. The details of the genealogies of the two clans have been given in Section 1.4 below.

1.4 People

The total population of the village as per the survey carried out by IRDWSI in 2004 was 90 (39 male and 51 female). However, survey conducted in June 2007 by the Research team shows an increase in the population which is now 97 people. This data has been updated upto April 2008. There is an increase of one person in the population making it 98 people. In June 2007, the number of household was 15. This has increased to 20 in April 2008.

Plate 1.2. Habitation Area of the Village.

The details of the expansion of the population in the village during the last eight generations are shown in a series of genealogies given in Appendix 1.

The village was first inhabited by late Bodu Hontal, eight generations ago. From the time Bodu Hontal inhabited, to the present eight generations have passed. There are 71 people (31 male and 40 female) descendents of Bodu Hontal presently living in 14 households in the village (Table 1.1).

Table 1.1. Lineages and Associated Descendents

Sl. No.	*Lineages*	*Descendents*			
		No. of Families	*Male*	*Female*	*Total*
1.	Bodu Hontal	14	31	40	71
2.	Somba Hontal	3	5	10	15
3.	Dasu Khora	2	4	3	7
4.	Malti Khora	1	3	2	5
	Total	**20**	**43**	**55**	**98**

About four generations ago, Somba Hontal came to live in this village. Presently, there are three households who are descendents of Somba Hontal numbering to 15 (five male and 10 female). As noted above four generations ago Dasu Khora, a Kondh migrated to this village. Presently Dasu Khora's descendents numbering seven (four male and three female) live in two households. More recently Malati Khora also a Kondh came to live in this village. Malati Khora with two sons, with one married live in one house.

Kondhpungar Household Map

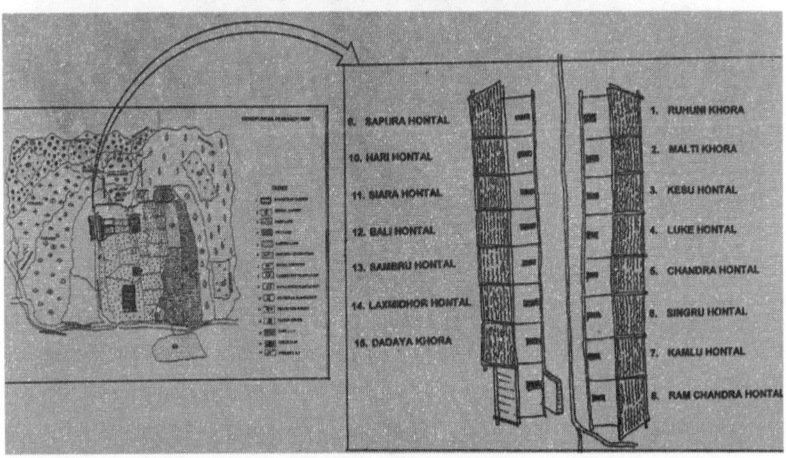

Fig. 1.2. Location of Fifteen Households in Kondhpungar.

The data analysed here pertains to 15 households. The location of the 15 households in the village is shown in Fig. 1.2. The household size varies from four to 13, the average being six (Table 1.2 and Fig. 1.3). Sixty per cent of the households have a size up to six members; twenty per cent between seven-eight members and significantly the remaining twenty per cent had more than eight members.

Plate 1.3: Tubewell in the Village.

Plate 1.4: A Typical Household in the Village.

Table 1.2: Distribution of Household Size

Household size	*No.*	*Percentage*
Up to 4	4	27
5 – 6	5	33
7 – 8	3	20
> 8	3	20
Total	**15**	**100**

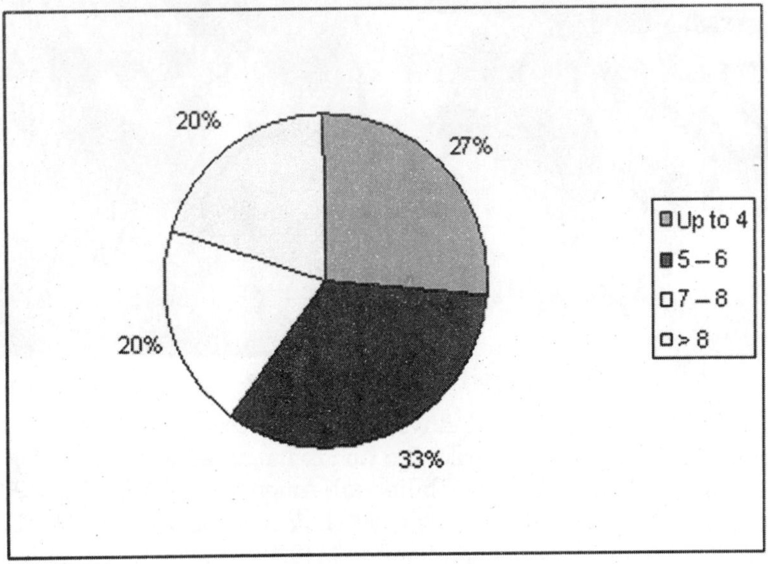

Fig. 1.3: Distribution of Household Size

Kondhs

It is appropriate that a brief overview about the Kondhs is given here. The review is drawn heavily from two publications: *The Scheduled Tribes* by K.S. Singh, Oxford University Press, 1994 and *Tribes of Odisha,* Harijan and Tribal Welfare Department, Government of Odisha, Bhubaneswar, 1990. The term Kondh is most probably derived from the Dravidian word *konda*, the hill. The Kondh are hilli people and they are divided into several sub-tribes, namely Dongria Kondh, Kutia Kondh, Desi Kondh, Penga Kondh and Kuvi Kondh etc.

A number of ethnographic accounts exist on the Kondhs. The Kondhs are distributed over the district of Phulbani, Koraput and Kalahandi of Odisha. They are also found in the districts of Visakhapatnam, Vizianagaram and Srikakulam of Andhra Pradesh

Plate 1.5: Kondh Women.

and Raigarh district of Madhya Pradesh. According to the 1961 census, 1,68,027 persons spoke the Kondh language, of which 68,865 persons (40.98 per cent) were bilingual. Among the bilingual 52,192 persons (75.79 per cent) had Oriya as their second language; 16,311 persons can speak Telugu and only 362 (0.52 per cent) speak other languages. In Odisha, the Kondhs are notified as a schedule tribe under the nomenclature Khond, grouped together with other groups, namely Kond, Kandha, Nanguli Kandha and Sitha Kandha. Their total population is 989,342 (as per 1981 census). They have a sex ratio of 1030 females per 1000 males. They speak the Kui or Kuvi language, belonging to the Dravidian family of languages.

Kuvi Kondh

Kondhs living in Koraput district including Kondhpungar of Odisha use Suanta as their surname. Their population figure is not available. These Kondhs are non-vegetarian, and they eat fish, egg, meat, including beef and pork. Ragi and rice are the staple cereals.

The Kuvi Kondhs have a number of exogamous clans (bansa) some of which are *Praska, Zumbeka, Wadoka (Wadaka), Muska, Tarika, Manding, Hikoka, Shikoka, Priska, Koleka and Melaka (Meloka).*

The Kondhs prefer adult marriage and acquire spouses by mutual consent or by capture. Bride price is paid in cash and kind. Monogamy is the common form of marriage, although instances of polygamy have been reported. Lac bangles and toe rings are the symbols of a married woman. The rule of residence after marriage is patri-local. Among them levirate, sororate and cross–cousin marriages are prevalent. Divorce can be sought by either spouse and remarriage is allowed for both sexes. A majority of Kondh families are of the nuclear type. Male equigeniture is the rule of inheritance and succession follows the male line. They observe a number of rituals in connection with birth, puberty, marriage and death.

The Kuvi Kondhs have their traditional council at the village level to maintain social control. Such council is headed by a *majhi, a nayak* and *a jani*. The other officials are *challan and barika*, the messenger. The traditional council solves inter-community disputes.

They follow a traditional form of religion and worship some family, village and regional deities. They also worship many Hindu gods and goddesses. Some of their sacred specialists are *disari, bejjini, pujari* and *gunia*. Their major festivals are *Dussehra, Pous Parab, Chaito Parab* and *Mandia Rani.*

The traditional as well as the present day's occupation of a majority of the Kuvi Kondhs is shifting cultivation, settled agriculture and animal husbandry. They also earn their livelihood as daily wage labourers.

1.5 Education

There is one primary school in the village established in 2004 under Education Guaranty Scheme located at the community center. There were 20 children (male six, female 14) enrolled in the school in 2008.

1.6 Languages Spoken

People in Kondhpungar speak Kuvi which belongs to the Dravidian language family and it is their mother tongue. Everyone in the village speaks Kuvi. In addition to it, Desia and Oriya are also spoken by all the villagers.

1.7 Land Holding Pattern

In Table 1.3 details of land holding pattern are given separately for each of the 15 households. There are five categories of land in the village, used for cultivation of crops, vegetables and trees. The five types are: (i) *Bada* (Homestead land); (ii) *Gudia kha* (Farm land); (iii) *Saria sabaiyan* (Rainfed land); (iv) *Sabaiyan* (Wet land); and (v) *Horkha kamma* (Shufting cultivation land).

Plate 1.6: Cultivation of Cabbage in Farm Lands.

Table 1.3: Land Holding (in acres) Pattern in the Village

Sl. No.	*Name of head of household*	*Family Size*	*Homestead*	*Farm land*	*Rainfed land*	*Wetland*	*Shifting cultivation*	*Total*
1.	Ruhuni Khora	4	0.03	0	1.0	0.10	3	4.1
2.	Malti Khora	5	0	0	0.10	0.20	2	2.3
3.	Kesu Hontal	6	0.10	1.0	1.0	0.40	1.00	3.5
4.	Luke Hontal	5	0.04	0.80	1.0	0.30	1.50	3.6
5.	Chandra Hontal	4	0.04	1.0	1.0	0.60	1.40	4.0
6.	Singru Hontal	4	0.05	0.90	1.0	0.60	1.80	4.4
7.	Kamblu Hontal	13	0.03	0.80	1.0	0.60	1.00	3.4
8.	Rama Chandra Hontal	9	0.06	0.90	1.0	0.60	0.50	3.1
9.	Sapura Hontal	8	0.08	0.80	0.80	0.60	0.60	2.9
10.	Hari Hontal	7	0.06	1.0	1.0	0.60	0.80	3.5
11.	Siara Hontal	9	0.09	0.70	1.0	0.30	0.90	3
12.	Bali Hontal	6	0.10	0.60	1.0	0.70	1.50	4
13.	Sambru Hontal	6	0.20	0.70	1.0	0.70	1.00	3.6
14.	Laxmidhar Hontal	7	0.10	0.70	1.0	0.68	1.50	4
15.	Dadeya Khora	4	0	0	0	0	0	0
Total (acre)		**97**	**0.98**	**9.9**	**12.9**	**6.98**	**18.5**	**49.4**
(Ha)			**0.396**	**4**	**5.22**	**2.82**	**7.5**	**20**

For the sake of convenience, each type of land holding is described separately.

(i) *Bada* (Homestead Land)

The distribution of size of *Badas* in 15 households is given in Table 1.4 and Fig. 1.4. Except for one household, the remaining 14 own small *Badas*. Two households (serial numbers 1 and 15) jointly own and manage a *Bada* of 0.025 acres. The area of *Badas* among the households varies from 0.025 to 0.20 acres. The total area under *Badas* in the village is 0.394 ha.

Plate 1.7: Bean cultivation recently introduced in Badas.

Table 1.4: Distribution of size of Badas in 15 households

Homestead size (acres)	*No.*	*Percentage*
0	1	6.7
0.01–0.05	6	40.0
0.06–0.09	4	26.7
>0.09	4	26.7
Total	**15**	**100**

(ii) *Gudia kha* (Farm land)

About four ha of such land are available in the village. There are three families that do not posses any farm land. Among the

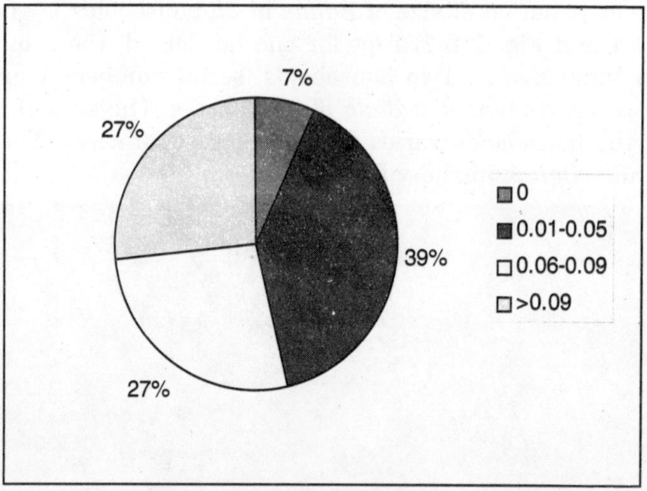

Fig. 1.4 Distribution of Size of Badas in 15 Households.

12 households who posses land, it varies from 0.60 acre to one acre. Only three families own one acre each, while all the remaining households own less than one acre.

Plate 1.8: Turmeric Cultivation in Farm Lands.

(iii) ***Saria sabaiyan*** (Rainfed land)

Except for one family, the remaining families own some piece of rainfed land. The holdings vary from 0.10 acres to one acre. Except for one household which owns 0.80 acres, the rest of the 12 households own one acre each. These lands are moderately undulating and are not capable of retaining water and moisture beyond the *Kharif* season. The total land under this category in the village is about 5.22 ha.

(iv) ***Sabaiyan*** (Wet land)

Except one household that does not own any wet land, the remaining 14 households own rather small size holdings. It varies from 0.10 acre to 0.70 acre. Five households own less than half an acre, while nine households own more than 0.5 acre but less than one acre. The total wet land in the village is about 2.82 ha.

Plate 1.9: Paddy Cultivation in Wet Land.

(v) ***Horkha Kamma*** (Shifting Cultivation Land)

Of the 15 households, 14 cultivate land under this category. It varies from a minimum of 0.5 acre to a maximum of three acres. The distribution of the shifting cultivation land among the households is given in Table 1.5 and Fig. 1.5. It is observed that a majority of the households (46 per cent) cultivate about 0.1 to one acre. Another substantial number of households (40 per cent) cultivate between 1.1 to two acres. Total land under this category in the village is about 7.5 ha. However, the amount of land that is actually cultivated varies from year to year as well as from family to family.

Table 1.5: Distribution of Shifting Cultivation Land (in acres)

Range	*No of Households*	*Percentage*
0	1	7
0.1 - 1	7	46
1.1 - 2	6	40
>2	1	7
Total	**15**	**100**

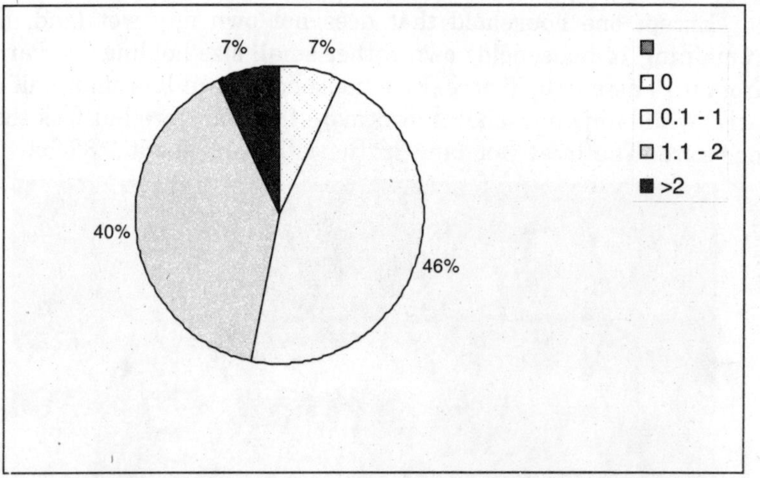

Fig. 1.5: Distribution of Shifting Cultivation Land.

1.7.1 Inter-household Variation in Total Land Holdings

From Table 1.6 and Fig. 1.6 the following main features with respect to inter-household variation in total land holdings emerge:

(i) Total land available for cultivation in the village is about 49.4 acres (20 ha);

(ii) There is one landless family in the village;

(iii) There is considerable variation between the households with respect to total land holdings; it varies from 2.3 acres to 4.35 acres;

(iv) Over 50 per cent of households own between three to four acres, while 20 per cent of the households own between two to three acres; and

(v) There are three families (20 per cent) that own more than four acres.

Table 1.6: Inter-household Variations in Total Land Holdings

Range	*No of Households*	*Percentage*
0	1	7
1 - 2	0	0
2.1 - 3	3	20
3.1 - 4	8	53
> 4	3	20
Total	**15**	**100**

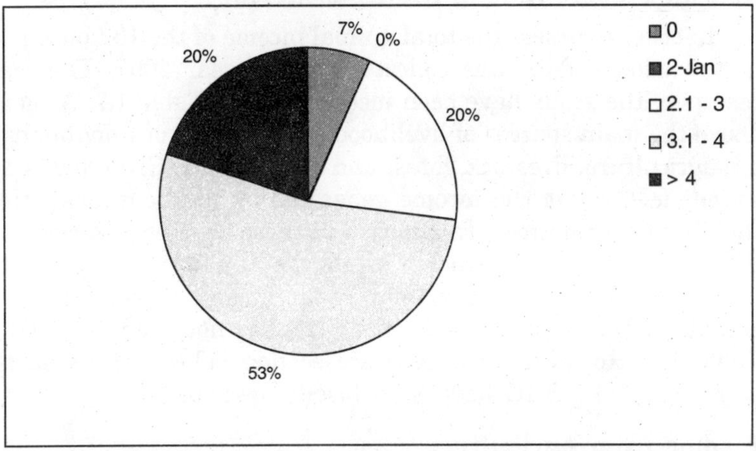

Fig. 1.6: Inter-household Variations in Total Land Holdings.

1.8 Sources of Livelihood

The main sources of livelihood of a majority of the people in the village are:

(i) Agriculture
(ii) Livestock
(iii) Forest, and
(iv) Wage labour

The details regarding the above livelihood sources are described in the subsequent chapters of the book. It is highly noteworthy that there is very little diversification in the village regarding livelihoods; there is one landless family who depend on wage labour and share cropping. Two persons Ramchandra Hontal and Singru Hontal since 2006 run a cycle repair shop at Kundli. However, it is highly noteworthy that a women's self-help group (SHG) was established in the village in 1993. The SHG has undertaken a few important economic activities described in detail later in this section.

IRDWSI conducted a survey in the village in 2003 regarding Secured Sustainable Livelihood (SSL). During 2003 there were only 16 households in the village. The survey revealed that the food produced by all the families in the village showed significant shortages. The estimated total food grains produced by the people of this village were 8547 kg. Whereas the requirement was 24660 kg. Thus, there was a significant shortage of food grains in the village.

Annual Income Among the Households

In order to assess the total annual income of the 15 households in the village, data was collected for the year 2007. The main results of the study have been incorporated in Table 1.7. As noted above the main sources of livelihood of the people of Kondhpungar are agriculture, livestock, forest and wage labour. Given below are salient features of the income generated by the households from the above four sources. In addition to these sources of income, an SHG comprising of 20 women established in 1993 also generates income through initiation of certain income generating (IG) activities. The profit made by the SHG has not been included in Table 1.7. However, in a separate section below details on the activities of the SHG have been briefly described.

Income from Agriculture

Data presented in Table 1.8 and Fig. 1.7 reveals the following main features with respect to income from agriculture:

(i) Annual income from agriculture varies considerably among the households from Rs 2,000 to Rs 21,700, average per household being Rs 12,577;

(ii) Except for one household number 15, all the rest of households income from agriculture is the main source and the contribution made by it to the total annual income of the households is enormous: the contribution varies from 24 to 100 per cent;

(iii) Twelve households generate more than 80 per cent of their total annual income from agriculture; and

(iv) Although the size of the *Badas* in the village are very small but as noted above they contribute very significantly to the overall income generated from agriculture.

Table 1.7: Main Sources of Livelihoods

Sl. No	Name of the Family	Agriculture			Livestock		Forest products		Wage		Total income
		Kind (kg)	Cash	Per cent	Cash	Per cent	Cash	Per cent	Cash	Per cent	
1.	Kamblu Hontal	890	12100	85.5	300	2.1	250	1.8	1500	10.6	**14150**
2.	Siara Hontal	370	15650	89.4	250	1.4	200	1.1	1400	8	**17500**
3.	Luke Hontal	230	11400	88.4	300	2.3	200	1.6	1000	7.75	**12900**
4.	Bali Hontal	425	21700	95.2	200	0.9	150	0.7	750	3.29	**22800**
5.	Laxmidhar Hontal	510	18000	93.8	200	1	250	1.3	750	3.91	**19200**
6.	Kesu Hontal	490	12250	96.5	250	2	200	1.6	0	0	**12700**
7.	Chandra Hontal	320	10450	100	0	0	0	0	0	0	**10450**
8.	Hari Hontal	570	12000	85.1	300	2.1	300	2.1	1500	10.6	**14100**
9.	Singru Hontal	250	19750	97.8	250	1.2	200	1	0	0	**20200**
10.	Sapura Hontal	100	15000	96.2	300	1.9	300	1.9	0	0	**15600**
11.	Sombru Hontal	337	17300	93.5	250	1.4	200	1.1	750	4.05	**18500**
12.	Ramo Hontal	395	7200	60	0	0	0	0	4800	40	**12000**
13.	Dadeya Hontal	190	2150	33.6	250	3.9	0	0	4000	62.5	**6400**
14.	Rohoni Khora	170	11700	91.1	300	2.3	0	0	850	6.61	**12850**
15.	Malti Khora	370	2000	24.1	4800	58	0	0	1500	18.1	**8300**
	Total	**5,617**	**188650**	**7950**			**2250**		**18800**		**217,650**
	Per cent		**86.7**		**3.65**		**1.03**		**8.64**		

Table 1.8: Distribution of Income (in thousands) from Agriculture Among 15 Households

Income range	*Number*	*Percentage*
up to 40	2	13.33
41 to 60	1	6.70
61 to 80	0	0.00
>80	12	80.00
Total	**15**	**100.0**

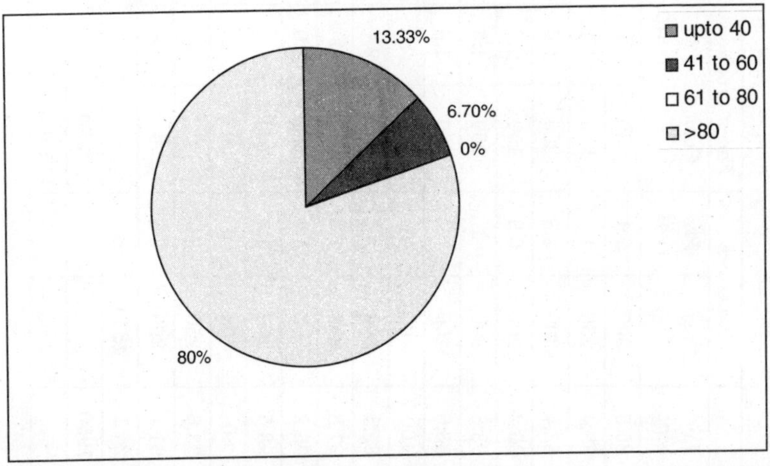

Fig. 1.7: Distribution of Income (in thousands) from Agriculture Among 15 Households.

Income from Livestock

Data presented in Table 1.9 and Fig. 1.8 in respect of income generated by the households from livestock reveal the following:

(i) The income generated from livestock varies from nil in household number 12 to Rs 4,800 in household number 15, the average annual income generated by a household from livestock being Rs 530;

(ii) There is not much inter-household variation with respect to the contribution made by the income from livestock to the total income, it varies from nil to 3.91 per cent (the only exception is household number 15 whose income from this source is 57.8 per cent of the total annual income); and

(iii) Over 66 per cent of the households generate income from this source that contributes between one to three per cent of the annual income.

Plate 1.10: A Flock of Goats in the Village.

Plate 1.11: Domesticated Country Fowl.

Table 1.9. Distribution of Income (in thousands) from Livestock Among 15 Households

Income / Range	*Number*	*Percentage*
0	2	13.33
upto 1	1	6.67
1.1 to 2	6	40.00
2.1 to 3	4	26.67
>3	2	13.33
Total	**15**	**100.0**

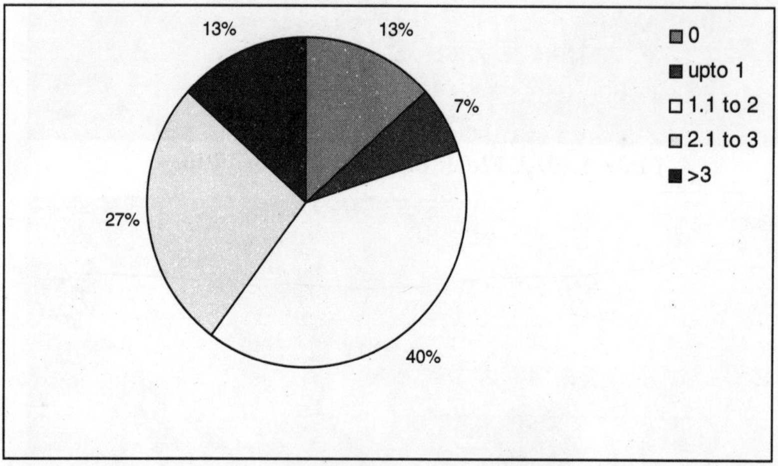

Fig. 1.8: Distribution of Income (in thousands) from Livestock Among 15 Households.

Income from Forest Products

Data presented in Tables 1.7 and 1.10 and Fig. 1.9 reveal the followings:

(i) Cash income from forest products is very low and varies from nil to Rs 300 among the households, average contribution made by it is only Rs 150 per households; and

(ii) There are five households that generate no income from the forest, whereas 60 per cent of the households generate from one to two per cent of their annual income.

Plate 1.12: Regenerating Pasiamba Protected Forest.

Plate 1.13: SHG Members being Trained in Broom Making.

Plate 1.14: SHG Members being Trained in Tamarind Processing.

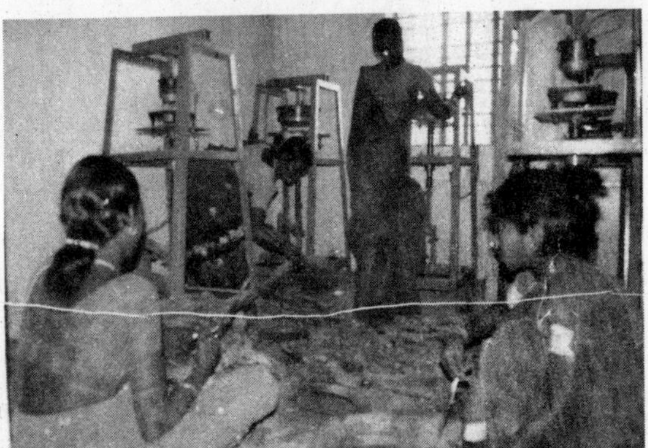

Plate 1.15: SHG Members making Siadi Leaf Plates.

Plate 1.16: Village Women Stitching Siadi Leaf Plates.

Table 1.10: Distribution of Income (in thousands) from Forest Products Among 15 Households

Income / range	*Number*	*Percentage*
0	5	33.33
up to 1	2	13.33
1.1 to 2	7	46.67
>2	1	6.67
Total	15	100.0

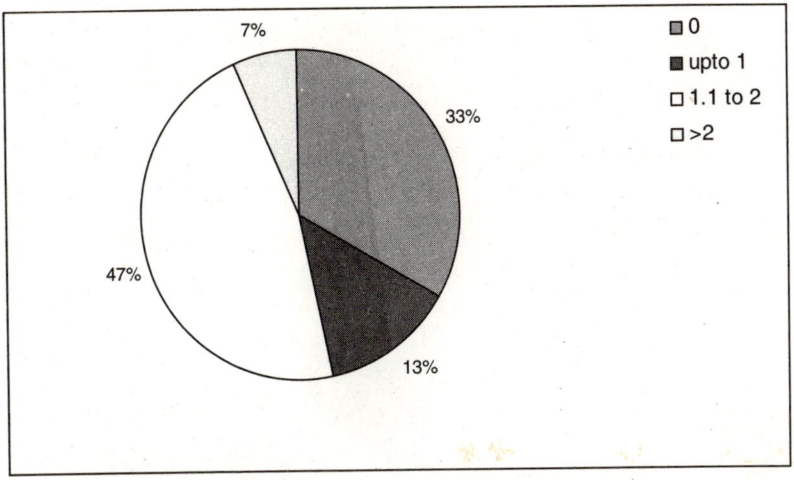

Fig. 1.9: Distribution of Income (in thousands) from Forest Products Among 15 Households.

Income from Wage Labour

An inspection of the data given in Tables 1.7 and 1.11 and Fig. 1.10 reveal the following main features in respect of income from wage labour :

(i) It varies from nil in four households to Rs 4,800 with an annual average income of Rs 1,253 per household;

(ii) Except for one family number 13 who has generated 62.5 per cent of its total annual income from wage labour, among the rest of the families contribution from this source varies from 0 to 18.1 per cent; and

(iii) Among over 50 per cent of the households contribution from this source to annual income is up to 10 per cent.

Table 1.11: Distribution of Income (in thousands) from Wage Labour Among 15 Households

Income / range	*Number*	*Percentage*
0	4	26.67
up to 5	3	20.00
5.1 to 10	3	20.00
>10	5	33.33
Total	15	100.0

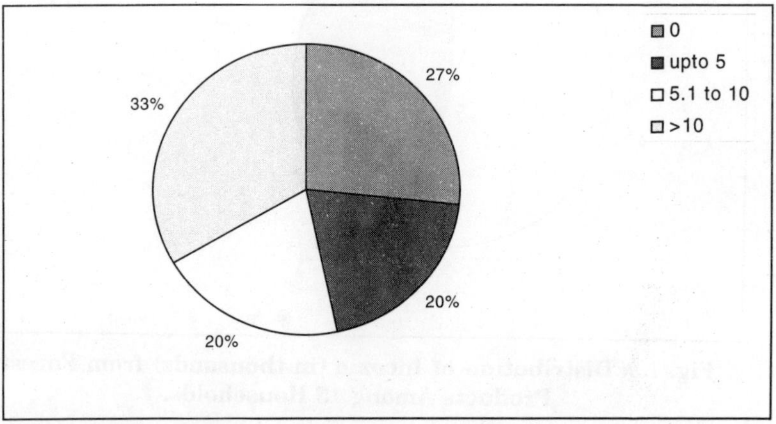

Fig. 1.10: Distribution of Income (in thousands) from Wage Labour Among 15 Households.

Distribution of Total Annual Income

Data presented in Tables 1.7 and 1.12 and Fig. 1.11 reveal the followings:

(i) Vast variation exists among the households with respect to the total annual income, it varies from Rs 6,400 to Rs 22,800 with an average of Rs 14,510;

(ii) A majority of the households annually generate between Rs 10,000 to Rs 20,000; there are however, two families that make more than Rs 20,000 annually; and

(iii) Thus all the families in the village are below poverty line.

Table 1.12: Distribution of Total Annual Income (in thousands) from all Sources Among 15 Households

Annual income/ range	*Number*	*Percentage*
up to 10	2	13.33
10.1 to 15	7	46.67
15.1 to 20	4	26.67
>20	2	13.33
Total	15	100.0

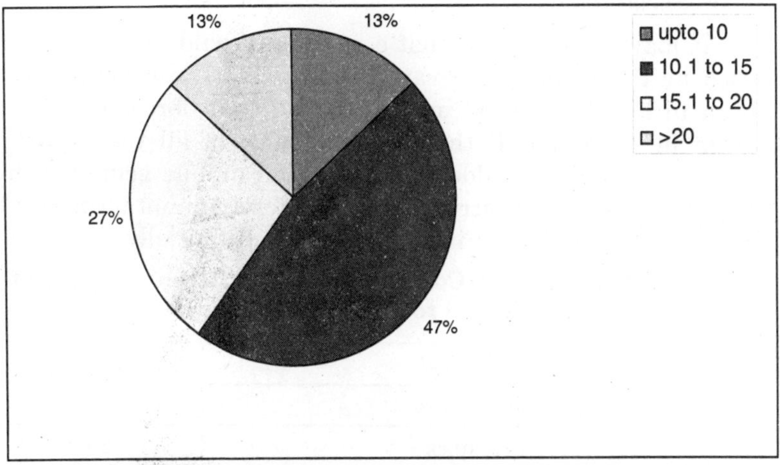

Fig. 1.11: Distribution of Total Annual Income (in thousands) from all Sources Among 15 Households.

Relative Contribution of Different Sources of Livelihood to Total Annual Income

From Tables 1.7 and 1.13 and Fig. 1.12 it is seen that agriculture is the main source of livelihood in the village and it contributes upto Rs 188,650, i.e., 86.7 per cent to the total annual revenue, i.e., Rs 2 17,650 generated by all the households in the village. The other source of income that contributes significantly is the income generated from wage labour; it contributes 8.65 per cent of the revenue. Livestock contributes only 3.65 per cent. It is highly noteworthy that the income from forest products is only a dismal 1.03 per cent.

It is appropriate to point out here that the income generated from forest products is rather underestimated. It does not include contribution made by grassing, fuel wood and timber. As we can see in Chapter 5 that a large number of plants are used for a variety of subsistence needs like:

- Food security
- Health care security
- Energy security
- Fodder security
- Timber
- Spiritual security, and
- Social bondage

It may also be noted that a number of wild animals are also used by the villagers for various purposes. These have also not been included in the income generated from forest products as given in Table 1.7. If the economic value of all these products were estimated and added to the annual income generated from forest products, its contribution to the total annual income of the households would have increased very substantially.

Table 1.13: Relative Contributions of Different Sources of Livelihood to Total Annual Income

Livelihood	*Percentage*
Agriculture	86.7
Livestock	3.65
Forest	1.03
Wage	8.65
Total	**100**

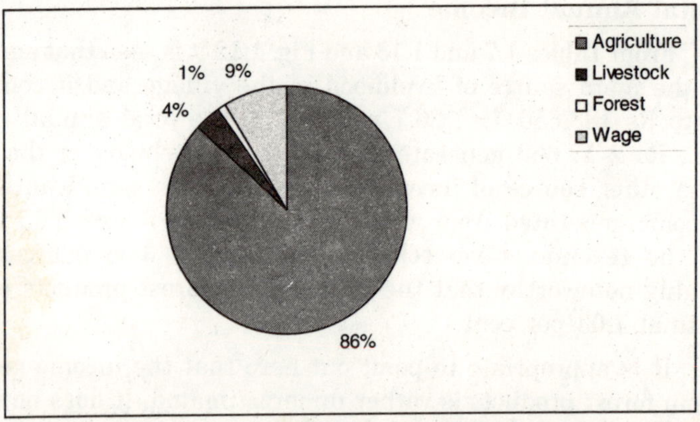

Fig. 1.12: Relative Contributions of Different Sources of Livelihood to Total Annual Income.

Income Generation Activities Undertaken by SHG in Kondhpungar

One SHG comprising of 20 women was established in 1993 in the village. Since then till recently the SHG has undertaken a number of income generating activities. The four activities undertaken i.e. ginger cultivation, vegetable cultivation, jute bag and herbal oil making have yielded some profit to the SHG. The SHG in future plans to undertake several new IG activities.

1. Ginger cultivation

Members involved	- 20
Cash invested for seeds	- 15,000 for five quintals
Compost	- Two truck loads–Rs 4,000
Total investment	- Rs 19,000
Ginger harvested	- 15 quintal
Sold in the market	- Rs 20 per kg
Amount received	- Rs 30,000
Profit	- Rs 11,000

2. Vegetable cultivation

Members involved	- 20
Cash invested for seeds	- Rs 20000
Compost	- Two and a half truck load–Rs 5000
Total investment	- Rs 25,000
Crop harvested and sold in the market	- Rs 50,000
Transportation cost	- Rs 4,000
Profit	- Rs 21,000

3. Jute bag making

Members involved	- 20
Cash invested @ Rs 6.50 per bag	- 3,300
No of bags prepared	- 200 Nos
Bag sold in the market	- Rs 22 per bag
Amount received	- Rs 4,400
Profit	- Rs 1,100

4. Herbal oil

Members involved	- 20
Cash invested	- Rs 1050 (oil and herbal medicine)
Oil extracted	- 9 litre
Sold in the market	- Rs 200 per kg
Amount received	- Rs 1800
Profit	- Rs 750

1.9 Annual Calendar of Main Festivals in the Village

In Table 1.14, the main festivals related to biodiversity celebrated in the village are listed. The last column in the table briefly gives the salient features of the various festivals in terms of the variety of domestic and wild biodiversity that is associated with the festivals.

Except for the month of June, it is highly noteworthy that at least one festival related to biodiversity is celebrated in each of the remaining eleven months. Although all the festivals listed in the table are culturally important for the villagers as well as biodiversity conservation, two festivals briefly described below deserve a special mention.

(i) *Rakhyas puja:* During the autumn seasons (September), while the crops grow in the fields, the growing crops often get damaged by insects and pests. People think that it is *Rakhyas* (demons) that destroy the crops. To prevent this, the people make two bullock carts and four bullocks with soft mud and also an idol, which symbolises the demon. People collect few insects from the niger, paddy and ragi fields.

The idol and insects are kept in the bullock carts they have prepared and put outside the village main road after performing elaborate rituals. This is done with the beliefs that the idol and the insects that damage crops leave out of the village and this ceremony will ensure that the crops are not damaged in that particular year.

(ii) *Spiritually empowered seeds:* *Chait Parabo* celebrated usually in April is a festival constituting of a series of events. *Bihu Puja* is an important event in the celebration of *Chait parabo.*

Empowering the seeds spiritually consists of two stages. The first stage consists of *Bihu* (seed) *Puja* in the *Jakhar (*sacred grove) and in the second stage the seeds are distributed to the community members.

Prior to the *Bihu Puja*, a fistful of seeds of all important crops cultivated by the community in the preceding year are collected. Each household contributes to this collection. This collection of seeds is then taken to the main *Jakhar* where a *Puja* is offered. Usually *Dishari* (Head Priest) assisted by *Jani (Priest)* performs the *puja*. The collection of seeds in a small bamboo basket is then placed under a small *pendal* (tent) decorated with mango leaves and flowers available in the village. *Jakhar debta* (deity in the sacred grove) and the other *debtas* (deities) in all directions are prayed and appealed to give divine power in the seeds. Water used for this *puja* is customarily collected from a perennial stream in the village. To propitiate the deities a black chicken and a goat are sacrificed. Women of the community are not allowed to attend this *puja*. Later the gathering enjoys a community feast prepared out of the sacrificed animals in the *Jakhar* itself. After the community feast the spiritually empowered seed collection is taken back to the village. The *puja* in *Jakhar* is usually carried out during the day time. On the evening of the same day the spiritually empowered seeds are distributed among the community members.

Second part of the celebrations starts after the sunset. The entire village community assembles at the *Sadar (*meeting place located at the centre usually under a banyan or peepal tree). The *Disari* and *Jani* place the spiritually empowered seeds and the water (collected in the earthen pot in the morning from the perennial stream) at the *Sadar*. A small *puja* that also includes sacrificing a black chicken is offered to the *Sadar debta* (deity). Later *Jani* pours the water of the earthen pot on *Disari* and at the end releases the pot on the ground for free fall so that it breaks into pieces. After making sure that earthen pot is broken, the drenched *Disari* tosses the seeds towards the community members gathered at the *Sadar*. While *Disari* is tossing the seeds, the community members try their best to collect as many seeds as possible. During the entire process of tossing of seeds, the *Disari* does not face the community members collecting the seeds. He continues chanting a *mantra* and throwing seeds towards the gathering with an overhead action. The community members later mix the spiritually empowered seeds with their stored seeds to be planted in the current year.

Plate 1.17: Bali Parab—Worship of Seeds, Mixing of Sed and Distribution of Mix Seeds Among Villagers.

Plate 1.18: Chaitra Parab being Celebrated in Neighbouring Village Kudi.

Table 1.14: Annual Calendar of Main Festivals Related to Domestic and Wild Biodiversity in the Village

Sl. No.	*Month*	*Festival*	*Significance*
1.	January	*Pus parab*	Collect *Pitkanda, Sindi Kida*, Honey (all from the wild) and feed to the cattle.
2.	February	*Biun topa*	Villagers go to *Jakari* with the accompaniment *dapu* a musical instrument and disperse seeds in it. This is followed by a community dance (*demsa*).
3.	March	*Ambo baulo puja*	Villagers tie threads around the wild mango trees for its good productivity.
4.	April	*Chaitra parab*	Start consuming wild mangos; go for annual ritual hunting.
5.	May	*Bali parab*	Worship seeds, mix seeds, distribute the mix seeds among villagers and start field preparation.
6.	July	*Taku parab*	After performing rituals they start eating mango kernel, *targa kanda*, Tamarind, and pumpkin leaves.
7.	August	*Sita puja*	Seedlings of Paddy, Ragi and Suan are worshiped, transplanted in the field and the blood of chicken mixed with castor oil is sprinkled in the crop area.
8.	September	*Rakhyas puja*	To prevent the crop from insects, they bring insects from fields and worship them and leave insects away from the village.
9.	October	*Dashara puja*	Collection of branches of *Kati* plant for making broom and start using the first harvest of cucumber.
10.	November	*Nua khai*	Worship harvested Rice and Turmeric.
11.	December	*Siadi poda parab*	Collection of hill broom starts and villagers start eating the *siadi* seeds.

1.10 Traditional Governance System

The village has a strong traditional governance structure. The village headman called *Nayak* occupies an important position in the village. The present *Nayak* is Shree Sombru Hontal. He has inherited the position from his father. He mostly takes administrative decisions. He also decides as to when festivals and other rituals should be performed in the village. He is assisted by the village *Challan* (messenger). The village has a priest (*Pujari*). The present *Pujari* in the village is Sapura Hontal. He performs various rituals in the village. *Gunia* is the traditional health practitioner. The other traditional functionary in the village is *Disari*. Hari Hontal is the current *Disari*. He is an astrologer and provides guidance to the villagers regarding various festivals and ceremonies like birth and death, naming of the new born child etc. Often *Pujari* and *Disari* work together especially if they anticipate danger from evil spirits.

Women in general do not play any substantive role in the traditional governance system of the village. Besides these traditional functionaries, the village also has a ward/panchayat member.

1.11 Present Governance System

While traditional governing institutions continue to play a significant role in managing the affairs of the village, the changed socio-economic and political scenario in the area necessitated crafting of new institutions for governance in the village. Presently, there are three such institutions in the village:

(i) People's Organisation,

(ii) Self Help Group, and

(iii) Rural Health and Environmental Programme (RHEP).

It is an appropriate to mention here that IRDWSI has been working in partnership with the people of this village since 1988 and has played a crucial facilitating role in setting up the above institutions (i) and (ii) RHEP has been crafted in the village by another NGO, Gram Vikas, Mohuda, Berhampur.

(i) People's Organisation

People's Organisation is a village level people's forum comprising of all the adult males and females of the village (Table 1.15). The organisation was formed way back in 1992. The organisation consists of 32 members (male 16, female 16). An executive committee comprising seven members (male four, female three) guides the functioning of the organisation. Mr Singru Hontal is the President, Mr. Kesu Hontal is the Secretary, Mrs Ratai Hontal is the Joint secretary and Mrs Rajmoni Hontal is the treasurer.

The executive committee meets on the tenth of every month and discusses the management and monitoring of the developmental activities initiated by the community related to natural resources such as land, water and forest.

The committee has formulated rules and regulations with respect to forest protection, planting of trees, establishment of grain fund, grassing, harvesting of wood for house construction and for making agricultural implements, collection of fire wood, wood required for cremation and demand for timber by the neighbouring villages. The committee negotiates with the Forest Department and other Government line departments for various developmental needs of the village. The committee reviews the progress of the activities undertaken by the community or other agencies and takes necessary actions (for details see Table 1.15).

Table 1.15: Details of People's Organisation (Loko Sangathan)

Name of the Organisation	*People's Organisation (Loko Sangathan)*	
Year of establishment	1993	
Composition of the Executive Committee (2008)		
Name	Gender	Designation
Singru Hontal	Male	President
Rupai Hontal	Female	Vice President
Kesu Hontal	Male	Secretary
Krusna Hontal	Male	Joint Secretary
Rajmoni Hontal	Female	Treasurer
Chandra Hontal	Male	Member
Laxmidhar Hontal	Male	Member
Ratai Hontal	Female	Member
Puse Khara	Female	Member
Jimlo Hontal	Female	Member
Kishore Hontal	Male	Member

The committee maintains minutes of all the meetings in a register. In order to meet the financial requirements the members contribute Rs 12 per year as membership fee. The amount is deposited in a bank. The balance in the bank at the time of this study in 2007 was Rs 2501. The fund is used for village developmental activities. The members actively participate in the *Palli Sabha* and *Gram Sabha* meetings.

General body meeting: The general body meets on the fifteenth of every month. The main functions of the general body are:

- Taking decisions on the village developmental activities
- Evolving strategies for accessing Government programmes
- Evolving strategies for:

  Child education,

  Health and sanitation,

  Agriculture development, and

  Forest protection and afforestation,
- Managing grain and seed banks,
- Generates awareness in the village regarding sustainable livelihoods, conservation of biodiversity, right to work, right to information etc.
- Disseminates information on marketing, wage rates and government schemes to the stakeholders.
- Monitors village development works,
- Resolves intra and inter village level conflicts,
- Takes decisions on proposals by NGOs and academic institutions for undertaking research projects in the village.

Conflicts resolved recently

(i) Water distribution conflicts between the neighbouring villages have been resolved, and

(ii) Tree felling by neighbouring villages has been amicably resolved.

(ii) Self-help group

The structure and function of the self-help group named *Sonidei Mahila Mandal* established in 1993 in the village are briefly given in Table 1.16.

Table 1.16: Details of Sonidei Mahila Mandal (SHG)

Name of the Organisation	Sonidei Mahila Mandal (SHG)	
Year of establishment	1993	
Composition of the Executive Committee (2008)		
Name	*Gender*	*Designation*
Jimlo Hontal	Female	President
Ratai Hontal	Female	Vice President
Rupai Hontal	Female	Vice President
Tikmo Hontal	Female	Secretary
Juali Hontal	Female	Joint Secretary
Rajmoni Hontal	Female	Treasurer
Member	Female	13

Functions of the executive committee:

- To hold monthly meetings,
- Collection of monthly membership fee,
- Planning, implementation and monitoring of SHG activities,
- To undertake income generating activities,
- Addressing women's issues,
- Promoting girl child's education,
- Promoting village agriculture development.

In addition to the functions mentioned above, the SHG members also take active part in the activities undertaken by the People's Organisation.

Periodic meeting: The SHG meets once in a month.

Membership fee: Monthly Rs 10 per member.

Amount in the bank as on April, 2007 is Rs 82,251 (includes own savings and support received from other agencies).

(iii) Rural Health and Environmental Programme (RHEP)

This committee was established in 2006 in the village by Gram Vikas, Mohuda, Berhampur to address issues related to drinking water and sanitation in the village. The structure and function of the RHEP committee are briefly given in Table 1.17. The committee meets once every month.

Plate 1.19: A toilet being constructed in the village under RHEP.

Table 1.17: Rural Health and Environmental Programme (RHEP)

Name of the Committee	*Rural Health and Environmental Programme (RHEP)*	
Year of establishment	2006	
Composition of the Executive Committee (2008)		
Name	*Gender*	*Designation*
Chandra Hontal	Male	President
Kesu Hontal	Male	Vice President
Singru Hontal	Male	Secretary
Krusnna Hontal	Male	Joint Secretary
Rajmoni Hontal	Female	Treasurer
Member	Female	Two

Functions of the executive committee

- Motivating families in the village to install toilets;
- Motivating families in the village to install drinking water facilities;
- Monitoring the progress of work;
- Collection of monthly membership fee;
- Ensuring that the community works in unity.

1.12 Growing Partnership: People of Kondhpungar and IRDWSI

IRDWSI was established in Semiliguda Block of Koraput district in 1981. It established partnership with the people of Kondhpungar in 1988 with the objective of jointly undertaking various developmental activities in the village. During the last twenty years the people of Kondhpungar and IRDWSI undertook several activities in the village in areas such as education, health, housing, energy, sericulture, community forestry, agriculture, irrigation, fisheries, crafting of social institutions like People's Organisation. etc. In Table 1.18 gives the salient features of the developmental activities undertaken by the people of Kondhpungar in partnership with IRDWSI.

Plate 1.20: IRDWSI and People of Kondhpungar are Discussing Sustainable Agricultural Practices.

Plate 1.21: Dialogue being Initiated for Forming People's Organisation, IRDWSI Personnel taking Part in the Deliberations.

Table 1.18: IRDWSI Facilitated the following Activities in Partnership with the People of Kondhpungar

Year	*Activity*
1988	First visit made by IRDWSI staff.
1989	Community meetings organised and explained about the work of IRDWSI.
1990	Staff continued visiting the village.
1991	Staff built rapport with the people and introduced People's Participatory Strategic Planning. Representatives from Kondhpungar attended the first Adivasi Mela held at Barakutni village.
1992	Formation of People's Organisation.
	Formation of Women's Organisation.
1993	Planning for building low cost houses and introducing stabilized mud block making with the help of local youth and women. The villagers organise a national youth camp in collaboration with IRDWSI, plantation work is undertaken in the village. Students from Sambalpur University stay at Kondhpungar and undertake anthropological study. Sericulture was introduced with women farmers.
1994	Housing programme; construction of houses.
	Establishment of community centre.
	Training of People's Organisation.
	Capacity building programme for the leaders of People's. Organisation and Women's Organisation.
	Establishment of grain and seed bank.
	Training of SHG.
1995	Help in securing land entitled to women's group of the village.
	Social forestry plantation.
	Leadership training.
	SHG formation and training.
	Training of traditional birth attendant.
	Training of village native doctor.
	Forest protection mechanisms.
2000	Training in tamarind processing and jute bag stitching.
	Entrepreneurship training.

Year	*Activity*
	Training in forest management.
	Transistor radios were given to the leaders of the village.
	Education materials given to school children.
2002	Land development.
	Compost pits installed.
	Training provided in sustainable agriculture.
	Training of ward members.
	Training of *Samiti* members and SHG.
	Participation in sustainable agriculture workshop.
	Support provided for construction of irrigation pond and community centre.
2003	Study on shifting cultivation by Raghu Velenkar, IIFM.
	Study on Ethno-botany By Franko Merlin of MCC Chennai.
	Participation in People's Biodiversity Register workshop.
	Assistance provided for repair of irrigation well.
	Micro capital support provided.
2004	Introduction of agro-forestry models by IIFM, Bhopal.
	Seeds support to farmers.
	Training in herbal shampoo processing.
	Training in food processing.
	Broom and community plantation.
	Vegetable cultivation and marketing.
	Orchard plantation.
	Poultry strengthened.
	Kitchen garden strengthened.
	Exposure visit arranged of the farmers on sustainable agriculture to Kokriguda watershed area.
	Vermi-composting introduced.
	Live fencing practice strengthened.
	Calamity preparedness workshop attended by Singru Hontal

Year	*Activity*
2004	Villages participated in World Social Forum, Mumbai.
	Villages participated in OAAA Rally at Bhubaneswar.
	Support for grain storage provided.
	Land development activities strengthened.
2005	Study on Agro-forestry by Anhsu Singh, IIFM, Bhopal.
	Check dam and irrigation canal support provided.
	Irrigation pond support provided.
	Herbal garden support provided.
2006	Training of PRIs.
	Support to children for Bridge course.
2007	Rural Health and Environment programme initiated among 15 families.
2008	Vermi compost introduced at community level.
	Solar lights provided to all families.

1.13 Glimpses of Kondhpungar's Journey 1988-2008

In Table 1.19 the glimpses of the journey that the people Kondhpungar have undertaken from 1988 to 2008 are given. The focus here is to show the significant changes that have occurred in the village with respect to:

(a) changes in number of families in the village,

(b) changes in means of livelihood,

(c) changes in vegetation cover in forests, and

(d) changes in domesticated plants.

In addition name of the agency that facilitated the process of change in the villages is given in the last column-"remarks". Significant changes that have made immense impact on the quality of life of the people of Kondhpungar are summarised below:

- In 1989 an earthen dam for irrigation was constructed that helped a few families to start growing *Rabi* crops for the first time in the village.
- Year 1992 was a watershed in the village as a number of new initiatives were undertaken.
    - sustainable agricultural practices introduced.
    - upgradation of the check dam helped many more families

to cultivate *rabi* crops in season, this enhanced the total productivity of grains in the village and considerably reduced dependence on market.

- establishment of cash and grain banks reduced the vulnerability of the poor households.
- new varieties of vegetable seeds introduced; this enhanced cash income.
- fruit bearing trees planted by many families and it continues till date.

- formation of People's Organisation and Women's Origination provided a strong social and political platform to the villagers that enabled them to negotiate with various government line departments for bringing in developmental schemes in the village.
- In year 1993 the following significant activities were started
- mixed cropping practices,
- sericulture,
- drinking water facilities,
- some mango trees grew naturally in the forest,
- In year 1994 the following important activities were undertaken.
- forest protection committee established,
- housing programme introduced,
- social forestry programme introduced,
- village road constructed,
- community centre established,
- In year 1995 the following activities were carried out.
- the village experienced unusual heavy rains that resulted in massive land slides and damaged cultivated fields. The villagers acted by restricting shifting cultivation area and accorded complete protection to the natural forest patches.
- shifting cultivation partially stopped;
- land entitlement to women group of the village procured;
- social forestry plantation started;
- SHG formed;
- regeneration of a variety of plant species started in the degraded forest.

- In year 1996 almost all the families started cultivation in the *rabi* season, thus a single crop village changed into a double crop village. This enhanced the overall crops as well as vegetable productivity enormously.
- In year 1997 the following activities were undertaken:
    - family forestry was introduced,
    - for the first time a women from the village was elected as *Samiti* member.
    - shifting cultivation stopped.
- In the year 1998, five per cent irrigation model was introduced.
- In the year 1999 transistor radio sets were given to three families; regeneration continued, forest canopy became dense.
- In year 2000 a number of new activities were initiated;
    - cashew plantation was undertaken;
    - water storage tank for irrigation during summer was constructed.
    - villagers were trained in tamarind processing and jute bag stitching.
    - villagers were trained in forest management practices.
- Year 2002 was very important for securing the livelihood of the villagers as a number of activities having far-reaching implications were introduced in the village.
    - integrated farming in homestead and farmland with perennial and seasonal vegetables introduced in large scale.
    - wet land and farm land used for double cropping;
    - new agricultural implements introduced-LLHP, water pump, sprayer, pick axe and weeding machineries
    - vermi-composting and compost pits introduced.
- In year 2003 three important activities were introduced:
    - Secure Sustainable Livelihood Programme (SSL) sponsored by Odisha Development Action Forum, Bhubaneswar was initiated.
    - check dam and irrigation channel were cemented .
    - drainage was made in the village.

- In 2004 the following main activities were carried out:
    - agro-forestry model introduced.
    - improved seed varieties of vegetables, spices and paddy were introduced.
    - villagers were trained in herbal shampoo making and food processing.
    - villagers participated in World Social Forum, Bombay.
    - degraded village forest became dense forest.
- In 2005 a fish pond was constructed and pisciculture started; dense forests emerged, wild animals increased.
- In 2007 three activities were undertaken:
    - Cement and concrete road laid in the village.
    - Rural Health and Environment Programme (RHEP) started by Gram Vikas.
    - study on biodiversity conservation and sustainable livelihoods initiated.
    - dense forest emerged, wild animals increased, crop damage increased.
- Rahul Gandhi with others visited the village on 7th March 2008 to see Rural Health and Environment programme.
- In year 2008, stand alone solar lighting systems were installed–street lights and every home was provided with one bulb connection.

The glimpses of Kondhpungar's journey listed above demonstrate that if the people wish, significant changes can be achieved even in a remote and backward village. It is remarkable that during the last two decades Kondhpungar, primarily perusing a subsistence economy has moved to fairly vibrant sustainable livelihoods. A village with rather dismal amenities has now cemented concrete roads, drinking water, durable housing, community centre, drainage, toilets, solar lights etc. In short, the economic status as well as the quality of life of the people of Kondhpungar has improved remarkably. With the formation of People's Organisation and Women's Organisation the future well-being of the people, animals and forest has been secured.

Table 1.19 Glimpses of Kondhpungar's Journey 1988-2008

Year	*No. of families in the village*	*Means of livelihood*	*Changes*		*Remarks*
			Wild	*Domestic*	
1988	8	Dependence on traditional agriculture and shifting cultivation in *kharif* season with single crop, low wages.	Forest areas degraded	Trees in the village decreased	
1989	10	Dependence on traditional agriculture and shifting cultivation in *kharif* season with single crop, an earthen dam for irrigation constructed, few families started growing *rabi* crops.	Forest areas degraded	Trees in the village decreased	
1990	10	Dependence on traditional agriculture and shifting cultivation in *kharif* season with single crop, more families started growing *rabi* crops.	Forest areas degraded	Trees in the village decreased	
1991	12	Almost all families started growing *rabi* crops.	Forest areas degraded	Trees in the village decreased	
1992	14	Sustainable agricultural practices introduced, check dam upgraded, cash and grain banks established, land used for double cropping, new varieties of vegetable seeds introduced. People's Organisation and Women's Organisation formed.	Forest degradation continues	Fruit bearing plants planted by many families	IRDWSI facilitated

Year	*No. of families in the village*	*Means of livelihood*	*Changes*		*Remarks*
			Wild	*Domestic*	
1993	14	Mixed cropping practices introduced, sericulture introduced, drinking water facilities established, shifting cultivation continues.	Some mango trees grew naturally in the forest	Plantation of fruit bearing trees continued	
1994	14	Forest protection committee established, drinking water facilities enhanced, housing programme introduced, social forestry programme introduced, village road constructed, shifting cultivation continues, community centre established, People's Organisation and Women's Organisation leaders trained.	Some mango trees grew naturally in the forest	Plantation of fruit bearing trees continued	IRDWSI facilitated
1995	14	The village experienced unusual heavy rains that resulted in massive land slides and damaged cultivated fields, shifting cultivation partially stopped, land entitlement to women group of the village procured, social forestry plantation started, leaders, TBAs and VND trained, SHG formed, forest protection measure streamlined.	Shifting cultivation area was restricted, complete protection accorded to forest patches, regeneration of a variety of plant species started in the degraded forest	Plantation of fruit bearing trees continued	IRDWSI facilitated

Year	*No. of families in the village*	*Means of livelihood*	*Changes*		*Remarks*
			Wild	*Domestic*	
1996	14	Focus on vegetable cultivation in large scale during *rabi* season, sericulture expanded, Participatory Strategic Plan programme initiated.	Regeneration of a variety of plant species started in the degraded forest	Plantation of fruit bearing trees continued	
1997	16	New varieties of improved paddy and family forestry introduced, extensive land used for double cropping, drinking water facilities further enhanced, women elected as *Samiti* member, shifting cultivation stopped.	Regeneration of a variety of plant species further enhanced	Plantation of fruit bearing trees continued	
1998	16	5% model introduced, extension of check dam undertaken, IG activities initiated.	Regeneration continues	Plantation of fruit bearing trees continued	
2000	16	Cashew plantation undertaken, farmers trained, water storage tank constructed for irrigation during summer, IG activities further enhanced, training in tamarind processing and jute bag stitching given, villagers trained in forest management, education materials provided to school children.	Regeneration continues, canopy became dense	Plantation of fruit bearing trees continued	IRDWSI facilitated

Year	No. of families in the village	Means of livelihood	Changes		Remarks
			Wild	Domestic	
2002	16	Integrated farming in homestead and farm land with perennial and seasonal vegetables introduced, wet land and farm land used for double cropping, new agricultural implements introduced -LLHP, water pump, sprayer, pick axe and weeding machineries, vermi -composting introduced, cashew plantation increased, IG activities enhanced, land development undertaken, compost pits introduced, farmers, ward members and *samiti* members trained, villagers participated in workshop on sustainable agriculture held at IRDWSI.	Regeneration continues, canopy became dense	Plantation of fruit bearing trees continued	IRDWSI facilitated
2003	16	Introduction of Secure Sustainable Livelihood Programme (SSL), check dam and irrigation channel cemented, drainage made inside the village.	Regeneration continues, canopy became further dense	Plantation of fruit bearing trees continued	IRDWSI facilitated
2004	16	Agro-forestry model and farm designing in 5 families, improved seed varieties of vegetables, spices and paddy introduced in large scale, hedgerow plantations undertaken, villagers trained in herbals	Dense forest emerged	Plantation of fruit bearing trees continued	IRDWSI facilitated

Year	*No. of families in the village*	*Means of livelihood*	*Changes*		*Remarks*
			Wild	*Domestic*	
		shampoo and food processing, broom plantation undertaken, vegetables and poultry marketed, kitchen gardens strengthened, villagers visited Kokriguda watershed area to see sustainable agriculture, study on shifting cultivation carried out by Raghu Velenkar, IIFM, Bhopal, Franko Merlin of MCC Chennai studied Ethno-botany of the village, villagers participated in PBR workshop at IRDWSI, Singru Hontal participated in Calamity Preparedness Workshop at Bhubaneswar villagers participated in World Social Forum, Bombay, and Evaluation team from ODAF visited the village in 2004.			

Year	*No. of families in the village*	*Means of livelihood*	*Changes*		*Remarks*
			Wild	*Domestic*	
2005	16	Fish pond constructed, pisciculture started, study on agro-forestry carried out by Anhsu Singh, IIFM, Bhopal, irrigation pond constructed, herbal garden established.	Dense forest emerged, wild animals increased	Plantation of fruit bearing trees continued, plants planted in homestead and farm land area as bio-fencing	IRDWSI facilitated
2006	16	Agro-forestry model replicated by all the families, one more drain constructed.	Dense forest emerged, wild animals increased, crop damage increased	Plantation of fruit bearing trees continued, plants planted in homestead and farm land area as bio-fencing	
2007	18	Cement-concrete road laid in the village, Rural Health and Environment Programme (RHEP) by Gram Vikas, started, study on biodiversity conservation and sustainable livelihoods initiated.	Communication and sanitation improved	Plantation of fruit bearing trees continued, plants planted in homestead and farm land area as bio-fencing	RHEP jointly undertaken by Gram Vikas and IRDWSI

Year	*No. of families in the village*	*Means of livelihood*	*Changes*		*Remarks*
			Wild	*Domestic*	
2008	20	Study on biodiversity conservation and sustainable livelihoods continue.	Dense forest emerged, wild animals increased, crop damage increased	Plantation of fruit bearing trees continued, plants planted in homestead and farm land area as bio-fencing	Rahul Gandhi with others visited Kondhpungar on 7th March 2008 to see RHEP.

Glimpses of Kondhpungar's Journey

Inauguration of housing project (1994).

Inauguration of housing project (1994).

Kondhpungar village (1994).

Mulberry plantation (1995).

Women involved in Sericulture (1995).

Villagers involved in Sericulture (1995).

Mulberry plantation (1995).

Training in processing of spices (1999).

Training in processing of spices (1999).

Ginger harvesting (2002).

Drilling of borewell (2002).

Grain bins provided by UNDP (2002).

Managing homegarden (2002).

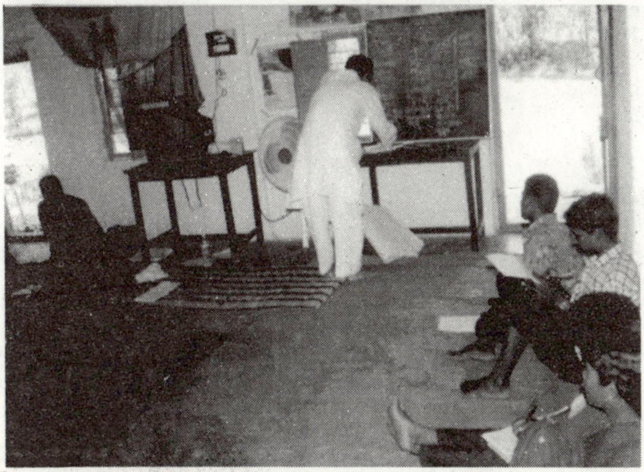

Leadership training programme at Jhimkiguda-Singru Hontal participated (2003).

Carrot harvesting (2003).

Deomali Women Federation (2003).

Farmers visiting Kondhpungar (2003).

Cashew nut plantation (2003).

Water storage tank under construction (2004).

Villagers being trained in jute bag making (2004).

SHG members from Andhra Pradesh visiting Kondhpungar (2004).

Coriander cultivation (2004).

ODAF evaluation (2004).

A view of check dam (2004).

Boko sakadi stream (2004).

Soil bunding (2004).

Education assistance to children (2004).

Capacity building training-Singru Hontal participated (2004).

ODAF evaluation (2004).

Water storage structure (2004).

Live fencing in homegardens (2005).

A view of forest in Kondhpungar (2005).

A view of forest in Kondhpungar (2005).

A view of forest in Kondhpungar (2005).

Mixed cultivation (2005).

Fruit trees planted in farm lands (2005).

Land preparation (2005).

Papaya plantation (2005).

Banana cultivation (2005).

Turmeric cultivation (2005).

Village mapping (2006).

Village mapping (2006).

Plate 1.22 Glimpses of Kondhpungar's journey.

Kondhpungar attracted numerous dignitaries from India and Abroad

2

Objectives, Concepts and Methods

2.1 Objectives of the Study

As noted in Chapter 1, the genesis of the study began from two workshops that were conducted by IRDWSI. The workshops among other aspects related to biodiversity conservation and livelihoods also deliberated on Biological Diversity Act (2002), with an emphasis on Chapter X of the act. This chapter deals with the constitution of Biodiversity Management Committees (BMC). In clause 41(i), it says, "Every local body shall constitute a Biodiversity Management Committee within its area for the purpose of promoting conservation, sustainable use and documentation of biological diversity including preservation of habitat, conservation of land races, folk varieties and cultivaters, domesticated stocks and breeds of animals and micro-organisms and chronicling of knowledge relating to biological diversity".

The study team discussed at length in the above provisions and observed that:

(i) the formal process of establishing State Biodiversity Board (SBB), and subsequently BMCs in the state of Orissa and the implementation of provisions of Biodiversity Act (2002), and Rules (2004) will take some more time to become operational;

(ii) a review of the strength and weaknesses of the human and financial resources available either in Kondhpungar village and IRDWSI revealed that neither in the village nor among the staff of IRDWSI-trained (formally qualified) biologist, taxonomist or ecologist were available to undertake various aspects mentioned in clause 41(i) of the act;

(iii) further available financial resources would not permit engaging such personnel in the study;

(iv) the existing institutional arrangements in the village needed clear perspective and strengthening for better management of the biodiversity; and

(v) in view of the above, it became clear to the study team that it will not be able to carry out all the provisions mentioned in clause 41 (i).

Therefore, the research team decided to undertake the study with the following objectives:

(i) To set up institutional arrangement in the village to promote conservation of existing domesticated and wild biodiversity occurring in all landscape and waterscape elements within the geographical boundary of the village;

(ii) To promote enhancement of biodiversity in degraded land and waterscape elements in the village;

(iii) To prepare a short-term and long-term biodiversity management plan to promote sustainable livelihoods; and

It may be emphasised that the above three objectives are integral part of clause-41(i).

2.2 Various Concepts Used

Having set the objectives of the study, the research team further deliberated about developing a shared understanding among all the team members regarding the various concepts to be used in the study. Essentially three main concepts have been used in the study:

- Biodiversity;
- Sustainable use of biodiversity; and
- Sustainable livelihoods.

Biodiversity

The Biological Diversity Act defines "biological diversity" as given in section 2(b) of the act—"biological diversity" means the variability among living organisms from all sources and the ecological complexes of which they are part and includes diversity within species or between species and of eco-systems. This definition is quite similar to the one proposed under the Convention of Biological Diversity, 1992.

The Act further defines biological resources in 2(c) as "biological resources" means plants, animals and micro-organisms are parts thereof, their genetic material and by-products (excluding value added products) with actual or potential use or value, but does not include human genetic material.

After detailed deliberations, and as mentioned above, in the absence of trained biologist or ecologist, it was decided that only the biodiversity (domesticated and wild) with which the people of Kondhpungar are familiar with (regarding various usages) will be documented, instead of all the biodiversity that exists in the village. The domesticated biodiversity with which the people are familiar is fairly complete and comprehensive in the study. In contrast, the wild biodiversity both flora and fauna is as expected rather incomplete; in particular ground flora, insects and invertebrates.

In short, the method used in the present study is primarily based on the knowledge and the relationship that the people of Kondhpungar have with the biodiversity occurring in their village.

Sustainable Use of Biodiversity

The study, has followed and adopted the definition given in Biodiversity Act (2002) under clause 2(o):

"Sustainable use" means the use of components of biological diversity in such manner and at such rate that does not lead to long-term decline of the biological diversity thereby maintaining its potential to meet the needs and aspirations of present and future generations.

Sustainable Livelihoods

Sustainable livelihoods has received enormous attention during the last two decades. There are a number of definitions proposed by different scholars and organisations. The word Livelihood can be and has been used in many different ways. Although it is beyond the scope of the present study to present a detailed review of the literature on sustainable livelihoods, it is appropriate that a brief description of some of the definitions widely used in the development of the sector is presented here.

Definition Advanced by Department for International Development (DFID)

"A livelihood comprises the capabilities, assets (including both material and social resources) and activities required for a means of living. A livelihood is sustainable when it can cope with and recover from stresses and shocks and maintain or enhance its capabilities and assets both now and in the future, while not undermining the natural resource base" [Adopted from Chambers R and G. Conway (1992). *Sustainable rural livelihoods: Practical concepts for the 21st century*. IDS discussion paper 296. Brighton: IDS]. In Fig. 2.1 the essential features of sustainable livelihoods framework as used by DIFID are given.

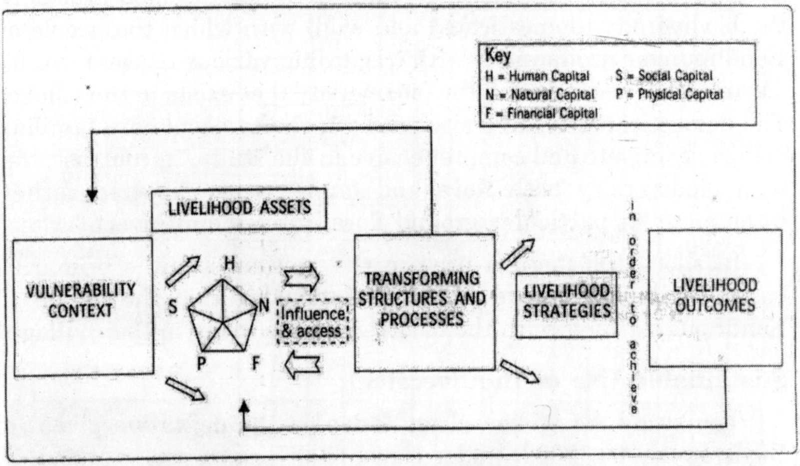

Fig. 2.1. Essential Features of Sustainable Livelihood Framework as Developed by DFID.

Definition Advanced by Oxfam UK

By a livelihood Oxfam means how people make their living. People need to have reliable and permanent sources of food, income and employment. Oxfam's livelihood programme seeks to help poor people have a sustainable livelihood, including making a living, living in a safe environment, with housing, clean water and sufficient food.

Definition Advanced by WWF

Sustainable livelihoods is a holistic approach to conservation which enables people and communities to analyse, decide and act to achieve fair and sustainable management and use of natural resources, and improved individual and community well-being.

An analysis of the various definitions on sustainable livelihoods given above show that there are a lot of similarities between these definitions, though they differ often in the degree of emphasis about certain features of sustainable livelihoods. In the present study, we have adopted in principle all the above definitions with an emphasis on the definition proposed by DFID. In the present study however, of the five capitals given in Fig. 2.1, emphasis was given to human capital, natural capital and social capital.

2.3 Methodology Adopted

The methodology use in the documentation of biodiversity occurring in different areas of the village had the following components.

(i) Formation of study team: The first step was to constitute the research team with advisors and the support team. The team thus, constituted is given earlier in the document.

(ii) Capacity building: The next step was to build the capacity of the study team to undertake biodiversity documentation process. For this purpose a selected number of men, women and youth of the village and the staff of IRDWSI were trained in various aspects of documenting the biodiversity by KCM. The topics covered were:

- Drawing of village map,
- Delineation of biodiversity bearing areas in the village,
- Determining the status of land and waterscape elements,
- Conducting group discussions,
- Designing data collection formats,
- Development of microplans.

Plate 2.1. Land and Waterscape Map of Kondhpungar Being Drawn.

(iii) Sub group formation: Depending on the nature of the habitat and the capacities of the study team, a few sub-groups were formed comprising people of the village and the staff of IRDWSI.

Plate 2.2. Mapping of Biodiversity Bearing Areas in Kondhpungar.

Data collection: The following four methods were used in inventorising biodiversity:

- *Field observation of all the landscape and waterscape elements*: Several field visits were made to all the biodiversity bearing areas in the village by different research teams. They combined the well-known method of *walk, talk, and see.* The local knowledgeable persons play a critical role in the identification and usages of plants and animals occurring in the village.
- *Group discussions*: After visiting each of the biodiversity bearing areas in the village, the team shared the findings with the full research team; doubts were clarified, gaps identified and future field strategy planned.

- *Interviews with individual families*: Detail discussions were held with the members of each family with regard to the use of biodiversity, pattern of consumption at home and nature and extent of products marketed.

Plate 2.3. Preparation of This Book Being Discussed.

- *Interviews with knowledgeable persons*: There are a number of knowledgeable persons in the village, detailed interviews were held with them to document special usages of biodiversity like medicinal use of plants etc.

(iv) Nomenclature: The names of biodiversity occurring in the village have been recorded wherever possible in three languages:

(i) Kuvi is mother tongue of the people of Kondhpungar;

(ii) Oriya is official language of the state of Orissa; and

(iii) Common English names.

(v) Validation of nomenclature: In 2003 Raghunandan Velenkar on behalf of the Indian Institute of Forest Management, Bhopal and IRDWSI had undertaken a detailed floristic study of the flowering plants in the village. The same has been used in establishing scientific names of the plants in this study. As will be seen in the subsequent chapters, the scientific identification and validation of a large number of wild plants and animals is incomplete. It may be emphasised here that for the purpose of use of this document by the people of Kondhpungar, in principle it is not necessary to know the scientific names of the biodiversity occurring in the village. For the management of biodiversity in the village, it is good enough to have a proper documentation of the biodiversity in respect of its distribution in the village, its conservation status, its contribution to the livelihoods of the people and future opportunities.

(vi) Duration of Study: The materials presented in this document were gathered from late September 2006 to the end of December 2006. Although the intensive field work was over by December, 2006 certain information continued to be gathered until as late as August, 2008.

(vii) Photo Documentation: A number of visits were made by the members of the research team in different seasons to document the photos:

- People in the village
- Agricultural implements, musical instruments, hunting implements,
- Houses,
- Infrastructure and amenities,
- Domesticated animals,
- Domesticated agricultural biodiversity including crops, vegetables and trees.
- Documentation of agricultural and horticultural practices.
- Documentation of wild plants and animals.
- Documentation of aquatic biodiversity.
- Status of various land and waterscape elements.

Collections of photographic materials at IRDWSI were scanned and relevant photographs taken in the past were selected and included in the document.

3

Biodiversity Bearing Areas in Kondhpungar

3.1 Introduction

This Chapter has two extensive sections. Section 3.2 lists relevant details of the various biodiversity bearing areas in the village, and in Section 3.3 data for each of the elements such as location, area and inventory of biodiversity have been given.

3.2 Identification of Biodiversity Bearing Areas

A team of youth, men and women of the village with staff of IRDWSI initially prepared a rough map delineating biodiversity bearing areas in Kondhpungar. The team then surveyed the village and prepared a final map given in Fig. 3.1. The map shows all the identified biodiversity bearing landscape and waterscape elements in the village. The map drawn is not to scale and the sizes of areas are also approximate. In Table 3.1 the names are in Kuvi; the mother tongue of the people of Kondhpungar, as well as in Oriya where every relevant and the English names of all the identified landscape and waterscape elements. In addition, the approximate size of the areas is also given. Further details are given separately for each of the elements in Chapter 4.

It may be noted that in the individual 20 landscapes and waterscape elements the names of the biodiversity that exists are given mostly in Oriya language. In Appendices 2-5 wherever possible the names are given in Oriya, Kuvi, English and as well as scientific names of domesticated and wild biodiversity found in the village are also given.

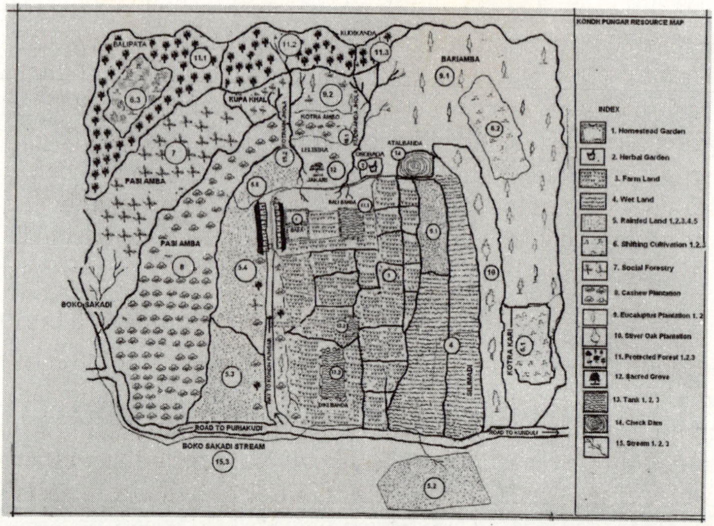

Fig. 3.1. Landscape and Waterscape Biodiversity Bearing Areas Delineated in the Village.

Table 3.1. Landscape and Waterscape Biodiversity Bearing Areas Delineated in the Village

Sl. No.	*English*	*Kuvi*	*Oriya*	*Area (acres)*	*Ha*
Landscape elements					
1.	Homestead gardens	Bada	Ghoro badi	0.975	0.394
2.	Herbal gardens	Osobada	Ousodho bogicha	0.15	0.06
3.	Farm lands	Gudia kha	Bogicha	9.9	4
4.	Wetland	Sabaiyan	Bilojomi	6.98	2.82
5.	Rainfed lands	Saria sabaiyan	Dhipojomi	12.9	5.22
6.	Shifting cultivation	Horkha kamma	Pahadojomi chaso	18.50*	7.5
6.1.	Kotra kari	Kotra kari			
6.2.	Bariamba	Bariamba			
6.3.	Balipata	Balipata			
7.	Social forestry plantations		Samajiko bonikorono	60	24.28
8.	Cashew plantations		Kaju Brukhya ropono	18	7.28
9.	Eucalyptus plantations		Niliogri chaso	45	18.21

Contd...

Sl. No.	*English*	*Kuvi*	*Oriya*	*Area (acres)*	*Ha*
9.1.	Kotra kari	Kotra kari		25	
9.2.	Kudi kanda	Kudi kanda		20	
10.	Silver oak plantations		Rupagocho chara ropono	3	1.21
11.	Protected forest		Surokhito jongolo	105	42.5
11.1.	Balipata	Balipata		55	
11.2.	Puligunta	Puligunta		20	
11.3.	Kudi kanda	Kudi kanda		30	
12.	Sacred groves	Jakari	Pujostoli	0.02	0.008
Waterscape elements					
13.	Tank 1	Balibanda	Bondho		0.014
14.	Tank 2	Baminiband ha	Bondho	25 m^2	
15.	Tank 3	Dikibanda	Bondho	500 m^2	
16.	Check dam	Atalbanda	Adibondho	70 m^2	
17.	Streams		Jhoro		
17.1.	Kotra jhola	Kotra jhola			
17.2.	Kudi kanda jhola	Kudi kanda jhola			
17.3.	Boko sakadi	Boko sakadi			
Other elements					
18.	Road side plantations		Rastakodo brukhyarop ono		
19.	Domesticated animals		Gruhopalito posu		

*Actual area cultivated. Although the total area under shifting cultivation is much more, the area put under shifting cultivation, however varies considerably between the years.

3.3 Description of Biodiversity Bearing Areas

As noted in Table 3.1 there are in all 20 distinct areas in the village that harbour domesticated and/or wild biodiversity. Out of these, 12 elements pertain to landscapes; several of these occur in more than one patch. If these patches are counted separately then the number of landscape elements increases to 17. In addition, biodiversity also occurs along the roadside in the village. There are seven waterscape elements that harbour aquatic fauna and flora. Following are descriptions of the observed biodiversity in each of the elements described above.

3.3.1 Landscape Biodiversity Bearing Areas

3.3.1.1 Homestead Gardens

The village has a strong tradition of having homestead gardens called *Badas*. All *Badas* are privately owned and managed. In these *Badas* a variety of vegetables, fruit trees as well as other useful plants are grown. The *Badas* are mostly live fenced. The species used as fence include *Sidi, Jiu, Siju, Bilia Kanta, Lantana,* etc. The domesticated fowl, dog and occasionally other domesticated animals also use *Badas*. Several wild animals that include mammals, reptiles and birds are also often sighted in *Badas*. Some of the wild animals like *Bhalu (sloth bear), Baria (wild boar), Salim (porcupine)*, often damage cultivated crops. The *Badas* are primarily looked-after by women and children, men usually provide a supportive role. The *Badas* of a majority of the households contribute significantly to its annual income.

Variation in Size of *Badas*

The distribution of the size of *Badas* in 15 households in the village is given in Table 3.2 and Fig. 3.2. Except for one household, the remaining 14 own small *Badas.* Two households (serial number. 1 and 15) jointly own and manage a *Bada* measuring 0.025 acres. The area of *Badas* among the households varies from 0.025 to 0.20 acres. The total area under Badas in the village is 0.394 ha.

Table 3.2. Size Distribution of Badas in 15 Households

Homestead size (acres)	*No. of Households*	*Percentage*
0	1	6.6
0.01–0.05	6	40.0
0.06–0.09	4	26.7
>0.09	4	26.7
Total	**15**	**100**

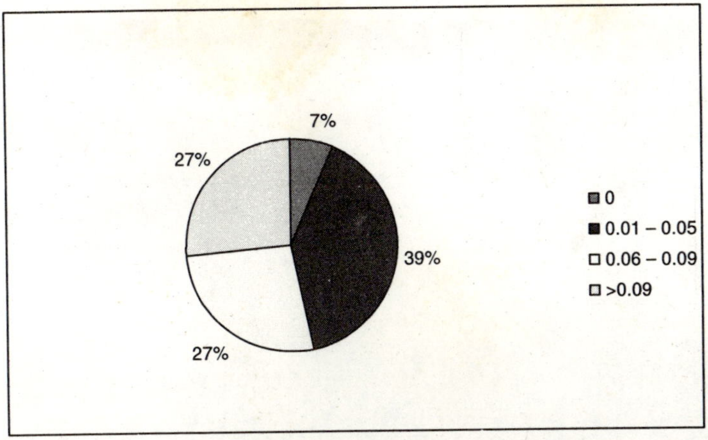

Fig. 3.2. Size Distributions of Badas in 15 Households.

Biodiversity in Individual Homestead Gardens

In this section are given, separate details for each of the 14 households, such as the house hold numbers (corresponding with Fig. 1.2), name of the head of the household, area of *Bada*, list of domesticated plants and animals, and wild animals sighted. Wherever relevant the season i.e. *kharif* and *rabi* is also given along with the cultivated plants.

Plate 3.1. Banana Cultivation in Home Gardens.

Plate 3.2. Pomegranate Cultivation in Home Gardens.

Household No. 1

Name of the head of household: Ruhini Khora

Area of *Bada*: 0.025 acres

(a) Domesticated Plants

(i) Trees

Sl. No.	*Name*	*Sl. No.*	*Name*
1.	Ambo	6.	Sapta
2.	Bileikanta	7.	Semili
3.	Jafra	8.	Sitaphol
4.	Kodoli	9.	Solop
5.	Panasa		

(ii) Vegetables and other plants

Sl. No.	Name	Growing season	
		Kharif	Rabi
1.	Dhania	✓	✓
2.	Gajor		✓
3.	Gendu phul		✓
4.	Guanr		✓
5.	Kakudi	✓	
6.	Rasuno		✓
7.	Saru	✓	
8.	Simbo	✓	

(b) Domesticated Animals

Name	Cow	Bullock	Pig	Sheep	Goat	Hen	Dog	Cat	Total
Numbers	0	0	0	0	0	0	0	0	0

(c) Wild Animals Sighted in Homestead Garden

Sl. No.	Name	Sl. No.	Name
1.	Salim	7.	Kolia
2.	Bag	8.	Kua
3.	Bariha	9.	Pandka
4.	Chia	10.	Rabbit
5.	Golia	11.	Rambi
6.	Gunduri	12.	Sindi katra

Household No. 2

Name of the head of household: Malti Khora

Area of *Bada*: 0

(a) Domesticated plants - nil

(b) Domesticated animals - nil

Household No. 3

Name of the head of household: Kesu Hontal

Area of *Bada*: 0.10 acres

(a) Domesticated Plants

(i) Trees

Sl.No.	*Name*	*Sl.No.*	*Name*
1.	Ambo	4.	Kodoli
2.	Bileikanta	5.	Sajna
3.	Kamala	6.	Sapta

(ii) Vegetables and Other Plants

Sl. No.	*Name*	*Growing season*	
		Kharif	*Rabi*
1.	Baigonoo	✓	✓
2.	Bhejiri	✓	✓
3.	Bilati Baigonoo	✓	✓
4.	Boit alu	✓	
5.	Bunda beans	✓	
6.	Ganti kobi		✓
7.	Janhi	✓	
8.	Khosla sago	✓	
9.	Palango sago	✓	
10.	Saru	✓	
11.	Simbo	✓	

(b) Domesticated Animals

Name	*Cow*	*Bullock*	*Pig*	*Sheep*	*Goat*	*Hen*	*Dog*	*Cat*	*Total*
Numbers	0	1	2	0	0	2	0	1	0

(c) Wild Animals Sighted in Homestead Garden

Sl. No.	*Name*	*Sl.No.*	*Name*
1.	Bago	7.	Kua
2.	Bariha	8.	Pandka
3.	Chia	9.	Thekua
4.	Gholia	10.	Rambi
5.	Gunduri	11.	Salim
6.	Kolia	12.	Sindikatri

Plate 3.3. Lemon Cultivation in Home Gardens.

Plate 3.4. Luxurient Fruiting of Jackfruit in Farm Land.

Household No. 4

Name of the head of household: Luke Hontal

Area of *Bada*: 0.04 acres

(a) Domesticated Plants

(i) Trees

Sl. No.	*Name*	*Sl. No.*	*Name*
1.	Ambo	5.	Jamkoli
2.	Amrutbhanda	6.	Khojuri
3.	Bileikanta	7.	Panasa
4.	Jafra		

(ii) Vegetables and other plants

Sl No.	*Name*	*Growing season*	
		Kharif	*Rabi*
1.	Ada	✓	
2.	Banda kobi		✓
3.	Boit alu	✓	
4.	Dhania		✓
5.	Gajor		✓
6.	Gendu phul		✓
7.	Khomb alu		✓
8.	Kolora	✓	✓
9.	Mati konda	✓	
10.	Phul kobi		✓
11.	Saru	✓	
12.	Simili konda	✓	
13.	Soriso		✓

(b) Domesticated Animals

Name	*Cow*	*Bullock*	*Pig*	*Sheep*	*Goat*	*Hen*	*Dog*	*Cat*	*TOTAL*
Numbers	0	0	0	0	2	6	1	0	9

(c) Wild Animals Sighted in Homestead Garden

Sl. No.	*Name*	*Sl. No.*	*Name*
1.	Bani	12.	Kau
2.	Bengo	13.	Kolia
3.	Bhalu	14.	Mandal
4.	Chiti	15.	Musa
5.	Dhadka	16.	Nago
6.	Dhamana	17.	Neulo
7.	Endua	18.	Pandka
8.	Gunduri	19.	Pimpudi
9.	Janda	20.	Saru nago
10.	Jea	21.	Thekua
11.	Jhintika		

Household No. 5

Name of the head of household: Chandra Hontal

Area of *Bada*: 0.04 acres

(a) Domesticated Plants

(i) Trees

Sl. No.	*Name*	*Sl.No.*	*Name*
1.	Bileikanta	6.	Mandar
2.	Borda	7.	Panasa
3.	Jafra	8.	Solop
4.	Karanjo	9.	Toba
5.	Kodoli	10.	Tutkoli

(ii) Vegetables and Other Plants

Sl. No.	*Name*	*Growing season*	
		Kharif	*Rabi*
1.	Ada	✓	
2.	Banda kobi		✓
3.	Bhendi		✓
4.	Bhejiri	✓	
5.	Dhania		✓
6.	Gajor		✓

Sl. No.	Name	Growing season	
		Kharif	Rabi
7.	Khada sago	✓	✓
8.	Khomb alu	✓	
9	Kolora	✓	✓
10.	Makka	✓	
11.	Maricho	✓	✓
12.	Palango sago	✓	✓
13.	Phul kobi		✓
14.	Rasuno		✓
15.	Saru	✓	
16.	Simili konda	✓	

(b) Domesticated Animals

Name	*Cow*	*Bullock*	*Pig*	*Sheep*	*Goat*	*Hen*	*Dog*	*Cat*	*Total*
Numbers	0	0	0	0	0	1	1	0	2

(c) Wild Animals Sighted in Homestead Garden

Sl No.	*Name*	*Sl. No.*	*Name*
1.	Bani	12.	Kau
2.	Bengo	13.	Kolia
3.	Bhalu	14.	Mandal
4.	Chiti	15.	Musa
5.	Dhadka	16.	Nago
6.	Dhamana	17.	Neulo
7.	Endua	18.	Pandka
8.	Gunduri	19.	Pimpudi
9.	Janda	20.	Saru nago
10.	Jea	21.	Thekua
11.	Jhintika		

Household No. 6

Name of the head of household: Singru Hontal

Area of *Bada*: 0.05 acres

(a) Domesticated Plants

(i) Trees

Sl. No.	*Name*	*Sl. No.*	*Name*
1.	Ambo	11.	Kodoli
2.	Amrutbhanda	12.	Kontagocho
3.	Baunso	13.	Lembu
4.	Bileikanta	14.	Murga
5.	Borda	15.	Niligiri
6.	Chitramul	16.	Panasa
7.	Dalimbo	17.	Rupa
8.	Gombari	18.	Sajna
9.	Jamkoli	19.	Solop
10.	Joda	20.	Tua

(ii) Vegetables and Other Plants

Sl No.	*Name*	*Growing season*	
		Kharif	*Rabi*
1.	Bhendi		✓
2.	Boit alu	✓	
3.	Ganti kobi	✓	✓
4.	Gendu phul	✓	
5.	Holdi	✓	
6.	Janhi	✓	
7.	Kunduri	✓	✓
8.	Mirlo	✓	✓
9.	Saru	✓	
10.	Simili konda	✓	

(b) Domesticated Animals

Name	*Cow*	*Bullock*	*Pig*	*Sheep*	*Goat*	*Hen*	*Dog*	*Cat*	*Total*
Numbers	0	0	0	0	0	5	1	0	6

(c) Wild Animals Sighted in Homestead Garden

Sl No.	*Name*	*Sl. No.*	*Name*
1.	Bani	12.	Kau
2.	Bengo	13.	Kolia
3.	Bhalu	14.	Mandal
4.	Chiti	15.	Musa
5.	Dhadka	16.	Nago
6.	Dhamana	17.	Neulo
7.	Endua	18.	Pandka
8.	Gunduri	19.	Pimpudi
9.	Janda	20.	Saru nago
10.	Jea	21.	Thekua
11.	Jhintika		

Household No. 7

Name of the head of household: Kamblu Hontal

Area of *Bada*: 0.03 acres

(a) Domesticated Plants

(i) Trees

Sl. No.	*Name*	*Sl. No.*	*Name*
1.	Ambo	6.	Panasa
2.	Amrutbhanda	7.	Saguan
3.	Baunso	8.	Sitaphol
4.	Bileikanta	9.	Solop
5.	Borda	10.	Tentuli

(ii) Vegetables and Other Plants

Sl. No.	*Name*	*Growing season*	
		Kharif	*Rabi*
1.	Banda kobi		✓
2.	Bhendi	✓	✓
3.	Boit alu	✓	
4.	Dhania		✓
5.	Gajor		✓
6.	Gendu phul		✓
7.	Holdi	✓	
8.	Kolora	✓	✓
9.	Maricho	✓	✓
10.	Mirlo	✓	✓
11.	Saru	✓	
12.	Simili konda	✓	

(b) Domesticated Animals

Name	*Cow*	*Bullock*	*Pig*	*Sheep*	*Goat*	*Hen*	*Dog*	*Cat*	*Total*
Numbers	0	4	0	0	4	3	0	0	11

(c) Wild Animals Sighted in Homestead Garden

Sl. No.	*Name*	*Sl. No.*	*Name*
1.	Bani	12.	Kau
2.	Bengo	13.	Kolia
3.	Bhalu	14.	Mandal
4.	Chiti	15.	Musa
5.	Dhadka	16.	Nago
6.	Dhamana	17.	Neulo
7.	Endua	18.	Pandka
8.	Gunduri	19.	Pimpudi
9.	Janda	20.	Saru nago
10.	Jea	21.	Thekua
11.	Jhintika		

Household No. 8

Name of the head of household: Ramo Ch. Hontal

Area of *Bada*: 0.06 acres

(a) Domesticated Plants

(i) Trees

Sl. No.	*Name*	*Sl. No.*	*Name*
1.	Ambo	7.	Khojuri
2.	Bileikanta	8.	Kodoli
3.	Borda	9.	Mandar
4.	Dalimbo	10.	Panasa
5.	Joda	11.	Sajna
6.	Karanjo	12.	Toba

(ii) Vegetables and Other Plants

Sl. No.	*Name*	*Growing season*	
		Kharif	*Rabi*
1.	Ada	✓	
2.	Boit alu	✓	
3.	Guanr	✓	
4.	Jhota	✓	
5.	Lau		✓
6.	Malo beans	✓	✓
7.	Mati konda	✓	
8.	Mula	✓	
9.	Saru	✓	
10.	Soriso		✓

(b) Domesticated Animals

Name	*Cow*	*Bullock*	*Pig*	*Sheep*	*Goat*	*Hen*	*Dog*	*Cat*	*Total*
Numbers	0	0	0	0	6	10	1	1	18

(c) Wild Animals Sighted in Homestead Garden

Sl. No.	*Name*	*Sl. No.*	*Name*
1.	Ada gundicha	13.	Kankada bicha
2.	Bago	14.	Kirngeli
3.	Baria	15.	Kiskeri
4.	Bauli	16.	Kolia
5.	Bhalu	17.	Mayur
6.	Chitti	18.	Musa
7.	Dhamana	19.	Pandaka
8.	Endua	20.	Paranda
9.	Girna	21.	Parjapati
10.	Gunduri	22.	Pecha
11.	Gungi	23.	Rambi
12.	Jea	24.	Tekor Machi

Household No. 9

Name of the head of household: Sapura Hontal

Area of *Bada*: 0.08 acres

(a) **Domesticated Plants**

(i) Trees

Sl. No.	*Name*	*Sl. No.*	*Name*
1.	Baunso	7.	Pijuli
2.	Bileikanta	8.	Sajna
3.	Khojuri	9.	Solop
4.	Kodoli	10.	Toba
5.	Kofi	11.	Tutkoli
6.	Nadia		

(ii) Vegetables and Other Plants

Sl. No.	*Name*	*Growing season*	
		Kharif	*Rabi*
1.	Ada	✓	
2.	Kakudi		✓
3.	Khosla sago	✓	✓
4.	Mirlo	✓	✓
5.	Simili konda	✓	

(b) Domesticated Animals

Name	*Cow*	*Bullock*	*Pig*	*Sheep*	*Goat*	*Hen*	*Dog*	*Cat*	*Total*
Numbers	6	1	0	3	0	1	0	0	11

(c) Wild Animals Sighted in Homestead Garden

Sl. No.	*Name*	*Sl. No.*	*Name*
1.	Rambi	11.	Girna
2.	Pandaka	12.	Kiskeri
3.	Kau	13.	Jhịntika
4.	Chia pata	14.	Endu
5.	Tumba	15.	Nago
6.	Pubuli	16.	Ada gundicha
7.	Paranda	17.	Mandal
8.	Dhandia	18.	Kolia
9.	Jea	19.	Kosa neheudi
10.	Bengo		

Household No. 10

Name of the head of household: Hari Hontal

Area of *Bada*: 0.06 acres

(a) Domesticated Plants

(i) Trees

Sl. No.	*Name*	*Sl. No.*	*Name*
1.	Amrutbhanda	8.	Kodoli
2.	Bileikanta	9.	Kontagocho
3.	Borokoli	10.	Panasa
4.	Dimri	11.	Pijuli
5.	Jamkoli	12.	Solop
6.	Karanjo	13.	Toba
7.	Khojuri	14.	Tutkoli

(ii) Vegetable and Other Plants

Sl. No.	*Name*	*Growing season*	
		Kharif	*Rabi*
1.	Ada	3	
2.	Banda kobi		3
3.	Boit alu	3	
4.	Gajor	3	
5.	Malo beans		3
6.	Mirlo	3	3
7.	Motor channa		3
8.	Saru	3	
9.	Simili konda	3	

(b) Domesticated Animals

Name	*Cow*	*Bullock*	*Pig*	*Sheep*	*Goat*	*Hen*	*Dog*	*Cat*	*Total*
Numbers	2	3	0	0	3	2	0	0	10

(c) Wild Animals Sighted in Homestead Garden

Sl. No.	*Name*	*Sl. No.*	*Name*
1.	Baria	8.	Kochoti
2.	Chabara	9.	Maraa
3.	Chia pota	10.	Musa
4.	Dhamana	11.	Nago
5.	Endua	12.	Pandaka
6.	Gharachatia	13.	Salim
7.	Kebda		

Household No. 11

Name of the head of household: Siara Hontal

Area of *Bada*: 0.09 acres

(a) Domesticated Plants

(i) Trees

Sl. No.	*Name*	*Sl. No.*	*Name*
1.	Ambo	6.	Niligiri
2.	Amrutbhanda	7.	Panasa
3.	Bileikanta	8.	Pijuli
4.	Kodoli	9.	Solop
5.	Kontagocho		

(ii) Vegetable and Other Plants

Sl. No.	*Name*	*Growing season*	
		Kharif	*Rabi*
1.	Banda kobi		✓
2.	Boit alu	✓	
3.	Dhania		✓
4.	Gajor		✓
5.	Kolora	✓	✓
6.	Phul kobi		✓
7.	Saru	✓	
8.	Simili konda	✓	

(b) Domesticated Animals

Name	*Cow*	*Bullock*	*Pig*	*Sheep*	*Goat*	*Hen*	*Dog*	*Cat*	*Total*
Numbers	2	6	0	1	3	3	1	0	16

(c) Wild Animals Sighted in Homestead Garden

Sl. No.	*Name*	*Sl. No.*	*Name*
1.	Bani	12.	Kau
2.	Bengo	13.	Kolia
3.	Bhalu	14.	Mandal
4.	Chiti	15.	Musa
5.	Dhadka	16.	Nago
6.	Dhamana	17.	Neulo
7.	Endua	18.	Pandka
8.	Gunduri	19.	Pimpudi
9.	Janda	20.	Sahin
10.	Jea	21.	Saru nago
11.	Jhintika	22.	Thekua

Household No. 12

Name of the head of household: Boli Hontal

Area of Bada: 0.10 acres

(a) Domesticated Plants

(i) Trees

Sl. No.	*Name*	*Sl. No.*	*Name*
1.	Ambo	5.	Kodoli
2.	Baunso	6.	Kontagocho
3.	Bileikanta	7.	Panasa
4.	Jafra		

(ii) Vegetable and Other Plants

Sl. No.	*Name*	*Growing season*	
		Kharif	*Rabi*
1.	Ada	✓	
2.	Banda kobi		✓
3.	Boit alu	✓	
4.	Dhania		✓
5.	Gajor		✓
6.	Holdi	✓	
7.	Jhudonga	✓	
8.	Kolora	✓	✓
9.	Malo beans	✓	✓
10.	Paluo	✓	
11.	Phul kobi		✓
12.	Saru	✓	
13.	Simbo	✓	
14.	Simili konda	✓	

(b) Domesticated Animals

Name	*Cow*	*Bullock*	*Pig*	*Sheep*	*Goat*	*Hen*	*Dog*	*Cat*	*Total*
Numbers	1	2	2	0	10	3	1	0	19

(c) Wild Animals Sighted in Homestead Garden

Sl. No.	*Name*	*Sl. No.*	*Name*
1.	Bani	13.	Kau
2.	Bengo	14.	Kolia
3.	Bhalu	15.	Mandal
4.	Chiti	16.	Musa
5.	Dhadka	17.	Nago
6.	Dhamana	18.	Neulo
7.	Endua	19.	Pandka
8.	Gunduri	20.	Pimpudi
9.	Janda	21.	Sahin
10.	Jea	22.	Saru nago
11.	Jhintika	23.	Thekua
12.	Kankada bicha		

Household No. 14

Name of the head of household: Lamxidhar Hontal

Area of Bada: 0.10 acres

(a) Domesticated Plants

(i) Trees

Sl. No.	*Name*	*Sl. No.*	*Name*
1.	Bileikanta	6.	Pijuli
2.	Joda	7.	Sapta
3.	Khojuri	8.	Sitaphol
4.	Kodoli	9.	Tentuli
5.	Panasa		

(ii) Vegetable and Other Plants

Sl. No.	*Name*	*Growing season*	
		Kharif	*Rabi*
1.	Boit alu	✓	
2.	China badam	✓	
3.	Gendu phul	✓	✓
4.	Janhi	✓	✓

Sl. No.	*Name*	*Growing season*	
		Kharif	*Rabi*
5.	Makka	✓	
6.	Mula		✓
7.	Saru	✓	
8.	Simbo	✓	
9.	Simili konda	✓	

(b) Domesticated Animals

Name	*Cow*	*Bullock*	*Pig*	*Sheep*	*Goat*	*Hen*	*Dog*	*Cat*	*Total*
Num-Bers	1	2	0	9	3	5	0	0	20

(c) Wild Animals Sighted in Homestead Garden

Sl. No.	*Name*	*Sl. No.*	*Name*
1.	Bago	7.	Kua
2.	Bariha	8.	Pandka
3.	Chia	9.	Rambi
4.	Golia	10.	Sahin
5.	Gunduri	11.	Sindi katra
6.	Kolia	12.	Thekua

Household No. 15

Name of the head of household: Dadeya Khora

Area of *Bada*: 0.025 acres

Domesticated animals: Nil

Remarks: Dadeya Khora and Ruhuni Khora (household No. 1) jointly own the *Bada*. Details of domesticated plants and wild animals sighted in their *bada* have been given under household No. 1.

Biodiversity in Homestead Gardens: Salient Features and Summary

In the preceding section, the type of plants grown in *Badas* of every household, domestic animals maintained by the households, and wild animals sighted in *Badas* was given. In the following section an analysis of biodiversity found in *Badas* is provided. The materials have been presented under the following four heads:

(i) Trees grown in *Badas*;

(ii) Vegetables and other plants grown in *Badas*;

(iii) Wild plants found in *Badas*; and

(iv) Wild animals sighted in *Badas*.

(i) Trees grown in *Badas*

Table 3.3 gives a complete list of all the tree spices found in individual *Badas* during the period September 2006 and May 2007 when the field observations for the present study were made. From this Tables 3.4 and 3.5, the following main features emerge:

(a) Altogether 37 different tree species are grown in 14 *Bada* lands covering a rather small area measuring only 0.394 ha;

(b) Among the 14 households that own *Badas* the number of tree species grown varies from 0 to 19. Over 50 per cent of the households have grown between six to 10 species. Only four households (27 per cent) have grown more than 10 species (Table 3.4 and Fig. 3.3).

(c) In Table 3.5 and Fig. 3.4 are given the names and frequent occurrence of five tree species that occur in more than 50 per cent of the households. The most preferred species is *Bileikanta* found in 86.7 per cent households. It is used as a live fence. This is followed by *Kodoli* and *Panasa* (66.7 per

Table 3.3: Inventory of Domesticated Tree Species Occurring in Homesteads

Sl. No.	*Name in Oriya*	*H1*	*H2*	*H3*	*H4*	*H5*	*H6*	*H7*	*H8*	*H9*	*H10*	*H11*	*H12*	*H13*	*H14*	*H15*	*Total*	
																	No.	*Percentage*
1.	Ambo	✓		✓	✓		✓	✓	✓			✓	✓	✓			9	60
2.	Amrutbhanda				✓		✓	✓			✓	✓					5	33.33
3.	Baunso						✓	✓		✓				✓			4	26.66
4.	Bileikanta	✓		✓	✓	✓	✓	✓	✓	✓	✓	✓	✓	✓	✓		13	86.66
5.	Borda					✓	✓	✓	✓								4	26.66
6.	Borokoli										✓						1	6.66
7.	Chitramul						✓										1	6.66
8.	Dalimbo						✓		✓								2	13.33
9.	Dimri										✓						1	6.66
10.	Gombari						✓										1	6.66
11.	Jafra	✓			✓	✓								✓			4	26.66

Sl. No.	*Name in Oriya*	*H1*	*H2*	*H3*	*H4*	*H5*	*H6*	*H7*	*H8*	*H9*	*H10*	*H11*	*H12*	*H13*	*H14*	*H15*	*Total*	
																	No.	*Percentage*
12.	Jamkoli				✓		✓				✓						3	20
13.	Joda						✓		✓						✓		3	20
14.	Kamala			✓													1	6.66
15.	Karanjo					✓			✓		✓		✓				4	26.66
16.	Khojuri				✓				✓	✓	✓				✓		5	33.33
17.	Kodoli	✓		✓		✓	✓		✓	✓	✓	✓		✓	✓		10	66.66
18.	Kofi									✓							1	6.66
19.	Kontagocho						✓				✓	✓	✓	✓			5	33.33
20.	Lembu						✓										1	6.66
21.	Mandar					✓			✓								2	13.33
22.	Murga						✓										1	6.66

Sl. No.	*Name in Oriya*	*H1*	*H2*	*H3*	*H4*	*H5*	*H6*	*H7*	*H8*	*H9*	*H10*	*H11*	*H12*	*H13*	*H14*	*H15*	*Total*	
																	No.	*Percentage*
23.	Nadia									✓							1	6.66
24.	Niligiri						✓					✓					2	13.33
25.	Panasa	✓			✓	✓	✓	✓	✓		✓	✓		✓	✓		10	66.66
26.	Pijuli									✓	✓	✓			✓		4	26.66
27.	Rupa						✓										1	6.66
28.	Saguan							✓									1	6.66
29.	Sajna			✓			✓		✓	✓							4	26.66
30.	Sapta	✓		✓											✓		3	20
31.	Semili	✓															1	6.66
32.	Sitaphol	✓						✓							✓		3	20
33.	Solop	✓				✓	✓	✓		✓	✓	✓	✓				8	53.33

Sl. No.	*Name in Oriya*	*H1*	*H2*	*H3*	*H4*	*H5*	*H6*	*H7*	*H8*	*H9*	*H10*	*H11*	*H12*	*H13*	*H14*	*H15*	*Total*	
																	No.	*Percentage*
34.	Tentuli							✓							✓		2	13.33
35.	Toba					✓			✓	✓	✓						4	26.66
36.	Tua						✓										1	6.66
37.	Tutkoli					✓				✓	✓						3	20
	Total	**9**	**0**	**6**	**7**	**10**	**20**	**10**	**12**	**11**	**14**	**9**	**5**	**7**	**9**	**0**		

Note: Household No. 2 does not posses a *Bada;* household Nos. 16 and 1 jointly manage a *Bada*.

Table 3.4: Distribution of Number of Tree Species in Badas

Range of tree species grown	*No.*	*Percentage*
0	2	13
1 – 5	1	7
6 – 10	8	53
11 – 15	3	20
> 15	1	7
Total	**15**	**100**

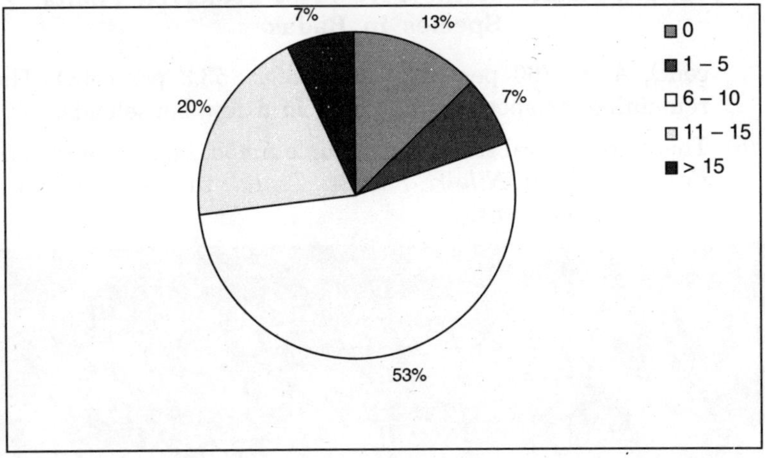

Fig. 3.3. Distribution of Number of Tree Spices in Badas.

Table 3.5: Names of the Five Most Preferred Plants Species in Badas

Sl. No.	*Plant species*	*No of households*	*Percentage*
1.	Bileikanta	13	86.7
2.	Kodoli	10	66.7
3.	Panasa	10	66.7
4.	Ambo	9	60.0
5.	Solop	8	53.3

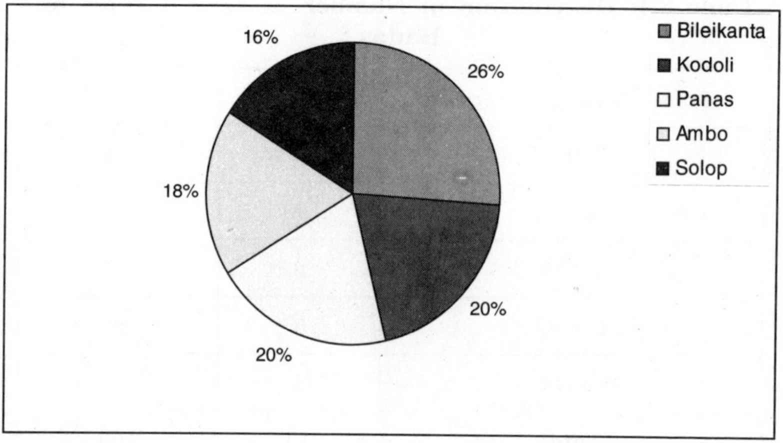

Fig. 3.4. Names of the Five Most Preferred Plants Species in Badas.

cent), *Ambo* (60 per cent) and *Solop* (53.3 per cent). The remaining 32 species occur only in a few households.

(d) There are several trees, for example *Ambo*, *Baunso*, *Jamkoli*, *Karanjo*, *Kodoli*, *Nilgiri*, *Panasa*, *Tentuli* that are used for a variety of purposes.

Plate 3.5. Mango Orchard in Home Gardens.

Plate 3.6. Recently Introduced Papaya Plantation in Home Gardens.

Vegetables and Other Plants Grown in *Badas*

(a) In Table 3.6 a list of 42 vegetables and other plants grown in *Badas* are given.

(b) A majority of the plants are annual in nature and comprise vegetables, tubers, bulbs, climbers and creepers. A majority of these plants are used at home and some of them are also sold.

Table 3.6: Names in Oriya and Kuvi of Vegetables and Other Plants grown in Badas

Sl. No.	*Oriya*	*Kuvi*
1.	Ada	Alami
2.	Baigonoo	Heyan
3.	Banda kobi	Puda kobi
4.	Bhendi	Bendi
5.	Bhejiri	Peja (Una)
6.	Bilati Baigonoo	Pejal (Kajai)
7.	Boit alu	Kumuda
8.	Bunda beans	Gocha kanga

Sl. No.	*Oriya*	*Kuvi*
9.	China badam	Bhumi sana
10.	Dhania	Dhania
11.	Gajor	Gajori
12.	Ganti kobi	Gati kobi
13.	Gendu phul	Tala bonda
14.	Guanr	Guanr
15.	Holdi	Hinga
16.	Janhi	Chichoni
17.	Jhota	Bailo
18.	Jhudonga	Kala kanga
19.	Jhudonga	Kala kanga
20.	Kakudi	Mundra
21.	Khada sago	Matakucha
22.	Khomb alu	Nangeli kuna
23.	Khosla sago	Matakucha
24.	Kolora	Karla
25.	Kunduri	Kunduru
26.	Lau	Tini lau
27.	Makka	Jona
28.	Malo beans	Ranja benisi
29.	Maricho	Mirsi
30.	Mati konda	Rani Kuna
31.	Mirlo	Mirlo
32.	Motor channa	Sana
33.	Mula	Mula
34.	Palango sago	Matakucha
35.	Paluo	Bateri
36.	Phul kobi	Puyu kobi
37.	Piajo	Ulli
38.	Rasuno	Doblauli
39.	Saru	Hopa
40.	Simbo	Hurwe
41.	Simili konda	Lakakuna
42.	Soriso	Harsu

Wild Plants Found in *Badas*

In Table 3.7 are given a list of wild plants that are found in homesteads. There are 35 such wild plant species.

Table 3.7: Wild Plants Found in Badas

Sl. No.	*Name*	*Sl. No.*	*Name*
1.	Ambo	19.	Lajokuli
2.	Apama rongo	20.	Mirchinga
3.	Bajramali	21.	Modoi
4.	Baunso	22.	Munch kondh
5.	Borkoli	23.	Muniga
6.	Dakli	24.	Paldua
7.	Didendimada	25.	Panasa
8.	Dubo ghas	26.	Patpadandi
9.	Gatamarka	27.	Patro goja
10.	Gereda	28.	Pijuli
11.	Ghantia	29.	Poyan
12.	Gombari	30.	Puruda
13.	Jamkoli	31.	Sindur
14.	Kadruhirsa	32.	Tangiachina
15.	Karanjo	33.	Tentuli
16.	Koi hirsa	34.	Thalkudi
17.	KoNo.ir	35.	Usku buta
18.	Kukur langudi		

In short, from the above description and analysis, it is evident that although the sizes of *Badas* are very small but the plants that are grown in these *Badas* as well as wild plants found in these *Badas* not only cater to the various subsistence needs of the people, but also contribute significantly to the annual household income.

Wild Animals Sighted in *Badas*

1. In Table 3.8 the list of 56 wild animals are given that are frequently sighted in the *Badas*. These include mammals, birds, reptiles, amphibian, insects etc.
   (a) It is observed that at least a few of the wild animals visit all the *Badas*.

Table 3.8: Inventory of Wild Animals in Oriya Occuring in Homesteads

Sl. No.	*Name*	*H1*	*H2*	*H3*	*H4*	*H5*	*H6*	*H7*	*H8*	*H9*	*H10*	*H11*	*H12*	*H13*	*H14*	*H15*	*Total*	
																	No.	*Per-centage*
1.	Azgor								✓	✓							2	0.6
2.	Badudi	✓		✓	✓	✓		✓		✓		✓		✓			8	2.4
3.	Bago	✓		✓	✓	✓		✓		✓	✓	✓	✓	✓	✓		11	3.3
4.	Bahurupi endua				✓	✓	✓	✓				✓		✓			6	1.8
5.	Bani	✓		✓	✓	✓	✓	✓	✓	✓	✓	✓	✓	✓	✓		13	4.0
6.	Baria	✓		✓					✓		✓						4	1.2
7.	Baya chodhai	✓		✓		✓			✓		✓	✓		✓	✓		8	2.4
8.	Bengo	✓		✓	✓	✓	✓	✓	✓	✓	✓	✓	✓	✓	✓		13	4.0
9.	Bhalu				✓	✓	✓	✓	✓			✓	✓	✓			8	2.4
10.	Biradi				✓												1	0.3
11.	Bono bilei								✓								1	0.3
12.	Budiani	✓		✓													2	0.6
13.	Chabara	✓		✓											✓		3	0.9
14.	Chanchana										✓						1	0.3
15.	Chia chadei	✓		✓											✓		3	0.9
16.	Chita bagh	✓		✓	✓	✓	✓	✓	✓	✓	✓	✓		✓	✓		12	3.6
17.	Chiti				✓	✓	✓	✓	✓			✓	✓	✓			8	2.4
18.	Dhadka	✓							✓	✓					✓		4	1.2

Sl. No.	Name	H1	H2	H3	H4	H5	H6	H7	H8	H9	H10	H11	H12	H13	H14	H15	Total	
																	No.	Per-centage
19.	Dhamana				✓	✓	✓	✓	✓	✓		✓	✓	✓			8	2.4
20.	Dhandia				✓	✓	✓	✓				✓	✓	✓			7	2.1
21.	Dingiri	✓			✓		✓		✓	✓		✓		✓			7	2.1
22.	Dud boda	✓		✓		✓	✓	✓		✓		✓		✓			8	2.4
23.	Endua				✓	✓	✓	✓	✓	✓	✓	✓	✓	✓			10	3.0
24.	Gharchatia	✓		✓	✓	✓	✓		✓	✓	✓	✓	✓	✓			11	3.3
25.	Girna								✓								1	0.3
26.	Gobar pok									✓							1	0.3
27.	Gunduchi			✓	✓	✓	✓				✓	✓	✓	✓			8	2.4
28.	Gunduri	✓		✓		✓	✓	✓	✓	✓	✓	✓	✓	✓	✓		12	3.6
29.	Gungi								✓								1	0.3
30.	Holdi basanta			✓		✓	✓		✓	✓	✓		✓	✓			8	2.4
31.	Jhiji pok									✓	✓						2	0.6
32.	Jhitipiti				✓												1	0.3
33.	Jia				✓	✓	✓	✓	✓	✓		✓	✓	✓			9	2.7
34.	Kala nago					✓	✓	✓		✓		✓	✓	✓	✓		8	2.4
35.	Kalet									✓							1	0.3
36.	Kankada bicha								✓					✓			2	0.6

Sl. No.	*Name*	*H1*	*H2*	*H3*	*H4*	*H5*	*H6*	*H7*	*H8*	*H9*	*H10*	*H11*	*H12*	*H13*	*H14*	*H15*	*Total*	
																	No.	*Per-centage*
37.	Kia chadei								✓								1	0.3
38.	Koili														✓		1	0.3
39.	Kojolpati			✓													1	0.3
40.	Kopta										✓						1	0.3
41.	Kua	✓		✓	✓		✓	✓	✓	✓		✓	✓	✓	✓		11	3.3
42.	Mayur								✓								1	0.3
43.	Musa				✓	✓	✓	✓	✓	✓	✓	✓	✓				8	2.4
44.	Nago			✓	✓	✓	✓		✓			✓	✓	✓			8	2.4
45.	Nago				✓	✓		✓		✓	✓	✓	✓	✓			8	2.4
46.	Odho	✓		✓	✓	✓	✓	✓	✓			✓	✓		✓		10	3.0
47.	Parja pati	✓		✓	✓	✓	✓	✓	✓	✓	✓	✓	✓	✓	✓		13	4.0
48.	Pecha	✓		✓	✓	✓	✓	✓	✓	✓	✓	✓	✓	✓	✓		13	4.0
49.	Pecha								✓								1	0.3
50.	Pimpudi				✓		✓	✓				✓					4	1.2
51.	Potra sap									✓							1	0.3
52.	Sailm	✓									✓	✓		✓	✓		5	1.5
53.	Saru nago					✓	✓	✓				✓	✓	✓			6	1.8
54.	Sungo poko	✓		✓	✓	✓	✓	✓	✓	✓	✓	✓	✓	✓	✓		13	4.0
55.	Tekor								✓								1	0.3
56.	Thekua			✓	✓	✓	✓	✓				✓	✓	✓	✓		9	2.7
	Total	**21**	**0**	**23**	**27**	**28**	**27**	**25**	**30**	**25**	**20**	**31**	**24**	**30**	**18**	**0**	**329**	**100**

(b) The distribution of the number of wild animals sighted in *Badas* varies from 18 to 31 (Table 3.8).

(c) The distribution of wild animals in different classes is shown in Table 3.9 and Fig. 3.5. Almost 50 per cent of the *Badas* are visited by more than 25 wild animals and in 27 per cent of the *Badas* 21 to 25 animals are sighted.

Table 3.9. Distribution of Number of Wild Animals in Badas

Wild Animals (range)	*Number*	*Percentage*
0	2	13
1 to 20	2	13
21 to 25	4	27
> 25	7	47
Total	**15**	**100**

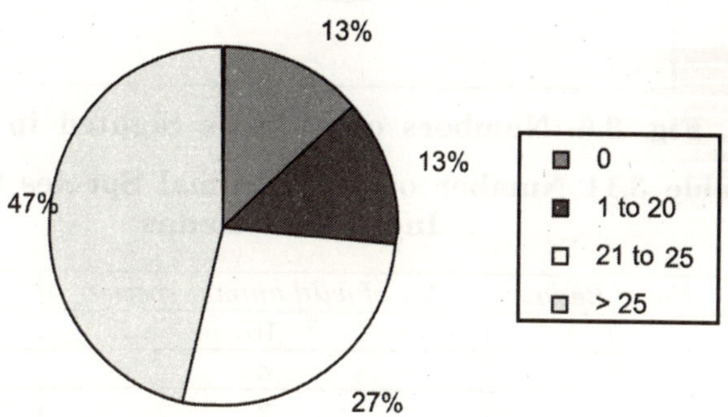

Fig. 3.5. Distribution of Number of Wild Animals in Badas.

(d) From Tables 3.10 and 3.11 and Figs. 3.6 and 3.7, it is observed that there are 16 (28.6 per cent) wild animals (*Bana bilei, Bilei, Chanchana, Girna, Gobar pok, Gungi, Jhitipiti, Kalet, Kia chadhei, Koili, Kojolpati, Kopta, Mayur, Pecha, Potra sap, Tekor*) that are sighted only in one of the *Badas*. There are 12 species that are sighted in more than 50 per cent of the *Badas*. There are five species, namely *Bani, Bengo, Pandka, Parjapati and Jhintika* that have been sighted in all the 13 *Badas*, followed by two species *Chita bagh* and *Gunduri*, three species *Bago, Gharchatia* and *Kua* in two *Badas* each.

Table 3.10. Number of Animals Sighted in Badas

Wild Animals (range)	*Number*	*Percentage*
1 to 5	26	47
6 to 10	18	32
> 10	12	21
Total	**56**	**100**

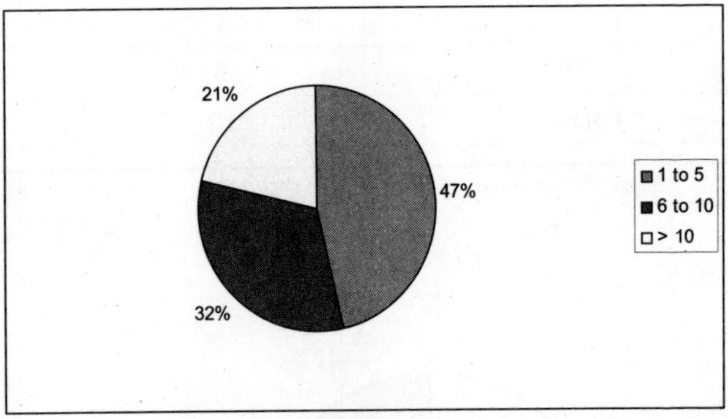

Fig. 3.6. Numbers of Animals Sighted in Badas.

Table 3.11 Number of Wild Animal Species Sighted in Individual Badas

No. of Badas	*No. of wild animal species*	*Percentage*
1.	16	28.6
2.	4	7.1
3.	2	3.6
4.	3	5.4
5.	1	1.8
6.	2	3.6
7.	2	3.6
8.	12	21.4
9.	2	3.6
10.	2	3.6
11.	3	5.4
12.	2	3.6
13.	5	8.9
Total	**56**	**100**

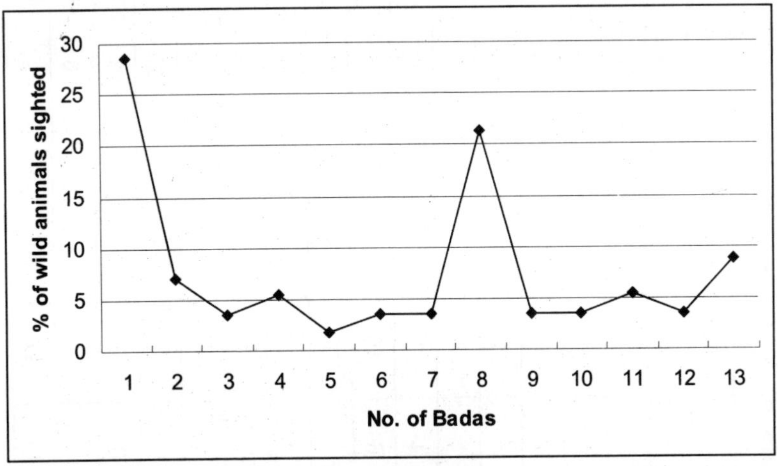

Fig. 3.7. Number of Wild Animal Species Sighted in Individual Badas.

3.3.1.2 Domesticated Animals

In Table 3.12 are given the number of various animals domesticated by each of the households in the village. There are three households without any livestock. Among the remaining 12 households there are 137 animals. The salient features with regard to livestock in the village are:

Cows: Only seven households maintain cows and their numbers vary from one to six. The total number of cows in the village is only 14.

Bullocks: There are eight households that maintain 22 bullocks. The number of bullocks among these households varies from one to six.

Pigs: There is only one household that has two pigs.

Sheep: The total numbers of sheep in the village are 13 and these are maintained by three households.

Goats: There are 36 goats owned by nine households. The number of goats among the households varies from two to 10.

Fowl: Total number of fowls in the village is 41. These are maintained by 11 households. The number among household varies from one to 10.

Dogs: There are eight dogs in the village which belong to eight households i.e. one dog per household.

Cats: There is only one household that has just one cat.

Table 3.12. Inter-household Variation in Type and Numbers of Animals maintained

Sl.No.	*Households*	*Cow*	*Bullock*	*Pig*	*Sheep*	*Goat*	*Fowl*	*Dog*	*Cat*	*Total*
1.	Ruhuni Khora									0
2.	Malti Khora									0
3.	Kesu Hontal	1	2			2		1		6
4.	Luke Hontal					2	6	1		9
5.	Chandra Hontal						1	1		2
6.	Singru Hontal						5	1		6
7.	Kamlu Hontal		4			4	3			11
8.	Ramachandra Hontal					6	10	1	1	18
9.	Sapura Hontal	6	1		3		1			11
10.	Hari Hontal	2	3			3	2			10
11.	Siara Hontal	2	6		1	3	3	1		16
12.	Bali Hontal	1	2			3	2	1		9
13.	Sambru Hontal	1	2	2		10	3	1		19
14.	Laxmidhar Hontal	1	2		9	3	5			20
15.	Dadaya Khora									0
	Total	**14**	**22**	**2**	**13**	**36**	**41**	**8**	**1**	137

Plate 3.7. Domesticated Cattle in the Village.

Inter-household Variation in Total Numbers of Animals Maintained

Data presented in Table 3.12 shows that there are three households without any livestock. Five households (33 per cent) own between 6-10 animals and six households (40 per cent) maintain above 10 animals.

Preferred Domesticated Animals

In Table 3.13 and Fig. 3.8, the animals domesticated in the village are arranged in descending order of preference. The most preferred animals are country fowl; numbering 41 (29.9 per cent), followed by goats (26.3 per cent), bullocks (16.1 per cent) and cows (10.2 per cent).

Table 3.13. Distribution of Domestic Animals in the Village

Domestic animals	*No.*	*Percentage*
Fowl	41	29.9
Goat	36	26.3
Bullock	22	16.1
Cow	14	10.2
Sheep	13	9.5
Dog	8	5.8
Pig	2	1.5
Cat	1	0.7
Total	**137**	**100.0**

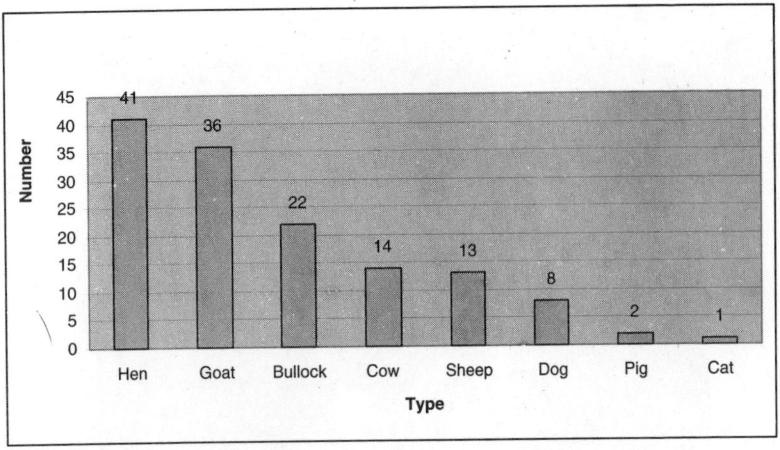

3.3.1.3 Herbal Garden

The herbal garden, known locally as *Osobada,* is located in the southeastern direction of the village (Fig. 3.1). It is about 500 meters from the habitation. The total area of the garden is 0.06 ha. The villagers with the support of IRDWSI and UNDP made the garden in June 2005. The status of the garden is good. Fencing is done with *Chiller, Sisal* and *Bileikonta*. The herbal garden is owned and managed by the native traditional healer Sapura Hontal and his son Singru Hontal. As the plantation is young Sapura Hontal is using the vacant space for intercropping by growing usually *ragi.*

Plate 3.8. Khadisiju Shrub in Herbal Gardens.

Plate 3.9. Begunia in Herbal Gardens.

Plate 3.10. Dohona in Herbal Gardens.

Plate 3.11. Nilgundi in Herbal Gardens.

Plate 3.12. Patalgarudo in Herbal Gardens.

Plate 3.13. A View of the Herbal Garden with Herbal Plants and Ragi Crop grown as Intercropping.

Table 3.14. Plants Planted in the Herbal Garden

Sl. No.	*Name in Oriya*	*Habit*	*Use*
1.	Posaruni	Creeper	Indigestion
2.	Khadisiju	Shrub	Joint pain
3.	Gudmari	Creeper	Diabetes
4.	Sibolingo	Shrub	Chest pain
5.	Akash garudo	Tree	Stomach pain
6.	Vrungoraj	Creeper	Joint pain, head cooling
7.	Ganggosiuli	Tree	Malaria
8.	Nilgundi	Creeper	Body pain
9.	Pipola	Tree	Cough, fever
10.	Biladona	Shrub	Stomach pain
11.	Ghe kunari	Shrub	Burning
12.	Potor Siju	Shrub	Joint pain
13.	Dalimo	Tree	Dysentery
14.	Vasmo potra	Shrub	Diarrhea
15.	Bono dhania	Creeper	Indigestion

Sl. No.	*Name in Oriya*	*Habit*	*Use*
16.	Daskerenga	Shrub	Headache
17.	Baya donda	Shrub	Dog bite
18.	Bhuinlimo	Shrub	Chronic fever
19.	Ashoganda	Shrub	Pneumonia, Worms, Menstrual problems
20.	Patal Garudo	Shrub	Stomach pain
21.	Agosti	Tree	White discharge

Note: Species with serial numbers 3, 7, 8, 9, 15 and 16 have died.

Medicinal Plants Planted in the Garden

Twentyone plants having medicinal value have been planted in the herbal garden (Table 3.14). Among these there are five trees, 11 shrubs and five creepers. These plants are used by the traditional healers not only in this village but also in the region for treatment of a variety of common as well as chronic diseases such as indigestion, dysentery, diarrhoea, joint pain, diabetes, chest pain, stomach pain, head cooling, malaria, body pain, cough, fever, burning, dog bite, chronic fever, pneumonia, worms, menstrual problems, white discharge etc.

Survival Status of Planted Species

Out of the 21 species planted, six species (Gudmari, Gangagosiuli, Nigundi, Pipola, Bono dhania and Daskerenga) have died. Therefore, the species presently standing in the garden are only 15. It may be mentioned that recently one more species (Menjuati) has been added in the garden.

Wild Plants Species found in Herbal Garden

In Table 3.15 are given the names of seven wild plants that are found in the herbal garden.

Table 3.15. Wild Plants Species Found in Herbal Garden

Sl. No.	*Name*
1.	Dubo ghas
2.	Kukur langudi
3.	Lajokuli
4.	Patro goja
5.	Puruda
6.	Thalkudi
7.	Usku buta

Wild Animals Sighted in Herbal Garden

In Table 3.16 the names of 38 wild animals often sighted in the herbal garden are given.

Table 3.16. Wild Animals Sighted in Herbal Garden (Names in Oriya)

Sl. No.	*Name*	*Sl. No.*	*Name*
1.	Bonbilie	20.	Jhitipiti
2.	Budinia	21.	Kala nag
3.	Bago	22.	Kalet
4.	Bohurupi anduo	23.	Kalia
5.	Bani	24.	Kankada bicha
6.	Bengo	25.	Kapto
7.	Chabara	26.	Kia chadei
8.	Chanchana	27.	Koili
9.	Chia	28.	Kua
10.	Dhamana	29.	Musa
11.	Dhulia nago	30.	Nago
12.	Dud boda	31	Parja pati
13.	Endua	32.	Pecha
14.	Girna	33.	Pimpudi
15.	Gobor poko	34.	Potra sap
16.	Gunduchi	35.	Sailm
17.	Holdi basanta	36.	Saru nago
18.	Jia	37.	Sua chadei
19.	Jhiji pok	38.	Sungo poko

The farm lands are spread over from the southeast towards the western side *i.e.* at the right side of the village entrance. The distance of the land is within 500 meters from the habitation area. All the farm lands are in one patch. The total farm land in the village is four ha. There are three households that do not posses farm land. Among the household that own farm lands there is not much variation. In all the households, the size of the farm land does not exceed more than 0.40 ha. All the farm lands are owned privately by individual families and are demarcated by stone bunding and live fencing. Some farmers have introduced the in-situ soil nutrient management through on-field compost pits and by planting green manure yielding plants on the bunds. To irrigate the farm land there is a check dam and canal constructed by the villagers with support from the government. In addition, a storage water tank for irrigation has also been constructed by the villagers with the support of IRDWSI. The farmers have developed a mutual understanding by which all the farmers are able to irrigate their lands by the canal and tank water. Some farmers lift the water by the KB Pump and kerosene pump from the irrigation tank. The crops grown in irrigated lands are primarily for consumption at home. However, some crops are also marketed.

Plate 3.14. Gourd Cultivation in Farm Land.

Plate 3.15 Chilly Cultivation in Farm Land.

Domesticated Plant Species

From Table 3.17, it is observed that 71 different types of plant species that include crops, trees, medicinal plants, etc. are grown in farm lands.

Table 3.17. Inventory of Domesticated Plant Species Found in Farm Lands

Sl. No.	*Name*	*Sl. No.*	*Name*
1.	Alami	2.	Khedjonna
3.	Alsi	4.	Khojuri
5.	Ambo	6.	Kodoli
7.	Amrutbhanda	8.	Koloth
9.	Arjun	10.	Kontagocho
11.	Banda kobi	12.	Kumunda
13.	Bhendi	14.	Kunduru
15.	Bileikanta	16.	Lembu
17.	Borda	18.	Mandia
19.	Chilor	20.	Matakucha
21.	China badam	22.	Matakucha
23.	Dhania	24.	Matakucha
25.	Dhano	26.	Matikonda
27.	Doblauli	28.	Mirlo
29.	Gajori	30.	Mirsi
31.	Gati kobi	32.	Motor channa
33.	Gendu phul	34.	Mula
35.	Gocha kanga	36.	Mundra (Kakudi)
37.	Guanr	38.	Murga
39.	Heyan	40.	Nangeli kuna
41.	Hinga	42.	Panasa
43.	Saru	44.	Peja (Kajai)
45.	Simbo	46.	Pijuli
47.	Jafra	48.	Puyu kobi
49.	Jamkoli	50.	Ranja benisi

Sl. No.	*Name*	*Sl. No.*	*Name*
51.	Janhi	52.	Sajna
53.	Joda	54.	Similikonda
55.	Makka	56.	Solap
57.	Jota	58.	Soriso
59.	Kala kanga	60.	Suan
61.	Kala kanga	62.	Tentuli
63.	Kamala	64.	Tini lau
65.	Kandul	66.	Toba
67.	Kangu	68.	Tutkoli
69.	Karla	70.	Ulli
71.	Valia		

Wild Plants Species Occurring in Farm Lands

From Table 3.18 it is observed that there are at least 25 species of wild plants that occur on the farm lands. These are mostly found on the bunds.

Table 3.18. Wild Plant Species Occurring in Farm Lands

Sl. No.	*Name*	*Sl. No.*	*Name*
1.	Ambo	14.	Kukur langudi
2.	Apama rongo	15.	Lajokuli
3.	Arjun	16.	Muniga
4.	Bajramali	17.	Panasa
5.	Baunso	18.	Poyan
6.	Dabpiri	19.	Puruda
7.	Dubo ghas	20.	Simili
8.	Gatamarka	21.	Solop
9.	Gereda	22.	Tentuli
10.	Ghantia	23.	Thalkudi
11.	Gna mandia	24.	Tutkoli
12.	Jamkoli	25.	Usku buta
13.	Karanjo		

Wild Animals Sighted in Farm Lands

In Table 3.19 the list of 48 differnet wild animals that are often sighted in the farm lands is given.

Table 3.19. Wild Animals Sighted in Farm Lands

Sl. No.	*Name*	*Sl. No.*	*Name*
1.	Ada gundicha	25.	Holdi basanta
2.	Badudi	26.	Jea
3.	Bago	27.	Jhiji pok
4.	Bani	28.	Jhitipiti
5.	Baya chodhai	29.	Kala nag
6.	Bengo	30.	Kalet
7.	Bhalu	31.	Kalia
8.	Bilei	32.	Kankada bicha
9.	Bohurupi anduo	33.	Kapto
10.	Bonbilie	34.	Kosa nuheudi
11.	Budinia	35.	Kia chadei
12.	Chabara	36.	Koili
13.	Chanchana	37.	Kojolpati
14.	Chia	38.	Kua
15.	Chita bagh	39.	Musa
16.	Chopeda	40.	Nago
17.	Dhamana	41.	Parja pati
18.	Dhulia nago	42.	Pecha
19.	Dud boda	43.	Pimpudi
20.	Endua	44.	Potra sap
21.	Gharchatia	45.	Sailm
22.	Girna	46.	Saru nago
23.	Gobor poko	47.	Sua chadei
24.	Gunduchi	48.	Sungo poko

Plate 3.16. Rainfed Land Converted into Terraces with Irrigation; Crops Being Grown During Rabi Season.

Plate 3.17. Irrigation Facility Brought to Rainfed Land: Crops Being Grown During Rabi Season.

Plate 3.18. Water Channel Made in Farm Land.

Plate 3.19. Land Development Undertaken in Rainfed Land.

Plate 3.20. A Stone Bund Separating Bada (Right) from Farm Land (Left).

3.3.1.5 Wet Lands

The wet lands are located in the southern and western direction of the village. The total area under this category of land type is about 2.82 ha. Except one family, all the remaining 14 own some wet lands. The size of the wet land is very small and varies among the families from 0.04 ha to 0.28 ha. The wet lands are privately owned.

Crop Grown in Wet Lands

Wet lands are used exclusively for growing paddy varieties. Farmers grow two different varieties of paddy *i.e.,* Lachey dhan and Lalat dhan.

Wild Plants Species Occurring in Wet Lands

Only seven wild plant species have been observed in wet lands (Table 3.20).

Table 3.20. Wild Plants Species Occurring in Wet Lands

Sl. No.	*Name*
1.	Apama rongo
2.	Dubo ghas
3.	Gereda
4.	Ghantia
5.	Panasa
6.	Thalkudi
7.	Ambo

Wild Animals Sighted in Wet Lands

In Table 3.21 gives the list of 25 wild animals that are often seen in the wet lands.

Table 3.21. Wild Animals Sighted in Wet Lands

Sl. No.	*Name*	*Sl. No.*	*Name*
1.	Ada gundicha	14.	Kapto
2.	Bonbilie	15.	Kia chadei
3.	Budinia	16.	Machronka
4.	Bago	17.	Musa
5.	Bengo	18.	Nago
6.	Chanchana	19.	Parja pati
7.	Chia	20.	Pecha
8.	Dhadka	21.	Sailm
9.	Dhandia	22.	Saru nago
10.	Gunji	23.	Singoti
11.	Jea	24.	Sua chadei
12.	Kalia	25.	Sungo poko
13.	Kankada bicha		

3.3.1.6 Rainfed Lands

The total land under this category in the village is about 5.22 ha. The land lies in a fragmented form in three directions—east, west and south. However, the bulk of it lies in the west of the habitated area of the village. Except for one family, all the remaining 14 own some rainfed land not exceeding more than 0.4 ha. Individual families manage their own patch of land. To retain soil fertility, organic manure and pesticides are used like-cow dung, green leaves, wood ash, koranjo leaf, neem leaf, ranbeli leaf, cattle urine etc.

Plate 3.21. Bamboo Clump on Embankment of Bali Banda Tank.

Crops and Trees Grown in Rainfed Lands

From Table 3.22, it is observed that 28 different types of crops and trees are grown in rainfed lands.

Table 3.22. Crops and Trees Grown in Rainfed Lands (Names in Kuvi)

Sl. No.	*Name*	*Sl. No.*	*Name*
1.	Aalsi	15.	Kawa janna
2.	Alami	16.	Kopa kucha
3.	Arka	17.	Krusnnachuda
4.	Bhumi sana	18.	Kuliyan
5.	Bileikanta	19.	Kumuda
6.	Chichoni	20.	Mahaaa
7.	Deru	21.	Marnu kanga
8.	Hinga	22.	Mirsi
9.	Hurwe	23.	Mundra
10.	Jafra	24.	Peja (kajai)
11.	Jona	25.	Peja (una)
12.	Kala kanga	26.	Pura kobi
13.	Karla	27.	Tala bonda
14.	Kawa janna	28.	Tini lau

Wild Plant Species Found on Rainfed Lands

There are 23 species of wild plants seen in rainfed lands (Table 3.23).

Table 3.23. Wild Plant Species Found in Rainfed Lands

Sl. No.	*Name*	*Sl. No.*	*Name*
1.	Ambo	13.	Koi hirsa
2.	Apama rongo	14.	Kukur languid
3.	Bajramali	15.	Lajokuli
4.	Baunso	16.	Mirchinga
5.	Didendimada	17.	Mota ghas
6.	Dubo ghas	18.	Panasa
7.	Gereda	19.	Patal garudo
8.	Ghantia	20.	Puruda
9.	Gna mandia	21.	Tentuli
10.	Gugunimal	22.	Thalkudi
11.	Kadruhirsa	23.	Usku buta
12.	Karanjo		

Wild Animal Species Sighted in Rainfed Lands

In Table 3.24 the list of 52 wild animals that are often sighted in the rainfed lands is given.

Table 3.24. Wild Animals Species Sighted in Rainfed Lands.

Sl. No.	*Name*	*Sl. No.*	*Name*
1.	Bonbilie	27.	Jea
2.	Budinia	28.	Jhiji pok
3.	Badudi	29.	Jhitipiti
4.	Bago	30.	Kala nag
5.	Bohurupi anduo	31.	Kalet
6.	Ban kukuda	32.	Kalia
7.	Bani	33.	Kankada bicha
8.	Bengo	34.	Kapto
9.	Bhalu	35.	Kia chadei
10.	Chabara	36.	Koili
11.	Chanchana	37.	Kosa nuheudi
12.	Chia	38.	Kua
13.	Chita bagh	39.	Kutra
14.	Chopeda	40.	Mankodo
15.	Dhadka	41.	Mayur
16.	Dhamana	42.	Musa
17.	Dhulia nago	43.	Nago
18.	Dingiri	44.	Parja pati
19.	Dud boda	45.	Pecha
20.	Endua	46.	Pimpudi
21.	Gharchatia	47.	Potra sap
22.	Girna	48.	Sailm
23.	Gobor poko	49.	Saru nago
24.	Gunduchi	50.	Sua chadei
25.	Gunduri	51.	Sungo poko
26.	Holdi basanta	52.	Thekua

3.3.1.7 Shifting Cultivation

The total area under shifting cultivation in the village is

approximately 7.5 ha. The shifting cultivation fields are located in three different hill ranges, locally known as Balipata, Bariamba and Kotrakari. This type of agricultural practice is locally known as Horkha kamma. Except for one household, all the remaining families practice shifting cultivation. The area under shifting cultivation among the households varies from 0.2 to 1.2 ha. However, the area under cultivation varies from one year to another.

It is appropriate to emphasise that shifting cultivation of fields represent an interesting mosaic of biodiversity that includes a variety of cultivated crops and trees, and a variety of wild plants and wild animals.

Crops Grown in Shifting Cultivation Fields

In Table 3.25 there are listed the names of the 16 crops that are grown in shifting cultivation fields. The crops include vegetables, pulses, oil seeds, cereal, millets and a special variety of upland rice (Horu kulian).

Table 3.25. Crops Grown in Shifting Cultivation Fields

Sl. No.	*Name in Kuvi*	*Name in Oriya*	*Type*
1.	Alsian	Alsi	Oil seed
2.	Arka	Kangu	Millet
3.	Borda	Saga	Vegetable
4.	Dongoroni	Dongorani	Pulse
5.	Gocha kanga	Buta simbi	Pulse
6.	Hinga	Holdi	Spice
7.	Horu kulian	Dhano	Cereal
8.	Hurwe	Simbo	Vegetable
9.	Jona	Makka	Millet
10.	Jota	Jhota	Pulse
11.	Kaja kohoda	Bada suan	Millet
12.	Kala kanga	Jhudungo	Pulse
13.	Kawajana	Khedjonna	Millet
14.	Kohoda	Suan	Millet
15.	Kolthayan	Koloth	Pulse
16.	Kumunda	Boit alu	Vegetable
17.	Mandia	Mandia	Millet
18.	Marnu kanga	Kandul	Pulse
19.	Mundra	Kakudi	Vegetable
20.	Tila	Rasi	Oil seed

Trees Grown in Shifting Cultivation Fields

In some shifting cultivation fields there are also a few trees grown, mostly yielding fruits (Table 3.26).

Table 3.26. Trees Grown in Shifting Cultivation Fields

Sl No.	*Name*
1.	Ambo
2.	Chandan
3.	Panasa
4.	Valia

Plate 3.22. Farm Land in the foreground and Shifting Cultivation Fields in the Background.

Plate 3.23. Shifting Cultivation in Pasiamba.

Plate 3.24. Shifting Cultivation in Kupa Khal.

Wild Plants Occurring in Shifting Cultivation Fields

From Table 3.27, it is seen that at least 43 wild species of plants occur in the shifting cultivation fields. These plants include a variety of trees, shrubs, creepers, grasses etc.

Table 3.27. Wild Plants Occurring in Shifting Cultivation Fields

Sl. No.	*Name*	*Sl. No.*	*Name*
1.	Ambo	14.	Dudmal
2.	Amla	15.	Orka
3.	Apama rongo	16.	Gandi buta
4.	Hatimal	17.	Gandiri
5.	Baidonko	18.	Gereda
6.	Bajramali	19.	Ghantia
7.	Belo	20.	Gna mandia
8.	Bileikanta	21.	Kadruhirsa
9.	Dakli	22.	Karanjo
10.	Damon	23.	Kathi badni
11.	Deruharja	24.	Koi hirsa
12.	Didendimada	25.	Kukudi sago
13.	Dubo ghas	26.	Kukur langudi

Sl. No.	*Name*	*Sl. No.*	*Name*
27.	Lajokuli	36.	Pitmari
28.	Mirchinga	37.	Puruda
29.	Modoi	38.	Sika ghas
30.	Mota ghas	39.	Simili
31.	Pakua	40.	Sorenda
32.	Palsi	41.	Targa
33.	Panasa	42.	Thalkudi
34.	Pardamal	43.	Usku buta
35.	Patal garudo		

Wild Animals Sighted in Shifting Cultivation Fields

In Table 3.28 the names of the 51 wild animals that are often seen in shifting cultivation fields are given.

Table 3.28. Wild Animals Sighted in Shifting Cultivation Fields

Sl. No.	*Name*	*Sl. No.*	*Name*
1.	Bonbilie	18.	Dingiri
2.	Budinia	19.	Dud boda
3.	Badudi	20.	Endua
4.	Bohurupi anduo	21.	Girna
5.	Ban kukuda	22.	Gobor poko
6.	Bani	23.	Gunduchi
7.	Baria	24.	Gunduri
8.	Bengo	25.	Holdi basanta
9.	Bhalu	26.	Jea
10.	Chabara	27.	Jhiji pok
11.	Chanchana	28.	Jhitipiti
12.	Chia	29.	Kala nag
13.	Chita bagh	30.	Kalet
14.	Chiti	31.	Kalia
15.	Chopeda	32.	Kankada bicha
16.	Dhamana	33.	Kapto
17.	Dhulia nago	34.	Kia chadei

Sl. No.	*Name*	*Sl. No.*	*Name*
35.	Koili	43.	Pecha
36.	Kosa nuheudi	44.	Pimpudi
37.	Kua	45.	Potra sap
38.	Kutra	46.	Sailm
39.	Mankodo	47.	Saru nago
40.	Mayur	48.	Sua chadei
41.	Musa	49.	Sungo poko
42.	Nago	50.	Thekua

3.3.1.8 Social Forestry Plantation

The social forestry initiative was undertaken in a patch of degraded forest land measuring approximately 24.28 ha in Pasiamba in 1994. The patch lies in the southern side of the village. This effort was supported by IRDWSI. The area is demarcated by stone bunding. Soil and water conservation measures have also been undertaken in this area. This patch is being managed by the community as a whole.

1.1 The land on which social forestry plantations have been undertaken belongs to the revenue department and was entered as a waste land. The women of the village formed an informal group and approached the revenue department and requested that the waste land may be handed over to them for plantation purposes. The villagers would like to record in this document their deep appreciation and gratitude to the revenue department who readily accepted their request. The men of the village gave all their support and help to the women in all the operations for the plantation programme. Although the plantation is owned collectively by all the women of the village, men continue to play a very significant role in the protection and management of the plantation.

Names of the Plant Species Planted

The villagers had a series of meetings and discussions among themselves and with the staff of IRDWSI regarding the choice of the species and their numbers to be planted. Keeping in view the kind of needs of the village, the community decided to plant 16 species listed in Table 3.29.

Table 3.29. Name of the Plant Species Planted

Sl. No.	*Name*
1.	Ambo
2.	Baunso
3.	Borda
4.	Borokoli
5.	Chakunda
6.	Gombari
7.	Jafra
8.	Jamkoli
9.	Kamala
10.	Mahaa neem
11.	Murga
12.	Pijuli
13.	Radhachuda
14.	Semili
15.	Tentuli
16.	Valia

Plate 3.25. Social Forestry Plantation of Chakunda and Fifteen Other Species in Pasiamba Hills.

Wild Plants Occurring in Social Forestry Patch

The villagers took utmost precaution of not removing the existing root stocks of different wild plants while planting the 16 species. However, lantana and other weeds were removed. The villagers are very happy that after 14 years of sustained efforts, a large number of wild plants have also got established in the area. Table 3.30 gives us the list of 83 wild plant species found in the area. These species include a variety of trees, shrubs, climbers and grasses.

Table 3.30. Wild Plants Occurring in Social Forestry Patch

Sl. No.	*Name*	*Sl. No.*	*Name*	*Sl. No.*	*Name*
1.	Ambo	23.	Deruharja	45.	Kadruhirsa
2.	Amla	24.	Dhopki	46.	Kalikochandi
3.	Apama rongo	25.	Didendimada	47.	Karakuta
4.	Bahada	26.	Dondera	48.	Karseli
5.	Bajramali	27.	Dubo ghas	49.	Kathi badni
6.	Bandona	28.	Dudmal	50.	Koi hirsa
7.	Bansaru	29.	Dumri	51.	Kontakoli
8.	Baunso	30.	Gadel	52.	Kukur langudi
9.	Bernga	31.	Gali morka	53.	Lajokuli
10.	Bhalu dar	32.	Gandi buta	54.	Mirchinga
11.	Bhalu jam	33.	Gandiri	55.	Modoi
12.	Bhui amla	34.	Gereda	56.	Mota ghas
13.	Bichhauati	35.	Ghantia	57.	Musa kani
14.	Bila	36.	Girli	58.	Muturimala
15.	Bileikanta	37.	Gna mandia	59.	Pakua
16.	Bisalya korani	38.	Golaki	60.	Palsi
17.	Borkoli	39.	Gombari	61.	Panasa
18.	Boruwa	40.	Gorudo	62.	Pardamal
19.	Chandan	41.	Hatimal	63.	Patal garudo
20.	Chilli	42.	Hirsi	64.	Pengo
21.	Chitini	43.	Horida	65.	Phul jhadu
22.	Dakli	44.	Jamkoli	66.	Pijuli

Sl. No.	*Name*	*Sl. No.*	*Name*	*Sl. No.*	*Name*
67.	Pitmari	73.	Sika ghas	79.	Tangiachina
68.	Pordi	74.	Simili	80.	Targa
69.	Puruda	75.	Sindur	81.	Tentuli
70.	Puti karla	76.	Sitakuti	82.	Thalkudi
71.	Ranbeli	77.	Sonari	83.	Usku buta
72.	Sata bari	78.	Sorenda		

Wild Animals Sighted in Social Forestry Patch

In Table 3.31 are given a list of 52 wild animals that are often seen in the social forestry patch.

Table 3.31. Wild Animals Sighted in Social Forestry Patch

Sl. No.	*Name*	*Sl. No.*	*Name*	*Sl. No.*	*Name*
1.	Bonbilie	19.	Dud boda	37.	Kua
2.	Budinia	20.	Endua	38.	Kutra
3.	Badudi	21.	Girna	39.	Mankodo
4.	Bohurupi anduo	22.	Gobor poko	40.	Mayur
5.	Ban kukuda	23.	Gunduchi	41.	Musa
6.	Bani	24.	Gunduri	42.	Nago
7.	Baria	25.	Holdi basanta	43.	Parja pati
8.	Bengo	26.	Jea	44.	Pecha
9.	Bhalu	27.	Jhiji pok	45.	Pimpudi
10.	Chabara	28.	Jhitipiti	46.	Potra sap
11.	Chanchana	29.	Kala nag	47.	Sailm
12.	Chia	30.	Kalet	48.	Saru nago
13.	Chita bagh	31.	Kalia	49.	Sua chadei
14.	Chiti	32.	Kankada bicha	50.	Sungo poko
15.	Chopeda	33.	Kapto	51.	Tekor
16.	Dhamana	34.	Kia chadei	52.	Thekua
17.	Dhulianago	35.	Koili		
18.	Dingiri	36.	Kosa nuheudi		

3.3.1.9 Cashew Nut Plantation

The cashew nut plantation area is situated adjacent to the habitation area and is located on the western side of the village.

Plate 3.26. Cashew Nut Plantation in Pasiamba Hills.

The total area of the cashew plantation is around 7.28 ha. The plantation was undertaken in the year 2003 and was supported by

Plate 3.27. Cashew Nut Plantation in Pasiamba Hills.

IRDWSI. A total of 945 saplings of predominantly cashew were planted; a small number of samplings of Mango (*Ambo)* and Tamarind (*Tentuli)* were also planted. Almost all the plants planted in the area have survived and are growing well.

The land on which cashew plantations have been undertaken belongs to the revenue department and was entered as waste land. The women of the village formed an informal group and approached the revenue department and requested that the waste land may be handed over to them for planting cashewnut trees. The revenue department readily accepted their request. The men of the village extended their support and help to the women.. The plantation is owned collectively by all the women of the village.

From the year 2008, the villagers will start harvesting cashew nuts. The village has decided that for next couple of years the fruits will be used for planting the area which is presently under Eucalyptus (*Bariamba*) plantation and shifting cultivation patches of *Balipata, Bariamba and Kotra kari*. Once this requirement is over, the cashew nut yields will be jointly harvested and shared equally among the women of the village.

Wild Plants Occurring in the Cashew Nut Plantation Patch

While the villagers began the plantation of the cashew trees, they took utmost precaution of not removing the existing root stocks of different wild plants as was done in the case of social forestry plantation. After five years a large number of wild plants have also got established in the area. In Table 3.32 are given the list of 26 wild plant species found in the area. These species include trees, shrubs, climbers and grasses.

Table 3.32. Wild Plants Occurring in Cashew Nut Plantation

Sl. No.	*Name*	*Sl. No.*	*Name*
1.	Ambo	14.	Kontakoli
2.	Apama rongo	15.	Kukur langudi
3.	Baidonko	16.	Lajokuli
4.	Bajramali	17.	Mirchinga
5.	Bileikanta	18.	Palsi
6.	Boruwa	19.	Pardamal
7.	Didendimada	20.	Patal garudo
8.	Dubo ghas	21.	Pitmari
9.	Gandi buta	22.	Puruda
10.	Gandiri	23.	Puti Karla
11.	Gereda	24.	Targa
12.	Ghantia	25.	Thalkudi
13.	Koi hirsa	26.	Usku buta

Wild Animals Sighted in Cashew Nut Plantation Area

In Table 3.33 we can see 51 wild animals listed that are often seen in cashew nut plantation area.

Table 3.33. Wild Animals Sighted in Cashew Nut Plantation Area

Sl. No.	*Name*	*Sl. No.*	*Name*
1.	Bonbilie	27.	Jhitipiti
2.	Budinia	28.	Kala nag
3.	Bohurupi anduo	29.	Kalet
4.	Ban kukuda	30.	Kalia
5.	Bani	31.	Kankada bicha
6.	Baria	32.	Kapto
7.	Bengo	33.	Kia chadei
8.	Bhalu	34.	Koili
9.	Chabara	35.	Kosa nuheudi
10.	Chanchana	36.	Kua
11.	Chia	37.	Kutra
12.	Chita bagh	38.	Mankodo
13.	Chiti	39.	Mayur
14.	Chopeda	40.	Musa
15.	Dhamana	41.	Nago
16.	Dhulia nago	42.	Parja pati
17.	Dingiri	43.	Pecha
18.	Dud boda	44.	Pimpudi
19.	Endua	45.	Potra sap
20.	Girna	46.	Sailm
21.	Gobor poko	47.	Saru nago
22.	Gunduchi	48.	Sua chadei
23.	Gunduri	49.	Sungo poko
24.	Holdi basanta	50.	Tekor
25.	Jea	51.	Thekua
26.	Jhiji pok		

3.3.1.10 Eucalyptus Plantation

The eucalyptus plantation in the village was undertaken in 1985 in collaboration with the Orissa State Forest Department. The total area under the plantation is about 18.21 ha. The plantation covers two distinct areas i.e. *Kotra kari* that lies in the eastern side of the village and *Bariamba* hills that lie on the northeastern side of the village.

The plantation is thus over 20 years old. Several eucalyptus trees have been periodically harvested for the bona fied needs of the villagers. Some trees have also been given on request to the neighbouring villages for their special needs such as cremation. This has resulted in considerable thinning of the plantation area. In several small patches lantana has invaded and got established. The villagers have consciously left behind kernels (seeds) of wild mangos found in the village in different areas of *Kotra kari* and *Bariamba*. Many of these have grown; some of them are even 10 years old.

The plantation is managed by the community as a whole. The people of the village have decided that in the coming years they shall replace eucalyptus plantation with cashew nut trees. The villagers are aware that by replacing eucalyptus by cashew they will not increase tree biodiversity in the village. Certain needs for which the villagers were earlier using eucalyptus can now be met by the plants from the protected forest areas, (*Balipata, Puligunta* and *Kudi kanda*) which has regenerated and became dense after strict forest protection measures were adopted by the villagers ever since 1995.

Wild Plant Species Occurring in Eucalyptus Plantation Area

While planting eucalyptus, the villagers took utmost precaution by not removing the existing root stocks of different wild plants as

Plate 3.28. Eucalyptus Plantation in Kudi Kanda.

they did in the case of other plantations. As a result, at least 27 wild plant species that include trees, shrubs, climbers and grasses are available in eucalyptus plantation patches (Table 3.34).

Table 3.34. Wild Plant Species Occurring in Eucalyptus Plantation Area

Sl. No.	*Name*	*Sl. No.*	*Name*
1.	Apama rongo	15.	Kontakoli
2.	Belo	16.	Kukur langudi
3.	Bhui amla	17.	Lajokuli
4.	Bichhauati	18.	Mirchinga
5.	Bileikanta	19.	Palsi
6.	Didendimada	20.	Pardamal
7.	Dubo ghas	21.	Patal garudo
8.	Gandi buta	22.	Pitmari
9.	Gandiri	23.	Puruda
10.	Gereda	24.	Puti karla
11.	Ghantia	25.	Targa
12.	Golaki	26.	Thalkudi
13.	Jamkoli	27.	Usku buta
14.	Koi hirsa		

Wild Animals Sighted in Eucalyptus Plantation Area

The plantation area provides a useful habitat for a number of wild animals. At least 52 wild animals are often sighted in the plantation patches (Table 3.35).

Table 3.35. Wild Animals Sighted in Eucalyptus Plantation Area

Sl. No.	*Name*	*Sl. No.*	*Name*	*Sl. No.*	*Name*
1.	Bonbilie	19.	Dud boda	37.	Kua
2.	Budinia	20.	Endua	38.	Kutra
3.	Badudi	21.	Girna	39.	Mankodo
4.	Bohurupi anduo	22.	Gobor poko	40.	Mayur
5.	Ban kukuda	23.	Gunduchi	41.	Musa
6.	Bani	24.	Gunduri	42.	Nago
7.	Baria	25.	Holdi basanta	43.	Parja pati
8.	Bengo	26.	Jea	44.	Pecha
9.	Bhalu	27.	Jhiji pok	45.	Pimpudi
10.	Chabara	28.	Jhitipiti	46.	Potra sap
11.	Chanchana	29.	Kala nag	47.	Sailm
12.	Chia	30.	Kalet	48.	Saru nago
13.	Chita bagh	31.	Kalia	49.	Sua chadei
14.	Chiti	32.	Kankada bicha	50.	Sungo poko
15.	Chopeda	33.	Kapto	51.	Tekor
16.	Dhamana	34.	Kia chadei	52.	Thekua
17.	Dhulia nago	35.	Koili		
18.	Dingiri	36.	Kosa nuheudi		

3.3.1.11 Silver Oak Plantation

The silver oak plantation was undertaken in 1985 in collaboration with the Orissa State Forest Department. The total area under the plantation is about 1.21 ha. The plantation has been undertaken in *Kotra kari* hills. In addition to silver oak plants a small number of eucalyptus plants were also planted.

Wild Plant Species Occurring in Silver Oak Plantation Area

There are 22 wild plant species that are found in the plantation area (Table 3.36).

Table 3.36. Wild Plant Species Occurring in Silver Oak Plantation Area

Sl. No.	*Name*	*Sl.No.*	*Name*
1.	Apama rongo	12.	Kukur langudi
2.	Bileikanta	13.	Lajokuli
3.	Didendimada	14.	Mirchinga
4.	Dubo ghas	15.	Palsi
5.	Gandi buta	16.	Pardamal
6.	Gandiri	17.	Patal garudo
7.	Gereda	18.	Pitmari
8.	Ghantia	19.	Puruda
9.	Golaki	20.	Targa
10.	Koi hirsa	21.	Thalkudi
11.	Kontakoli	22.	Usku buta

Wild Animals Sighted in Silver Oak Plantation Patch

As seen from Table 3.37, there are 51 wild animals that are frequently sighted in this plantation area.

Table 3.37. Wild Animals Sighted in Silver Oak Plantation Patch

Sl. No.	*Name*	*Sl. No.*	*Name*	*Sl. No.*	*Name*
1.	Bonbilei	9.	Bhalu	17.	Dingiri
2.	Budinia	10.	Chabara	18.	Dud boda
3.	Badudi	11.	Chanchana	19.	Endua
4.	Bohurupi anduo	12.	Chia	20.	Girna
5.	Ban kukuda	13.	Chita bagh	21.	Gobor poko
6.	Bani	14.	Chiti	22.	Gunduchi
7.	Baria	15.	Dhamana	23.	Gunduri
8.	Bengo	16.	Dhulia nago	24.	Holdi basanta

Sl. No.	*Name*	*Sl. No.*	*Name*	*Sl. No.*	*Name*
25.	Jea	34.	Koili	43.	Pecha
26.	Jhiji pok	35.	Kosa nuheudi	44.	Pimpudi
27.	Jhitipiti	36.	Kua	45.	Potra sap
28.	Kala nag	37.	Kutra	46.	Sailm
29.	Kalet	38.	Mankodo	47.	Saru nago
30.	Kalia	39.	Mayur	48.	Sua chadei
31.	Kankada bicha	40.	Musa	49.	Sungo poko
32.	Kapto	41.	Nago	50.	Tekor
33.	Kia chadei	42.	Parja pati	51.	Thekua

3.3.1.12 Protected Forest

The protected forest comprises three hills: 1. *Balipata*; 2. *Puligunta*; and 3. *Kudi kanda*.

These three hills form a continuous forest range and are located at about 150 meters from the habitation area. The total area is about 42.5 ha and falls under the ownership of the forest department. The community as a whole protects and manages the forest through People's Organisation. Initial survey in these three hills showed that there was not much variation in terms of either the status of the forest or the occurrence of plant species. Therefore, below here is presented a list of plants and animals for all the three hills taken together.

Plants Planted in the Protected Forests

Table 3.38 lists of the 13 species of trees planted. These have been planted on the lower slopes of the hills in the gaps.

Table 3.38. Plants Planted in the Protected Forests

Sl. No.	*Name*	*Sl. No.*	*Name*
1.	Ambo	8.	Jamkoli
2.	Baunso	9.	Karanjo
3.	Borda	10.	Niligiri
4.	Borokoli	11.	Pijuli
5.	Chandan	12.	Semili
6.	Chitramul	13.	Tentuli
7.	Dimri		

Wild Plant Species Occurring in Protected Forest

As expected, the protected forests contain a large number of wild plant species. All together 134 plant species were observed. The names of these plants are given in Table 3.39. These include mostly trees, shrubs, climbers, and some grasses. It may be re-emphasised here that this list is rather a conservative list and infact a lot more plant species especially herbs exist in these forests.

Table 3.39. Wild Plant Species Occurring in Protected Forest

Sl. No.	*Name*	*Sl. No.*	*Name*
1.	Ambo	29.	Bongordal
2.	Amla	30.	Borkoli
3.	Apama rongo	31.	Boruwa
4.	Bagonaki	32.	Chikni
5.	Bahada	33.	Chilli
6.	Baidonko	34.	Chitini
7.	Bajramali	35.	Dabpiri
8.	Ban jhudongo	36.	Dakli
9.	Bandona	37.	Damon
10.	Bansaru	38.	Deruharja
11.	Baria kanda	39.	Dhopki
12.	Bauso	40.	Didendimada
13.	Belo	41.	Dondera
14.	Bernga	42.	Dubo ghas
15.	Berongo	43.	Dudmal
16.	Bhaira bhuta	44.	Dumri
17.	Bhalu dar	45.	Gadel
18.	Bhalu jam	46.	Gali morka
19.	Bhui amla	47.	Gandi buta
20.	Bichhauati	48.	Gandiri
21.	Bila	49.	Gereda
22.	Bileikanta	50.	Ghantia
23.	Bisalya korani	51.	Girli
24.	Bod tetenka	52.	Gna mandia
25.	Bodkokodi	53.	Golaki
26.	Bojra mali	54.	Gorimenda
27.	Bon kodli	55.	Gorudo
28.	Bondari	56.	Gugunimal

Sl. No.	*Name*	*Sl. No.*	*Name*
57.	Gurdi sago	92.	Muturimala
58.	Harchand	93.	Orka
59.	Hatimal	94.	Pakodimala
60.	Hirsi	95.	Pakua
61.	Horida	96.	Palsi
62.	Jamkoli	97.	Pardamal
63.	Kadruhirsa	98.	Patal garudo
64.	Kalikochandi	99.	Patpadandi
65.	Karakuta	100.	Patro goja
66.	Karseli	101.	Pengo
67.	Kathi badni	102.	Phul jhadu
68.	Keu kanda	103.	Pijuli
69.	Khajuri niali	104.	Pit konda
70.	Kichi	105.	Pita konda
71.	Klia konda	106.	Pitmari
72.	Koi hirsa	107.	Podai
73.	Koicho	108.	Poroi buta
74.	Koineteri	109.	Poyan
75.	Kontakoli	110.	Puruda
76.	Kosa kanda	111.	Puti karla
77.	Kudei	112.	Ranbeli
78.	Kudupa	113.	Randuli
79.	Kukudi sago	114.	Reteli
80.	Kukur langudi	115.	Rupni
81.	Kuramal	116.	Sakra
82.	Lajokuli	117.	Sata bari
83.	Lohomada	118.	Siadi
84.	Mankodo kendu	119.	Sika ghas
85.	Marda mala	120.	Simili
86.	Mendha mal	121.	Sindi
87.	Mirchinga	122.	Sindur
88.	Modoi	123.	Sitakuti
89.	Monjorsulia	124.	Sonari
90.	Mota ghas	125.	Sorenda
91.	Musa kani	126.	Sua kanda

Sl. No.	*Name*	*Sl. No.*	*Name*
127.	Tangiachina	131.	Thakurani phulo
128.	Targa	132.	Thalkudi
129.	Tendka kanda	133.	Tirimundi
130.	Tentuli	134.	Usku buta

Plate 3.29. Puligunta Hills With Natural Dense Forest.

Plate 3.30. Shifting Cultivation in Bariamba Hills.

Plate 3.31. Eucalyptus Plantation in Lelisira Hill.

Plate 3.32. A View of Kupakhal Hills.

Wild Animals Sighted in Protected Forest

Table 3.40 gives us a list of 53 wild animals that are sighted in the protected forest.

Table 3.40. Wild Animals Sighted in Protected Forest

Sl. No.	*Name*	*Sl. No.*	*Name*	*Sl. No.*	*Name*
1.	Bonbilie	19.	Dud boda	37.	Kua
2.	Budinia	20.	Endua	38.	Kutra
3.	Badudi	21.	Girna	39.	Mankodo
4.	Bago	22.	Gobor poko	40.	Mayur
5.	Bohurupi anduo	23.	Gunduchi	41.	Musa
6.	Ban kukuda	24.	Gunduri	42.	Nago
7.	Bani	25.	Holdi basanta	43.	Odho
8.	Baria	26.	Jea	44.	Parja pati
9.	Bengo	27.	Jhiji pok	45.	Pecha
10.	Bhalu	28.	Jhitipiti	46.	Pimpudi
11.	Chabara	29.	Kala nag	47.	Potra sap
12.	Chanchana	30.	Kalet	48.	Sailm
13.	Chia	31.	Kalia	49.	Saru nago
14.	Chita bagh	32.	Kankada bicha	50.	Sua chadei
15.	Chiti	33.	Kapto	51.	Sungo poko
16.	Dhamana	34.	Kia chadei	52.	Tekor
17.	Dhulia nago	35.	Koili	53.	Thekua
18.	Dingiri	36.	Kosa nuheudi		

3.3.1.13 Sacred Grove

The sacred grove called locally *Jakari* is located around 50 metre away from the habitation area in the northeastern direction of the village. The total area of the sacred grove is about 0.008 ha (800 sq. ft.).

The sacred grove is managed by the village priests called *Pujari* and *Disari*. At the time of festivals the *Disari* and *Pujari* clean the surrounding areas of the grove and worship and perform rituals. Tree felling and collection of biomass from the grove is strictly prohibited.

Wild Plant Species Occurring in the Sacred Grove

In Table 3.41 a list of 23 plant species that occur in the grove are given. Except for a few plants of eucalyptus, the remaining 22 species are wild. For a select eight species their number in the grove was also counted as given in the Table 3.42.

Table 3.41. Wild Plant Species Occurring in the Sacred Grove

Sl. No.	*Name*	*Sl. No.*	*Name*
1.	Apama rongo	13.	Koi hirsa
2.	Bajramali	14.	Kukur langudi
3.	Bileikanta	15.	Lajokuli
4.	Dakli	16.	Mirchinga
5.	Didendimada	17.	Nilgiri
6.	Dubo ghas	18.	Panasa
7.	Dudmal	19.	Pitmari
8.	Gandi buta	20.	Puruda
9.	Gandiri	21.	Sindur
10.	Gereda	22.	Thalkudi
11.	Ghantia	23.	Usku buta
12.	Golaki		

Table 3.42. Number of a Select Eight Plant Species Found in the Sacred Grove

Sl. No.	*Name*	*Type*	*Number*
1.	Bissalya korani	Tree	2
2.	Bod kokodi	Tree	2
3.	Panasa	Tree	1
4.	Kudei	Tree	1
5.	Mankodo kendu	Tree	2
6.	Mirchinga	Tree	8
7.	Sindur	Tree	2
8.	Usku buta	Shrub	10

Plate 3.33. Sacred Grove in the Village.

Wild Animals Sighted in Sacred Grove

Although the size of the sacred grove is very small, as noted in Table 3.43, 46 wild animals are often sighted in the grove.

Table 3.43. Wild Animals Sighted in Sacred Grove

Sl. No.	*Name*	*Sl. No.*	*Name*	*Sl. No.*	*Name*
1.	Bonbilie	12.	Chita bagh	23.	Jhiji pok
2.	Budinia	13.	Chiti	24.	Jhitipiti
3.	Bohurupi anduo	14.	Dhulia nago	25.	Kala nag
4.	Ban kukuda	15.	Dingiri	26.	Kalet
5.	Bani	16.	Dud boda	27.	Kalia
6.	Baria	17.	Endua	28.	Kankada bicha
7.	Bengo	18.	Girna	29.	Kapto
8.	Bhalu	19.	Gobor poko	30.	Kia chadei
9.	Chabara	20.	Gunduchi	31.	Koili
10.	Chanchana	21.	Holdi basanta	32.	Kosa nuheudi
11.	Chia	22.	Jea	33.	Kua

Sl. No.	*Name*	*Sl. No.*	*Name*	*Sl. No.*	*Name*
34.	Kutra	39.	Parja pati	44.	Saru nago
35.	Mankodo	40.	Pecha	45.	Sungo poko
36.	Mayur	41.	Pimpudi	46.	Tekor
37.	Musa	42.	Potra sap		
38.	Nago	43.	Sailm		

3.3.1.14 Road Side Plantation

The village is about 100 metre from the road that comes from Kundli and goes to Puriakhudi. On both sides of the road in the year 1994, the villagers planted Chakunda, Gombari, Moha neembo and Bouganvilla.

Wild Plant Species Occurring on Road Side

Seventeen wild plant species have also got established on both sides of the road since the plantation was undertaken along the road (Table 3.44).

Table 3.44. Wild Plant Species Occurring on Road Side

Sl. No.	*Name*	*Sl. No.*	*Name*
1.	Ambo	10.	Koi hirsa
2.	Apama rongo	11.	Kukur langudi
3.	Bajramali	12.	Lajokuli
4.	Didendimada	13.	Pitmari
5.	Dubo ghas	14.	Puruda
6.	Gandi buta	15.	Targa
7.	Gandiri	16.	Thalkudi
8.	Gereda	17.	Usku buta
9.	Ghantia		

Plate 3.34. Avenue Trees Along the Village Road; Lots of Gaps are Seen.

Wild Animals Sighted on Road Side

Although as noted above the overall plant diversity is limited along the road side, yet atleast 48 wild animals frequent this area (Table 3.45).

Table 3.45. Wild Animals Sighted on Road Side

Sl. No.	*Name*	*Sl. No.*	*Name*	*Sl. No.*	*Name*
1.	Bonbilie	10.	Chia	19.	Girna
2.	Budinia	11.	Chita bagh	20.	Gobor poko
3.	Badudi	12.	Chiti	21.	Gunduchi
4.	Bohurupi anduo	13.	Dhamana	22.	Gunduri
5.	Bani	14.	Dhulia nago	23.	Holdi basanta
6.	Bengo	15.	Dingiri	24.	Jia
7.	Bhalu	16.	Dud boda	25.	Jhiji pok
8.	Chabara	17.	Endua	26.	Jhitipiti
9.	Chanchana	18.	Gharchatia	27.	Kala nag

Sl. No.	*Name*	*Sl. No.*	*Name*	*Sl. No.*	*Name*
28.	Kalet	35.	Kua	42.	Potra sap
29.	Kalia	36.	Mankodo	43.	Sailm
30.	Kankada bicha	37.	Musa	44.	Saru nago
31.	Kapto	38.	Nago	45.	Sua chadei
32.	Kia chadei	39.	Parja pati	46.	Sungo poko
33.	Koili	40.	Pecha	47.	Tekor
34.	Kosa nuheudi	41.	Pimpudi	48.	Thekua

3.3.2 Waterscape Elements Bearing Biodiversity

3.3.2.1 Tank 1

The tank locally known as *Bali banda* is situated about 100 ft from the habitation area in the northern direction. The total area of the tank is 0.014 ha and the depth of the tank is around 5.2 metre. The pond is rectangular in shape with an earthen embankment. In order to avoid soil erosion in the earthen embankment, a variety of plant species have been planted. The tank was constructed with the support of IRDWSI under the Food for Work (FFW) programme of United Nations World Food Programme (UNWFP) in the year 2001. The community manages this tank collectively.

Plants Planted on the Embankment of the Tank

In Table 3.46 a list of plants that have been planted on the embankment is given. As seen from these tables 16 types of plants that include fruit trees, vegetables, etc., have been planted. It is noteworthy that *Mendaphul* (Marigold) flower has been planted as a bio-repellent for the insects.

Table 3.46. Plants Planted on the Embankment of the Tank

Sl. No.	*Name*	*English name*	*Habit*
1.	Amrutabhanda	Papaya	Tree
2.	Baunso	Bamboo	Tree
3.	Jada	Castor	Shrub
4.	Jamkoli	Blackberry	Tree

Sl. No.	*Name*	*English name*	*Habit*
5.	Kodli	Banana	Tree
6.	Kumuda	Pumpkin	Creeper
7.	Mandara	Hibiscus	Shrub
8.	Mendaphul	Marigold	Shrub
9.	Morchi	Chilly	Shrub
10.	Panasa	Jackfruit	Tree
11.	Pijuli	Guava	Tree
12.	Semi	Simbo	Creeper
13.	Similikanda	Tapioca	Tuber
14.	Tini Lau	Bottle gourd	Creeper
15.	Tova	Grape fruit	Tree
16.	Tutkoli	Melbury	Tree

Plate 3.35. Bali Banda Tank.

Wild Plants Occurring on the Embankment of the Tank

Table 3.47 provids the list of wild plants occurring on the embankment of the tank.

Altogether 12 wild plants species have been observed.

Table 3.47. Wild Plants Occurring on the Embankment of the Tank

Sl. No.	*Name*
1.	Ambo
2.	Apama rongo
3.	Bauso
4.	Dubo ghas
5.	Gereda
6.	Karanjo
7.	Koi hirsa
8.	Kukur languid
9.	Lajokuli
10.	Pijuli
11.	Thalkudi
12.	Usku buta

Aquatic Fauna Found in the Tank

In Table 3.48 the names of the seven aquatic fauna found in the tank are given. Out of these, five are fishes; three varieties of fishes which are *Vakur*, *Rohu* and *Mirkali* have been introduced. *Magur* and *Godsi* fish species occur naturally in the tank. Besides fishes, frogs and crabs are also found in tank and its vicinity.

Table 3.48. Fishes Found in the Tank

Sl. No.	*Name*	*English Name*	*Introduced*	*Wild*
1.	Bengo	Frog		+
2.	Godsi	Fish		+
3.	Kankda	Crab		+
4.	Magur	Catfish		+
5.	Mirkali	Mrigal	+	
6.	Rohi	Rohu	+	
7.	Vakur	Catla	+	

Wild Animals Found in and Around the Tank

There are a number of both aquatic and terrestrial animals that are found in and around the tank. Altogether there are at least 34 animals as given in Table 3.49 that are found in and around the tank. This list includes frog and crab listed in Table 3.48.

Table 3.49. Wild Animals Found in and Around the Tank

Sl. No.	*Name*	*Sl. No.*	*Name*
1.	Ada gundicha	18.	Kia chadei
2.	Bago	19.	Koili
3.	Bohurupi anduo	20.	Kosa nuheudi
4.	Bani	21.	Kua
5.	Bengo	22.	Mankodo
6.	Chia	23.	Machronka
7.	Dhadka	24.	Musa
8.	Dhandia	25.	Nago
9.	Endua	26.	Odho
10.	Gunji	27.	Parja pati
11.	Jea	28.	Pecha
12.	Jhitipiti	29.	Pimpudi
13.	Kala nag	30.	Sailm
14.	Kalet	31.	Saru nago
15.	Kalia	32.	Singoti
16.	Kankada bicha	33.	Sua chadei
17.	Kapto	34.	Sungo poko

3.3.2.2 Tank 2

The tank is known as *Bamini banda* and is situated about 100 ft from the habitation area in the southern direction and was constructed in the year 2002 under the United Nations Development Programme (UNDP–Women in Agriculture programme). The area of the tank is 25 m^2. The depth of the tank is around 4.5 metre. The shape of the tank is rectangular with stone packing in the inner part. This tank has been constructed mainly for the purpose of irrigation during *Rabi* season. The villagers have constructed bund around the tank and planted trees like Banana, Gliricidia etc. The tank is managed by the community.

Aquatic Animals Found in and Around the Tank

In Table 3.50 the list of aquatic animals found in and around the tank is given. Out of the four animals, two are fishes and other two are frogs and crabs.

Table 3.50. Aquatic Animals Found in and Around the Tank

Sl. No.	*Name*	*English name*
1.	Bengo	Frog
2.	Godsi	Fish
3.	Kankda	Crab
4.	Magur	Catfish

Plants Raised on the Tank Bund

Four plant species have been planted on the tank bund (Table 3.51).

Table 3.51. Plants Raised on the Tank Bund

Sl. No.	*Name*	*English name*	*Type*
1.	Ambo	Mango	Tree
2.	Kodli	Banana	Tree
3.	Mendaphul	Marigold	Shrub
4.	Kumuda	Pumpkin	Creeper

Wild Plants Occurring on the Tank Bund

Eight wild plant species are found on the tank bund (Table 3.52).

Table 3.52. Wild Plants Occurring on the Tank Bund

Sl. No.	*Name*
1.	Ambo
2.	Apama rongo
3.	Dubo ghas
4.	Gereda
5.	Kukur langudi
6.	Lajokuli
7.	Thalkudi
8.	Usku buta

Wild Animals Seen Around the Tank

At least 33 species of wild animals are often sighted in and around the tank (Table 3.53).

Table 3.53. Wild Animals Seen Around the Tank

Sl. No.	*Name*	*Sl. No.*	*Name*	*Sl. No.*	*Name*
1.	Ada gundicha	12.	Jhitipiti	23.	Musa
2.	Bago	13.	Kala nag	24.	Nago
3.	Bohurupi anduo	14.	Kalia	25.	Odho
4.	Bani	15.	Kankada bicha	26.	Parja pati
5.	Bengo	16.	Kapto	27.	Pecha
6.	Chia	17.	Kia chadei	28.	Pimpudi
7.	Dhadka	18.	Koili	29.	Sailm
8.	Dhandia	19.	Kosa nuheudi	30.	Saru nago
9.	Endua	20.	Kua	31.	Singoti
10.	Gunji	21.	Mankodo	32.	Sua chadei
11.	Jia	22.	Machronka	33.	Sungo poko

Plate 3.36. Bamini Banda Tank.

3.3.2.3 Tank 3

The tank is situated about 50 ft from the habitation area in the southeast direction and is known as *Diki banda*. The area of the tank is about 500 m^2 and the depth of the tank is about 3.65 metre. The shape of the tank is rectangular with earthen embankment. The community constructed the pond with the support of Integrated Tribal Development Agency, Government of Orissa in the year 2005. Before the pond was constructed the area was used as a farm land and besides growing crops it had housed a number of wild plants as well. The tank was constructed primarily for water harvesting and for fish rearing. The tank is managed by the community.

Wild Aquatic Animals Found in and Around the Tank

In Table 3.54 are presented the list of eight aquatic animals found in the tank. Of these three are fishes e.g., *Vakur, Rohi* and *Mirkali* that have been introduced. The remaining five animals occur naturally in the tank.

Plate 3.37. Fishing Being Carried Out in Diki Banda Tank.

Plate 3.38. Plantation on Embankment of Diki Banda Tank.

Table 3.54. Wild Aquatic Animals Found in and Around the Tank

Sl. No.	*Name*	*English Name*	*Introduced*	*Wild*
1.	Bengo	Frog		+
2.	Godsi	Fish		+
3.	Kankda	Crab		+
4.	Magur	Catfish		+
5.	Mirkali	Mrigal	+	
6.	Panisap	Water snake		+
7.	Rohi	Rohu	+	
8.	Vakur	Catla	+	

Plants Raised on the Bund of the Tank

A number of plant species (17) comprising of trees, tubers and creepers have been planted on the bund with the twin objective of arresting soil erosion as well as raising supplementary income for the villagers (Table 3.55).

Table 3.55. Plants Raised on the Bund of the Tank

Sl. No.	*Name*	*English name*	*Type*
1.	Ambo	Mango	Tree
2.	Amrutu	Papaya	Tree
3.	Baunso	Bamboo	Tree
4.	Chandan	Sandal	Tree
5.	Chilor	Chillor	Shrub
6.	Jafra	Jafra	Shrub
7.	Jamkoli	Blackberry	Tree
8.	Kodli	Banana	Tree
9.	Kumuda	Pumpkin	Creeper
10.	Genduphul	Marigold	Shrub
11.	Panasa	Jackfruit	Tree
12.	Pijuli	Gouva	Tree
13.	Sajana	Drumstick	Tree
14.	Semi	Creeper beans	Creeper
15.	Simili	Semili cotton	Tree
16.	Similikanda	Tapioca	Tuber
17.	Valia	Cashew	Tree

Wild Plants Occurring on the Tank

Nine wild plants occur on the tank bund (Table 3.56).

Table 3.56. Wild Plants Occurring on the Tank

Sl. No.	*Name*
1.	Ambo
2.	Apama rongo
3.	Dubo ghas
4.	Gereda
5.	Kukur langudi
6.	Lajokuli
7.	Pijuli
8.	Thalkudi
9.	Usku buta

Wild Animals Seen Around the Tank

Thirty-one wild animals are often sighted around the tank area (Table 3.57).

Table 3.57. Wild Animals Seen Around the Tank

Sl. No.	*Name*	*Sl. No.*	*Name*	*Sl. No.*	*Name*
1.	Ada gundicha	12.	Jhitipiti	23.	Nago
2.	Bago	13.	Kalia	24.	Odho
3.	Bohurupi anduo	14.	Kankada bicha	25.	Parja pati
4.	Bani	15.	Kapto	26.	Pimpudi
5.	Bengo	16.	Kia chadei	27.	Sailm
6.	Chia	17.	Koili	28.	Saru nago
7.	Dhadka	18.	Kosa nuheudi	29.	Singoti
8.	Dhandia	19.	Kua	30.	Sua chadei
9.	Endua	20.	Mankodo	31.	Sungo poko
10.	Gunji	21.	Machronka		
11.	Jia	22.	Musa		

3.3.2.4 Check Dam

The tank is called *Atal banda* situated about 33 metre from the habitation in the southeast direction. The area of the tank is 70 m^2 and the depth of the tank is around one meter. The check dam is of square shape with earthen embankment. The community constructed the check dam with financial assistance from Integrated

Tribal Development Agency, Government of Orissa, 2003. The check dam was built for the purpose of irrigation of *Rabi* crop.

The management of the check dam rests with the community. Every year disiltation of the tank is carried out during the summer season.

Aquatic Animals Found in and Around the Check Dam

Table 3.58 presents the list of nine aquatic animals that are found in the check dam. Out of these three fishes, e.g., *Vakur, Rohi* and *Mirkali* have been introduced. The remaining six animals occur naturally in the check dam.

Table 3.58. Aquatic Animals Found in and Around the Check Dam

Sl. No.	*Name*	*English name*	*Introduced*	*Wild*
1.	Bengo	Frog		+
2.	Godsi	Fish		+
3.	Kankda	Crab		+
4.	Karandi	Fish		+
5.	Magur	Catfish		+
6.	Mirkali	Mrigal	+	
7.	Panisapo	Water snake		+
8.	Rohi	Rohu	+	
9.	Vakur	Catla	+	

Plate 3.39. A View of Check Dam.

Plate 3.40. A View of Check Dam.

Aquatic and Terrestrial Plant Species

In Table 3.59 a list of plants that occur in the check dam as well as around it are given; ten plant species have been observed. Out of these four are wild aquatic weeds. Six plant species have been planted around the check dam.

Table 3.59. Aquatic and Terrestrial Plant Species

Sl. No.	*Name*	*English name*	*Type*	*Wild*	*Introduced*
1.	Kodli	Banana	Tree		+
2.	Chakunda	Chakunda	Tree		+
3.	Pijuli	Gouva	Tree		+
4.	Karonjo	Pongamia	Tree		+
5.	Murga	Sisal	Shrub		+
6.	Genduphul	Marigold	Shrub		+
7.	Ghaso-1	Azolla	Weed	+	
8.	Ghaso-2	Pistia	Weed	+	
9.	Ghaso-3	Hydrilla	Weed	+	
10.	Ghaso-4	Salvinia	Weed	+	

Wild Plants Occurring on the Check Dam

There are 16 wild plants listed in Table 3.60 that have established themselves on the bund of check dam.

Table 3.60. Wild Plants Occurring on the Check Dam

Sl. No.	*Name*	*Sl. No.*	*Name*
1.	Ambo	9.	Kukur langudi
2.	Apama rongo	10.	Lajokuli
3.	Dandira	11.	Mirchinga
4.	Dubo ghas	12.	Phul jhadu
5.	Dumri	13.	Podai
6.	Gereda	14.	Puruda
7.	Kantakoli	15.	Thalkudi
8.	Koi hirsa	16.	Usku buta

Wild Animals Seen Around the Check Dam

In Table 3.61 the list of 30 wild animals that are often sighted around the check dam is given.

Table 3.61. Wild Animals Seen Around the Check Dam

Sl. No.	*Name*	*Sl. No.*	*Name*	*Sl. No.*	*Name*
1.	Ada gundicha	11.	Jhitipiti	21.	Machronka
2.	Budinia	12.	Kalia	22.	Musa
3.	Bago	13.	Kankada bicha	23.	Nago
4.	Bani	14.	Kapto	24.	Parja pati
5.	Bengo	15.	Kia chadei	25.	Pimpudi
6.	Chia	16.	Koili	26.	Sailm
7.	Dhamana	17.	Kosa nuheudi	27.	Saru nago
8.	Endua	18.	Kua	28.	Singoti
9.	Gunji	19.	Kutra	29.	Sua chadei
10.	Jia	20.	Mankodo	30.	Sungo poko

3.3.2.5 Streams

There are three streams that drain the village. Their names are 1. *Kotra am jhola*, 2. *Kudi kanda jhola* and 3. *Boko sakadi*. *Kotra am jhola* stream originates from *Puliganta* hills and drains through the middle of the village in the western direction and is seasonal. *Kudi kanda jhola* stream originates from the hill range *Kudi kanda* in the east and drains to the west direction and is seasonal in nature. The third stream *Boko sakadi* originates from the southern side of the village and drains in the eastern direction. It is perennial. Below are given the details regarding the aquatic fauna and flora found in the streams as well as the wild animals that are sighted around the streams. Domestic animals use these streams specially *Boko sakadi* for drinking purposes. Only water from *Boko sakadi* stream is used for irrigating fields located on the western border of the village.

Stream 1: *Kotra am Jhola*

Wild Plants Occurring along the Stream *Kotra am Jhola*

In Table 3.62 is presented a list of 37 wild plants that occur along the stream *Kotra am jhola.*

Table 3.62. Wild Plants Occurring along the Stream Kotra am Jhola

Sl. No.	*Name*	*Sl. No.*	*Name*	*Sl. No.*	*Name*
1.	Ambo	14.	Girli	27.	Kukur langudi
2.	Apama rongo	15.	Gna mandia	28.	Lajokuli
3.	Bajramali	16.	Gorimenda	29.	Mirchinga
4.	Dakli	17.	Gugunimal	30.	Pardamal
5.	Deruharja	18.	Kadruhirsa	31.	Phul jhadu
6.	Didendimada	19.	Kalikochandi	32.	Pijuli
7.	Dondera	20.	Karanjo	33.	Pitmari
8.	Dubo ghas	21.	Kathi badni	34.	Puruda
9.	Dudmal	22.	Keu kanda	35.	Sua kanda
10.	Gandi buta	23.	Koi hirsa	36.	Thalkudi
11.	Gandiri	24.	Koicho	37.	Usku buta
12.	Gereda	25.	Koineteri		
13.	Ghantia	26.	Kudupa		

Wild Animals Sighted Around Stream *Kotra am Jhola*

In Table 3.63 is given the list of 41 wild animals that are often sighted along the stream.

Table 3.63. Wild Animals Sighted Around Stream Kotra am Jhola

Sl. No.	*Name*	*Sl. No.*	*Name*	*Sl. No.*	*Name*
1.	Ban kukuda	15.	Gunduchi	29.	Kutra
2.	Bani	16.	Gunduri	30.	Mankodo
3.	Baria	17.	Gunji	31.	Mayur
4.	Bengo	18.	Holdi basanta	32.	Musa
5.	Bhalu	19.	Jhitipiti	33.	Nago
6.	Bonbilie	20.	Jia	34.	Odho
7.	Budinia	21.	Kalet	35.	Parja pati
8.	Chanchana	22.	Kalia	36.	Pimpudi
9.	Chia	23.	Kankada bicha	37.	Potra sap
10.	Chita bagh	24.	Kapto	38.	Sailm
11.	Dhandia	25.	Kia chadei	39.	Saru nago
12.	Dhulia nago	26.	Koili	40.	Sua chadei
13.	Endua	27.	Kosa nuheudi	41.	Sungo poko
14.	Gobor poko	28.	Kua		

Stream 2: *Kudi Kanda Jhola*

Wild Plants Occurring along the Stream *Kudi Kanda Jhola*

The wild plants occurring along the stream *Kudi kanda jhola* are by and large the same as observed along *Kotra am jhola* and are given in Table 3.62.

Wild Animals Sighted Around *Kudi Kanda Jhola*

In Table 3.64 is given the list of 36 wild animals that are often sighted along the stream.

Table 3.64. Wild Animals Sighted Kudi Kanda Jhola

Sl. No.	*Name*	*Sl. No.*	*Name*	*Sl. No.*	*Name*
1.	Ban kukuda	13.	Gobor poko	25.	Kua
2.	Bani	14.	Gunduchi	26.	Kutra
3.	Baria	15.	Gunduri	27.	Mankodo
4.	Bengo	16.	Gunji	28.	Mayur
5.	Bhalu	17.	Holdi basanta	29.	Musa
6.	Bonbilie	18.	Jea	30.	Nago
7.	Budinia	19.	Kalia	31.	Odho
8.	Chia	20.	Kankada bicha	32.	Parja pati
9.	Chita bagh	21.	Kapto	33.	Pimpudi
10.	Dhandia	22.	Kia chadei	34.	Potra sap
11.	Dhulia nago	23.	Koili	35.	Sailm
12.	Endua	24.	Kosa nuheudi	36.	Sua chadei

Plate 3.41. Water Being Diverted for Irrigation from Boko Sakadi Stream.

Stream 3: *Boko Sakadi*

Aquatic Wild Plants Found along the *Boko Sakdi* Stream

In Table 3.65 the list of four wild aquatic plants that are seen along the stream are given.

Table 3.65. Aquatic Wild Plants Found along the Boko Sakadi Stream

Sl. No.	*Name*	*Type*
1.	Bagh kokodi	Weed
2.	Duan sago	Creeper
3.	Puruda	Weed
4.	Sunsunia	Creeper

Wild Plants Occurring along the *Boko Sakadi* Stream

Both sides of this stream provide an excellent habitat for a wide varity of plants to colonise the area. There are atleast 40 plant species that include trees, shrubs, herbs, creepers and grasses are found along the *Boko sakadi* stream.

Table 3.66. Wild Plants Occurring along the *Boko Sakadi* Stream

Sl. No.	*Name*	*Sl. No.*	*Name*	*Sl. No.*	*Name*
1.	Ambo	15.	Gandiri	29.	Kukur langudi
2.	Apama rongo	16.	Gereda	30.	Lajokuli
3.	Bajramali	17.	Ghantia	31.	Mirchinga
4.	Bernga	18.	Girli	32.	Pardamal
5.	Bisalya korani	19.	Gna mandia	33.	Patal garudo
6.	Bon kodli	20.	Gorimenda	34.	Phul jhadu
7.	Dakli	21.	Gugunimal	35.	Pijuli
8.	Deruharja	22.	Kadruhirsa	36.	Pitmari
9.	Didendimada	23.	Karakuta	37.	Puruda
10.	Dondera	24.	Keu kanda	38.	Sua kanda
11.	Dubo ghas	25.	Koi hirsa	39.	Thalkudi
12.	Dudmal	26.	Koicho	40.	Usku buta
13.	Dumri	27.	Koineteri		
14.	Gandi buta	28.	Kudupa		

Wild Animals Sighted *Boko Sakadi* Stream

In Table 3.67 is given the list of 36 wild animals that are often sighted along the stream. In addition to these 36 wild animals, there are frogs and crabs that are found along, in some parts of the stream.

Table 3.67. Wild Animals Sighted along Boko Sakadi Stream

Sl. No.	*Name*	*Sl. No.*	*Name*	*Sl No.*	*Name*
1.	Ada gundicha	13.	Dhandia	25.	Kua
2.	Bonbilie	14.	Dhulia nago	26.	Kutra
3.	Budinia	15.	Gobor poko	27.	Mankodo
4.	Bago	16.	Gunduchi	28.	Mayur
5.	Ban kukuda	17.	Gunji	29.	Machronka
6.	Bani	18.	Gunduri	30.	Musa
7.	Baria	19.	Holdi basanta	31.	Nago
8.	Bengo	20.	Jea	32.	Odho
9.	Bhalu	21.	Kalia	33.	Parja pati
10.	Chia	22.	Kankada bicha	34.	Potra sap
11.	Chita bagh	23.	Kapto	35.	Sailm
12.	Dhadka	24.	Kia chadei	36.	Sua chadei

4

A Comparative Analysis of the Distribution of Biodiversity in Various Land and Waterscape Elements

In the preceeding Chapter, the names of different plant species were given, both cultivated and wild as well as wild animals occurring in 20 different biodiversity bearing areas in Kondhpungar. In this chapter, an analysis of the occurrence of each of the species in different land and waterscape elements as well as the number of species occurring in individual elements is presented. The material has been organised, analysed and described under the following four heads:

4.1 A comparative analysis of the occurrence of cultivated plant species in different land and waterscape elements;

4.2 A comparative analysis of the occurrence of wild plant species in different land and waterscape elements;

4.3 A comparative analysis of the occurrence of wild animal species in different land and waterscape elements; and

4.4 A comparative analysis of the occurrence of aquatic and wild animal species in different waterscape elements.

4.1 A Comparative Analysis of the Occurrence of Cultivated Plant Species in Different Land and Waterscape Elements

In Table 4.1 are given the names of cultivated plant species in different land and waterscape elements. Altogether at least 95 plant species are cultivated in the village. This list might contain only the generic names of crops and vegetables. Therefore, in fact the number of species and varieties of cultivated plants will be much higher than what is listed in Table 4.1. Although names of most of the plants are given in Oriya, for some plants however the names are given in Kuvi.

In a separate section below, are given varieties of a select number of crops and vegetables that are grown in the village.

Variation in Number of Cultivated Plants Occurring in Different Land and Waterscape Elements

In Table 4.2 the numbers of plant species occurring in 20 individual biodiversity bearing areas are given in the discending order. The data presented in Table 4.2 have been reanalysed in terms of occurrence of plants in different ranges and the results are presented in Table 4.3 and Fig. 4.1. The analysis reveals the following salient features:

(i) Altogether at least 95 plant species are cultivated in the village. These include crops, vegetables, fruit trees, culturally useful plants and ornamentals;

(ii) It is highly noteworthy that a maximum number of cultivated plant species, i.e., 81 (77 per cent) are found in homestead lands. This is followed by farm land (71 species; 67.45 per cent) and rainfed land (28 species; 26.6 per cent); these three areas account for 15 per cent of the total landscape and waterscape elements. In the remaining 17 biodiversity bearing areas the number of cultivated plants do not exceed more than 17 species;

(iii) As expected, the three streams are devoid of any cultivated plants; and

(iv) There are eight areas (40 per cent of total elements) that have between 1-10 cultivated plant species. They are check dam, road sides, tank two, cashew nut, eucalyptus and silver oak plantations, wet land and sacred grove.

In a summary, as expected a considerable inter-area variation occurs in the number of cultivated plant species. The observed variation is primarily a function of land capability, availability of water and distance from the habitation area.

Inter-area variation in cultivated tree species in 20 biodiversity bearing areas

As it is evident from Fig. 3.1, the village has different categories of land as well as water bearing areas with different characteristics. It is therefore, expected that different categories of land and water bodies, depending on their capabilities will support the growing of certain type of trees. Data given in Table 4.4 adequately supports this inference. Salient features emerging from Tables 4.1 and 4.4 are:

(i) Mango occurs in 11 out of 20 areas. Therefore, it is evident that it is indeed one of the most preferred species. Also, it is perhaps that mango can grow in a wide range of habitats;

(ii) Four species, Hurwe (simbo) a creeper yielding beans used both as food and fodder, Kumuda (boit alu) used as a vegetable, Pijuli (guava) a fruit bearing tree and Gendu phul (marigold) a flower, are found in as many as seven different areas out of 20 which is 35 per cent;

(iii) Four species-Baunso (bamboo), Boroda (a leafy vegetable), Jamkoli (black berry yielding tree) and Kodoli (banana) are found in six areas;

(iv) Jafra (a dye yielding plant) and Tentuli (tamarind) are found in five areas; and

(v) It is observed from Table 4.4 and Fig. 4.3 that 10.5 per cent of the 95 species occurred only in one area; 37.9 per cent in two areas; 26.3 per cent in three areas and 13.7 per cent in four areas. For each one of these categories although details of the name of the plants involved can be seen from Table 4.1, a few illustrative examples are given below:

Occurring in one area: *Arjun, Kofi, Nadia, Radhachuda, Saguan, Sapota, Tua, Batri, Dongor rani etc.*

Occurring in two areas: *Chandan, Chitramul, Rasuno, Gajor, Ganti kobi, Gam bhari, Baigono, Khojuri, Lembu etc.*

Occurring in three areas: *Ada, Borokoli, Banda kobi, Holdi, Joda, Jhota, Kolera, Sajana, Toba, Alsi, Kangu, etc.*

Occurring in four areas: *Amrutabhanda, Makka, Karanjo, Maricho, Murga, Panasa, Semilikonda, Lau, Kaju etc.*

Table 4.1: Cultivated Plant Species Occurring in Different Landscape and Waterscape Elements

Sl. No.	Local	Homestead	Herbal garden	Farm land	Wet land	Rainfed	Shifting cultivation	Plantations					Protected forest	Sacred grove	Tank 1	Tank 2	Tank 3	Check dam	Streams			Total	
								S. forestry	Cashew nut	Eucalyptus	Silver oak	Road side							Kotra am jhola	Kudi kanda jhola	Boko sakadi	No.	Percentage
		(1).	(2)	(3)	(4)	(5)	(6)	(7)	(8)	(9)	(10)	(11)	(12)	(13)	(14)	(15)	(16)	(17)	(18)	(19)	(20)		
1.	Ada	✓		✓		✓																3	1.1
2.	Alsi			✓		✓	✓															3	1.1
3.	Ambo	✓		✓		✓		✓	✓	✓		✓	✓			✓	✓	✓				11	3.9
4.	Amrut-bhanda	✓		✓											✓		✓					4	1.4
5.	Arjun			✓																		1	0.4
6.	Baigono	✓		✓																		2	0.7
7.	Banda kobi	✓		✓		✓																3	1.1
8.	Batapi	✓		✓											✓							3	1.1
9.	Baunso	✓				✓		✓					✓		✓		✓					6	2.1
10.	Bhendi	✓		✓																		2	0.7
11.	Bhrjiri (una)	✓				✓																2	0.7
12.	Bilaiti baigono	✓		✓		✓																3	1.1

Sl. No.	Local	Homestead	Herbal garden	Farm land	Wet land	Rainfed	Shifting cultivation	Plantations					Protected forest	Sacred grove	Tank 1	Tank 2	Tank 3	Check dam	Streams			Total	
								S. forestry	Cashew nut	Eucalyptus	Silver oak	Road side							Kotra am jhola	Kudi kanda jhola	Boko sakadi	No.	Percentage
		(1)	(2)	(3)	(4)	(5)	(6)	(7)	(8)	(9)	(10)	(11)	(12)	(13)	(14)	(15)	(16)	(17)	(18)	(19)	(20)		
13.	Bileikanta	✓		✓		✓						✓										**4**	**1.4**
14.	Boit alu	✓		✓		✓	✓								✓	✓	✓					**7**	**2.5**
15.	Borda	✓		✓		✓	✓	✓					✓									**6**	**2.1**
16.	Borokoli	✓						✓					✓									**3**	**1.1**
17.	Buda beans	✓		✓																		**2**	**0.7**
18.	Chakunda	✓						✓										✓				**3**	**1.1**
19.	Chandan												✓				✓					**2**	**0.7**
20.	Chilor	✓		✓													✓					**3**	**1.1**
21.	China badam	✓		✓		✓																**3**	**1.1**
22.	Chitramul	✓											✓									**2**	**0.7**
23.	Dhania	✓		✓																		**2**	**0.7**
24.	Dhano			✓	✓	✓	✓															**4**	**1.4**
25.	Dimri	✓											✓					✓				**3**	**1.1**
26.	Dongor rani						✓															**1**	**0.4**

Sl. No.	Local	Homestead	Herbal garden	Farm land	Wet land	Rainfed	Shifting cultivation	Plantations					Protected forest	Sacred grove	Tank 1	Tank 2	Tank 3	Check dam	Streams			Total	
								S. forestry	Cashew nut	Eucalyptus	Silver oak	Road side							Kotra am jhola	Kudi kanda jhola	Boko sakadi	No.	Percentage
		(1)	(2)	(3)	(4)	(5)	(6)	(7)	(8)	(9)	(10)	(11)	(12)	(13)	(14)	(15)	(16)	(17)	(18)	(19)	(20)		
27.	Gajor	✓		✓																		2	0.7
28.	Gam bhari	✓						✓														2	0.7
29.	Ganti kobi	✓		✓																		2	0.7
30.	Gendu phul	✓		✓		✓									✓	✓	✓	✓				7	2.5
31.	Guanr	✓		✓																		2	0.7
32.	Holdi	✓		✓																		3	1.1
33.	Jafra	✓		✓		✓		✓									✓					5	1.8
34.	Jamkoli	✓		✓				✓					✓		✓		✓					6	2.1
35.	Janhi	✓		✓		✓																3	1.1
36.	Jhota	✓		✓			✓															3	1.1
37.	Jhudongo	✓		✓		✓																3	1.1
38.	Jhudongo	✓		✓																		2	0.7
39.	Joda	✓		✓											✓							3	1.1
40.	Kaju			✓				✓	✓								✓					4	1.4

Sl. No.	Local	Homestead	Herbal garden	Farm land	Wet land	Rainfed	Shifting cultivation	Plantations					Protected forest	Sacred grove	Tank 1	Tank 2	Tank 3	Check dam	Streams			Total	
								S.forestry	Cashew nut	Eucalyptus	Silver oak	Road side							Kotra am jhola	Kudi kanda jhola	Boko sakadi	No.	Percentage
		(1)	(2)	(3)	(4)	(5)	(6)	(7)	(8)	(9)	(10)	(11)	(12)	(13)	(14)	(15)	(16)	(17)	(18)	(19)	(20)		
41.	Kakudi	✓		✓		✓																**3**	**1.1**
42.	Kamala	✓		✓				✓														**3**	**1.1**
43.	Kandul			✓		✓	✓															**3**	**1.1**
44.	Kangu			✓		✓	✓															**3**	**1.1**
45.	Karanjo	✓										✓	✓					✓				**4**	**1.4**
46.	Khada sago	✓		✓																		**2**	**0.7**
47.	Khed jonna			✓		✓	✓															**3**	**1.1**
48.	Khed jonna			✓		✓	✓															**3**	**1.1**
49.	Khoda			✓			✓															**2**	**0.7**
50.	Khojuri	✓		✓																		**2**	**0.7**
51.	Khomb alu	✓		✓																		**2**	**0.7**
52.	Khosla sago	✓		✓																		**2**	**0.7**
53.	Kodoli	✓		✓											✓	✓	✓	✓				**6**	**2.1**
54.	Kofi	✓																				**1**	**0.4**

Sl. No.	Local							Plantations											Streams			Total	
		Homestead	*Herbal garden*	*Farm land*	*Wet land*	*Rainfed*	*Shifting cultivation*	*S. forestry*	*Cashew nut*	*Eucalyptus*	*Silver oak*	*Road side*	*Protected forest*	*Sacred grove*	*Tank 1*	*Tank 2*	*Tank 3*	*Check dam*	*Kotra am jhola*	*Kudi kanda jhola*	*Boko sakadi*	*No.*	*Percentage*
		(1)	(2)	(3)	(4)	(5)	(6)	(7)	(8)	(9)	(10)	(11)	(12)	(13)	(14)	(15)	(16)	(17)	(18)	(19)	(20)		
55.	Kolera	✓		✓		✓																**3**	**1.1**
56.	Kontagocho	✓		✓																		**2**	**0.7**
57.	Krusnna chuda	✓				✓																**2**	**0.7**
58.	Kunduri	✓		✓																		**2**	**0.7**
59.	Lau	✓		✓		✓									✓							**4**	**1.4**
60.	Lembu	✓		✓																		**2**	**0.7**
61.	Mahaa neem	✓						✓				✓										**3**	**1.1**
62.	Makka	✓		✓		✓	✓															**4**	**1.4**
63.	Malo beans	✓		✓																		**2**	**0.7**
64.	Mandar	✓													✓							**2**	**0.7**
65.	Mandia			✓		✓																**2**	**0.7**
66.	Maricho	✓		✓		✓									✓							**4**	**1.4**
67.	Mati konda	✓		✓																		**2**	**0.7**

Sl. No.	Local	Homestead	Herbal garden	Farm land	Wet land	Rainfed	Shifting cultivation	Plantations: S. forestry	Plantations: Cashew nut	Plantations: Eucalyptus	Plantations: Silver oak	Plantations: Road side	Protected forest	Sacred grove	Tank 1	Tank 2	Tank 3	Check dam	Streams: Kotra am jhola	Streams: Kudi kanda jhola	Streams: Boko sakadi	Total: No.	Total: Percentage
		(1)	(2)	(3)	(4)	(5)	(6)	(7)	(8)	(9)	(10)	(11)	(12)	(13)	(14)	(15)	(16)	(17)	(18)	(19)	(20)		
68.	Mirlo	✓		✓																		2	0.7
69.	Motor channa	✓		✓																		2	0.7
70.	Mula	✓		✓																		2	0.7
71.	Murga	✓		✓				✓										✓				4	1.4
72.	Nadia	✓																				1	0.4
73.	Niligiri									✓	✓		✓	✓								4	1.4
74.	Palango sago	✓		✓																		2	0.7
75.	Paluo	✓																				1	0.4
76.	Panasa	✓		✓											✓		✓					4	1.4
77.	Phul kobi	✓		✓				✓					✓		✓		✓	✓				7	2.5
78.	Piajo	✓		✓																		2	0.7
79.	Puyu kobi	✓		✓																		2	0.7
80.	Radhachuda							✓														1	0.4
81.	Rasuno	✓		✓																		2	0.7

Sl. No.	Local	Homestead	Herbal garden	Farm land	Wet land	Rainfed	Shifting cultivation	Plantations					Protected forest	Sacred grove	Tank 1	Tank 2	Tank 3	Check dam	Streams			Total	
								S. forestry	Cashew nut	Eucalyptus	Silver oak	Road side							Kotra am jhola	Kudi kanda jhola	Boko sakadi	No.	Percentage
		(1)	(2)	(3)	(4)	(5)	(6)	(7)	(8)	(9)	(10)	(11)	(12)	(13)	(14)	(15)	(16)	(17)	(18)	(19)	(20)		
82.	Rupa	✓									✓											2	0.7
83.	Saguan	✓																				1	0.4
84.	Sajna	✓		✓													✓					3	1.1
85.	Sapta	✓																				1	0.4
86.	Saru	✓		✓																		2	0.7
87.	Semili	✓						✓					✓				✓					4	1.4
88.	Simbo	✓		✓		✓	✓								✓	✓	✓					7	2.5
89.	Similikonda	✓		✓											✓		✓					4	1.4
90.	Sitaphol	✓																				1	0.4
91.	Solop	✓		✓																		2	0.7
92.	Soriso	✓		✓																		2	0.7
93.	Tentuli	✓		✓				✓	✓				✓									5	1.8
94.	Tua	✓																				1	0.4
95.	Tutkoli	✓		✓											✓							3	1.1
	Total	**81**	**0**	**71**	**1**	**28**	**14**	**16**	**3**	**2**	**2**	**4**	**13**	**1**	**16**	**4**	**17**	**8**	**0**	**0**	**0**	**282**	**100**

Note: In herbal garden as detailed in Chapter 3, section 3.3.1.3, there are 21 medicinal plants that have been planted. However, those plants have not been incorporated in this table.

Table 4.2: Occurrence of Number of Cultivated Plant Species in Different Land and Waterscape Elements Arranged in Descending Order

Sl. No.	*Elements*	*No. of plant species*	*Percentage*
1.	Homestead	81	85.3
2.	Farm land	71	74.7
3.	Rainfed land	28	29.5
4.	Tank–3	17	17.9
5.	Social forestry	16	16.8
6.	Tank–1	16	16.8
7.	Shifting cultivation	14	14.7
8.	Protected forest	13	13.7
9.	Check dam	8	8.4
10.	Road side	4	4.2
11.	Tank-2	4	4.2
12.	Cashew nut plantation	3	3.2
13.	Eucalyptus plantation	2	2.1
14.	Silver oak plantation	2	2.1
15.	Wet land	1	1.1
16.	Sacred grove	1	1.1
17.	Herbal garden	0	0.0
18.	Kotra am jhola	0	0.0
19.	Kudi kanda jhola	0	0.0
20	Boko sakadi	0	0.0

Note: In herbal garden as detailed in Chapter 3, section 3.3.1.3, there are 21 medicinal plants that have been planted. However, those plants have not been incorporated in this table. That is why against Sl. No. 17, the number of plant mentioned is zero.

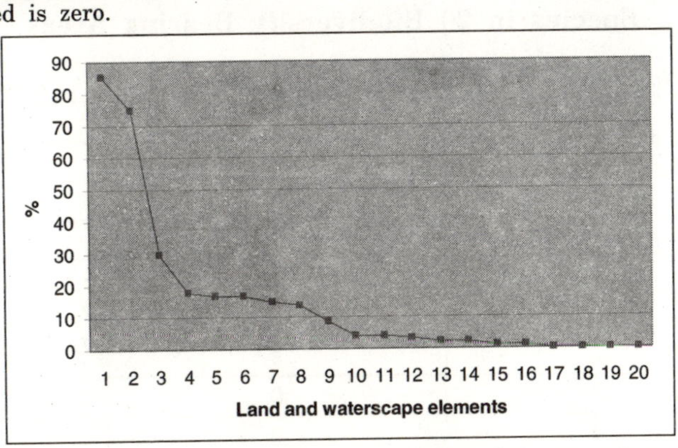

Fig. 4.1. Occurrence of number of cultivated plant species in different land and waterscape elements arranged in discending order. The numbers on the X-axis correspond with the numbers given in column 2 of Table 4.2.

Table 4.3: Distribution of Number of Plant Species in 20 Areas

No. of plant species	*No. of areas*	*%*
0	4	20
1–10	8	40
11–20	5	25
>20	3	15
Total	**20**	**100**

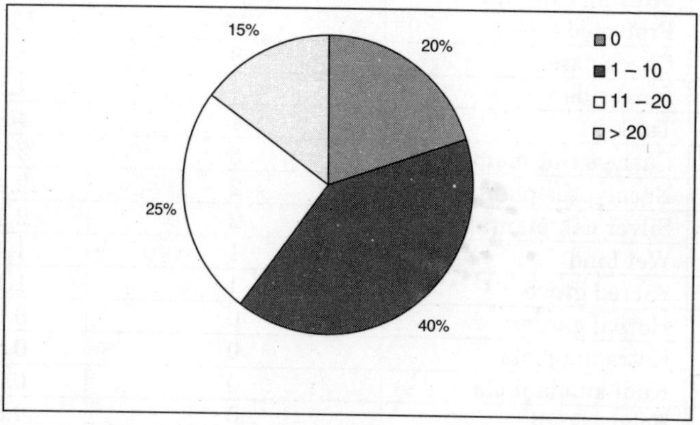

Fig. 4.2. Per cent Distribution of Plant Species in 20 Areas.

Table 4.4: Inter-area Variation in Cultivated Plant Species in 20 Biodiversity Bearing Areas

No. of elements	*No. of species*	*Percentage*
1.	10	10.5
2.	36	37.9
3.	25	26.3
4.	13	13.7
5.	2	2.1
6.	4	4.2
7.	4	4.2
8.	0	0
9.	0	0
10.	0	0
11.	1	1.0
Total	**95**	**100**

Varietal Diversity in Select Cultivated Crops

In Table 4.5 are given varietal diversity in select 26 cultivated crops. As seen from the table for almost each of the crops grown in the village, a number of varieties exist. For example, Kangu millet has five different verities; Jowar, Dongor rani and Arhar have two varieties each; mustard has two varieties; bottle gourd with three varieties; and five varieties of yam.

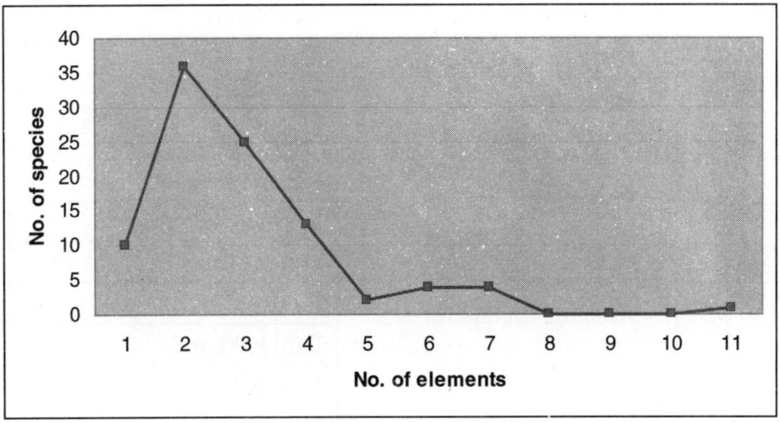

Fig. 4.3: Inter-area Variations in Cultivated Plant Species in 20 Biodiversity Bearing Areas.

In Table 4.5 are listed 26 crops. However, considering varieties of these crops the total number of varieties comes to 66 that means, on an average each crop has more than two varieties.

Table 4.5: Varietal Diversity in Select Cultivated Crops

	Name of plants in Oriya / English	
Sl. No.	*Plants*	*Varieties*
1.	Kangu (finger millet)	San kangu
		Bod kangu
		Rongo kangu
		Kola kangu
		Gonthia
2.	Jowar (sorghum)	Dhola khed jonna
		Kola khed jonna
3.	Dongor rani (green gram)	Bod Dongor rani
		San Dongor rani

Sl. No.	*Name of plants in Oriya / English*	
	Plants	*Varieties*
4.	Arhar	Siri kandul
		Biri
5.	Koloth (horse gram)	Bod koloth
		Kola koloth
		San koloth
6.	Niger	Alsi
7.	Makka (maize)	Dala moka
		Mami moka
8.	Kakudi (cucumber)	Mandia kakudi
		Khotgod kakudi
		Muna kakudi
9.	Kumuda (pumpkin)	Kakharu
		Pani kakharu
		Rani kakharu
10.	Malo (beans)	Malo beans
		Buda beans
		Rang buda beans
11.	Jhota	Dhola jhota
		Kola jhota
		Rani jhota
12.	Soriso (mustrad)	Soriso
		Rai soriso
13.	Simbo (beans)	Kedi simbo
		Gonti simbo
		Dhola simbo
14.	Jhudongo (cow pea)	Kola jhudongo
		Rango jhudongo
		Dhola jhudongo
15.	Lau (bottle gourd)	Lamba lau
		Gol lau
		Pita lau

Sl. No.	*Name of plants in Oriya / English*	
	Plants	*Varieties*
16.	*Karela* (bitter gourd)	Bon karla
		Dud karla
		Majia karla
17.	Baigon (brinjal)	Konta Baigono
		Nila Baigono
		Dhola Baigono
18.	Bhejiri (tomato)	Bhejiri
19.	Holdi (turmeric)	Desi holdi
20.	Ada (ginger)	Darada ada
		Kodi muti
21.	Sago (green leafy vegetables)	Nali sago
		Dhola sago
		Konta bhaji
		Kendesi sago
		Zelenga sago
22.	Lasuno (garlic)	Rasuno
23.	Maricho (chilly)	Desi muricho
		Dhanua muricho
24.	Piajo (onion)	Ulli piajo
25.	Saru (arum)	Rango saru
		Makdi saru
26.	Kanda (yam)	Nangal kanda
		Dhala nangal kanda
		Geileng nangal kanda
		Podsingia nangal kanda
		Semili kanda (nali)

Varietal Diversity in Paddy, Ragi and Suan

In Table 4.6 are given varieties of three important crops, i.e. paddy, ragi and suan traditionally grown in the village. All the three crops show remarkable richness in number of varieties. There are 11 varieties of paddy, 12 varieties of ragi and seven varieties of suan. However, presently not all the varieties are grown; some have been discontinued for a long time (for details see Section 6.2 of Chapter 6).

Table 4.6: Varietal Diversity in Paddy, Ragi and Suan

Name of Crops	*Varieties*	
	Oriya name	*Kuvi Name*
	Paddy	
1.	Lochoi	Lachoi
2.	Sopur lochoi	Jeema kulli
3.	Bhata dhan	Gudiakulli
4.	Amo dhan	Mahaaa kulli
5.	Karandi	Karandi
6.	Kandul kati	Kandul kathi
7.	Kola dhan	Balukuti
8.	Baigonoi	Heyapedka
9.	Poda lochoi	Gundia lochoi
10.	Gorda lochoi	Gorda lochoi
11.	Nili dhan	Nilikuli
	Ragi	
1.	Sonadei mandia	
2.	Bodeli	Bodeli
3.	Dasra bodeli	Dasra bodeli
4.	Marda mandia	Marda mandia
5.	Chilli mandia	Chilli mandia
6.	Telenga mandia	Telenga mandia
7.	Boddu	Boddu
8.	Karanga	Karanga
9.	Majhia mandia	Majhia mandia
10.	Majhia bodeli	Majhia bodeli
11.	Biri mandia	Biri mandia
12.	Modei mandia	Modei mandia

Name of crops	*Varieties*	
	Oriya Name	*Kuvi Name*
Suan		
1.	Mami suan	Kudji kohoda
2.	Bod suan	Kachak kohoda
3.	Mathili suan	Matli kohoda
4.	Kola suan	Kadini kohoda
5.	Jinjiri suan	Jinjiri kohoda
6.	Jurua jetili	Jurua jetili kohoda
7.	Laiseri	Laiseri kohoda

4.2 A Comparative Analysis of the Occurrence of Wild Plant Species in Different Land and Waterscape Elements

In Table 4.7 is given a list of the wild plants that are found in different land and waterscape elements in the village. At least 148 wild plants are found in the village. It may be re-emphasised here that the list is rather a partial one. Representation of perhaps tree species in the list is fairly comprehensive but ground flora comprising of grasses and herbs is rather sparsely represented.

It may be noted that several varieties of mushrooms also occur in the village. These however, have not been included in Table 4.7 and have been described in Table 4.11.

Plate 4.1: Konta Koli Plants in Puligunta.

Table 4.7: Wild plant species occurring in different landscape and waterscape elements

Sl. No.	Names[1]						Plantations											Streams			Total	
		Homestead (1).	Herbal garden (2)	Farm land (3)	Wet land (4)	Rainfed (5)	Shifting cultivation (6)	S.forestry (7)	Cashew nut (8)	Eucalyptus (9)	Silver oak (10)	Road side (11)	Protected forest (12)	Sacred grove (13)	Tank 1 (14)	Tank 2 (15)	Tank 3 (16)	Check dam (17)	Kotra am jhola (18)	Kudi kanda jhola (19)	Boko sakadi (20)	Number	Percentage
1.	Ambo	✓		✓	✓	✓	✓	✓	✓			✓	✓		✓	✓	✓	✓	✓	✓	✓	16	2.5
2.	Amla												✓									3	0.5
3.	Apama rongo	✓		✓	✓	✓	✓	✓	✓	✓	✓	✓	✓	✓	✓	✓	✓	✓	✓	✓	✓	19	3.0
4.	Arjun			✓																		1	0.2
5.	Bagonaki												✓									1	0.2
6.	Bahada							✓					✓									2	0.3
7.	Baidonko						✓		✓				✓									3	0.5
8.	Bajramali	✓		✓		✓	✓	✓	✓			✓	✓	✓					✓	✓	✓	12	1.9
9.	Ban jhudongo												✓									1	0.2
10.	Bandona							✓					✓									2	0.3
11.	Bansaru							✓					✓									2	0.3
12.	Baria kanda												✓									1	0.2
13.	Baunso	✓		✓		✓		✓					✓		✓							6	1.0
14.	Belo						✓			✓			✓									3	0.5

Sl No	Names[1]	Homestead	Herbal garden	Farm land	Wet land	Rainfed	Shifting cultivation	Plantations					Protected forest	Sacred grove	Tank 1	Tank 2	Tank 3	Check dam	Streams			Total	
								S. forestry	Cashew nut	Eucalyptus	Silver oak	Road side							Kotra am jhola	Kudi kanda jhola	Boko sakadi	Number	Percentage
		(1)	(2)	(3)	(4)	(5)	(6)	(7)	(8)	(9)	(10)	(11)	(12)	(13)	(14)	(15)	(16)	(17)	(18)	(19)	(20)		
15	Bernĝa							✓					✓								✓	2	0.3
16	Berongo												✓									1	0.2
17	Bhaira bhuta												✓									1	0.2
18	Bhalu dar							✓					✓									2	0.3
19	Bhalu jam							✓					✓									2	0.3
20	Bhui amla							✓		✓			✓									3	0.5
21	Bichhauati							✓		✓			✓									3	0.5
22	Bila							✓					✓									2	0.3
23	Bileikanta						✓	✓	✓	✓	✓		✓	✓								7	1.1
24	Bisalya korani							✓					✓								✓	3	0.5
25	Bod tetenka												✓									1	0.2
26	Bodkokodi												✓									1	0.2
27	Bojra mukhi												✓									1	0.2

Sl No	Names[1]	Homestead	Herbal garden	Farm land	Wet land	Rainfed	Shifting cultivation	Plantations: S.forestry	Plantations: Cashew nut	Plantations: Eucalyptus	Plantations: Silver oak	Plantations: Road side	Protected forest	Sacred grove	Tank 1	Tank 2	Tank 3	Check dam	Streams: Kotra am jhola	Streams: Kudi kanda jhola	Streams: Boko sakadi	Total: Number	Total: Percentage
		(1).	(2)	(3)	(4)	(5)	(6)	(7)	(8)	(9)	(10)	(11)	(12)	(13)	(14)	(15)	(16)	(17)	(18)	(19)	(20)		
28	Bon kodli												✓								✓	2	0.3
29	Bondari												✓									1	0.2
30	Bongordal												✓									1	0.2
31	Borkoli	✓						✓					✓									3	0.5
32	Boruwa							✓	✓				✓									3	0.5
33	Chandan							✓														1	0.2
34	Chikni												✓									1	0.2
35	Chilli							✓					✓									2	0.3
36	Chitini							✓					✓									2	0.3
37	Dabpiri			✓									✓									2	0.3
38	Dakli	✓					✓	✓					✓	✓					✓	✓	✓	8	1.3
39	Damon						✓						✓									2	0.3
40	Deruharja						✓	✓					✓						✓	✓	✓	6	1.0
41	Dhopki							✓					✓									2	0.3

Sl No	Names[1]	Homestead	Herbal garden	Farm land	Wet land	Rainfed	Shifting cultivation	Plantations					Protected forest	Sacred grove	Tank 1	Tank 2	Tank 3	Check dam	Streams			Total	
								S.forestry	Cashew nut	Eucalyptus	Silver oak	Road side							Kotra am jhola	Kudi kanda jhola	Boko sahadi	Number	Percentage
		(1).	(2)	(3)	(4)	(5)	(6)	(7)	(8)	(9)	(10)	(11)	(12)	(13)	(14)	(15)	(16)	(17)	(18)	(19)	(20)		
42	Didendimada	✓				✓	✓	✓	✓	✓	✓	✓	✓	✓					✓	✓	✓	14	2.2
43	Dondera							✓					✓						✓	✓	✓	5	0.8
44	Dubo ghas	✓	✓	✓	✓	✓	✓	✓	✓	✓	✓	✓	✓	✓	✓	✓	✓	✓	✓	✓	✓	20	3.2
45	Dudmal						✓	✓					✓	✓					✓	✓	✓	7	1.1
46	Dumri							✓					✓					✓			✓	4	0.6
47	Gadel							✓					✓									2	0.3
48	Gali morka							✓					✓									2	0.3
49	Gandi buta						✓	✓	✓	✓	✓	✓	✓	✓					✓	✓	✓	12	1.9
50	Gandiri						✓	✓	✓	✓	✓	✓	✓	✓					✓	✓	✓	11	1.7
51	Gatamarka	✓		✓																		2	0.3
52	Gereda	✓		✓	✓	✓	✓	✓	✓	✓	✓	✓	✓	✓	✓	✓	✓	✓	✓	✓	✓	18	2.9
53	Ghantia	✓		✓	✓	✓	✓	✓	✓	✓	✓	✓	✓	✓					✓	✓	✓	15	2.4
54	Girli							✓					✓						✓	✓	✓	5	0.8
55	Gna mandia			✓		✓	✓	✓					✓						✓	✓	✓	8	1.3

Sl No	Names[1]	Homestead	Herbal garden	Farm land	Wet land	Rainfed	Shifting cultivation	Plantations					Protected forest	Sacred grove	Tank 1	Tank 2	Tank 3	Check dam	Streams			Total	
								S.forestry	Cashew nut	Eucalyptus	Silver oak	Road side							Kotra am jhola	Kudi kanda jhola	Boko sakadi	Number	Percentage
		(1).	(2)	(3)	(4)	(5)	(6)	(7)	(8)	(9)	(10)	(11)	(12)	(13)	(14)	(15)	(16)	(17)	(18)	(19)	(20)		
56	Golaki							✓		✓	✓		✓	✓								5	0.8
57	Gombari	✓						✓														2	0.3
58	Gorimenda												✓						✓	✓	✓	4	0.6
59	Gorudo							✓					✓									2	0.3
60	Gugunimal					✓							✓						✓	✓	✓	5	0.8
61	Gurdi sago												✓									1	0.2
62	Harchand												✓									1	0.2
63	Hatimal						✓	✓					✓									3	0.5
64	Hirsi							✓					✓									2	0.3
65	Horida							✓					✓									2	0.3
66	Jamkoli	✓		✓				✓		✓			✓									5	0.8
67	Kadruhirsa	✓				✓	✓	✓					✓						✓	✓	✓	8	1.3
68	Kalikochandi							✓					✓						✓	✓		4	0.6
69	Karakuta							✓					✓								✓	3	0.5

Sl No	Names[1]	Homestead	Herbal garden	Farm land	Wet land	Rainfed	Shifting cultivation	Plantations					Protected forest	Sacred grove	Tank 1	Tank 2	Tank 3	Check dam	Streams			Total	
								S.forestry	Cashew nut	Eucalyptus	Silver oak	Road side							Kotra am jhola	Kudi kanda jhola	Boko sakadi	Number	Percentage
		(1)	(2)	(3)	(4)	(5)	(6)	(7)	(8)	(9)	(10)	(11)	(12)	(13)	(14)	(15)	(16)	(17)	(18)	(19)	(20)		
70	Karanjo	✓		✓		✓	✓								✓				✓	✓		7	1.1
71	Karseli							✓					✓									2	0.3
72	Kathi badni						✓	✓					✓						✓	✓		5	0.8
73	Keu kanda												✓						✓	✓	✓	4	0.6
74	Khajuri niali												✓									1	0.2
75	Kichi												✓									1	0.2
76	Klia konda												✓									1	0.2
77	Koi hirsa	✓				✓	✓	✓	✓	✓	✓	✓	✓	✓	✓			✓	✓	✓	✓	15	2.4
78	Koicho												✓						✓	✓	✓	4	0.6
79	Koineteri												✓						✓	✓	✓	4	0.6
80	Konior	✓																				1	0.2
81	Kontakoli							✓	✓	✓	✓		✓									5	0.8
82	Kosa kanda												✓									1	0.2
83	Kudei												✓									1	0.2

Sl No	Names[1]	Homestead	Herbal garden	Farm land	Wet land	Rainfed	Shifting cultivation	Plantations: S.forestry	Plantations: Cashew nut	Plantations: Eucalyptus	Plantations: Silver oak	Plantations: Road side	Protected forest	Sacred grove	Tank 1	Tank 2	Tank 3	Check dam	Streams: Kotra am jhola	Streams: Kudi kanda jhola	Streams: Boko sakadi	Total: Number	Total: Percentage
		(1)	(2)	(3)	(4)	(5)	(6)	(7)	(8)	(9)	(10)	(11)	(12)	(13)	(14)	(15)	(16)	(17)	(18)	(19)	(20)		
84	Kudupa												✓						✓	✓	✓	4	0.6
85	Kukudi sago						✓						✓									2	0.3
86	Kukur langudi	✓	✓	✓		✓	✓	✓	✓	✓	✓	✓	✓	✓	✓	✓	✓	✓	✓	✓	✓	19	3.0
87	Kuramal												✓									1	0.2
88	Lajokuli	✓	✓	✓		✓	✓	✓	✓	✓	✓	✓	✓	✓	✓	✓	✓	✓	✓	✓	✓	19	3.0
89	Lohomada												✓									1	0.2
90	Mankodo kendu												✓									1	0.2
91	Marda mala												✓									1	0.2
92	Mendha mal												✓									1	0.2
93	Mirchinga	✓				✓	✓	✓	✓	✓	✓		✓	✓				✓	✓	✓	✓	13	2.1
94	Modoi	✓					✓	✓					✓									4	0.6
95	Monjorsulia												✓									1	0.2
96	Mota ghas					✓	✓	✓					✓									4	0.6

Sl No	Names[1]	Homestead	Herbal garden	Farm land	Wet land	Rainfed	Shifting cultivation	Plantations					Protected forest	Sacred grove	Tank 1	Tank 2	Tank 3	Check dam	Streams			Total	
								S.forestry	Cashew nut	Eucalyptus	Silver oak	Road side							Kotra am jhola	Kudi kanda jhola	Boko sakadi	Number	Percentage
		(1)	(2)	(3)	(4)	(5)	(6)	(7)	(8)	(9)	(10)	(11)	(12)	(13)	(14)	(15)	(16)	(17)	(18)	(19)	(20)		
97	Munch kondh	✓																				1	0.2
98	Muniga	✓		✓																		2	0.3
99	Musa kani							✓					✓									2	0.3
100	Muturimala							✓					✓									2	0.3
101	Nilgiri													✓								1	0.2
102	Orka						✓						✓									2	0.3
103	Pakodimala												✓									1	0.2
104	Pakua						✓	✓					✓									3	0.5
105	Paldua	✓																				1	0.2
106	Palsi						✓	✓	✓	✓	✓		✓									6	1.0
107	Panasa	✓		✓	✓	✓	✓	✓						✓								7	1.1
108	Pardamal						✓	✓	✓	✓	✓		✓						✓	✓	✓	9	1.4
109	Patal garudo					✓	✓	✓	✓	✓	✓		✓								✓	8	1.3
110	Patpadandi	✓											✓									2	0.3

Sl No	Names[1]	Homestead	Herbal garden	Farm land	Wet land	Rainfed	Shifting cultivation	Plantations: S.forestry	Plantations: Cashew nut	Plantations: Eucalyptus	Plantations: Silver oak	Plantations: Road side	Protected forest	Sacred grove	Tank 1	Tank 2	Tank 3	Check dam	Streams: Kotra am jhola	Streams: Kudi kanda jhola	Streams: Boko sakadi	Total: Number	Total: Percentage
		(1).	(2)	(3)	(4)	(5)	(6)	(7)	(8)	(9)	(10)	(11)	(12)	(13)	(14)	(15)	(16)	(17)	(18)	(19)	(20)		
111	Patro goja	✓	✓										✓									3	0.5
112	Pengo							✓					✓									2	0.3
113	Phul jhadu							✓					✓					✓	✓	✓	✓	6	1.0
114	Pijuli	✓						✓					✓		✓		✓	✓	✓	✓	✓	9	1.4
115	Pit konda												✓									1	0.2
116	Pita konda												✓									1	0.2
117	Pitmari						✓	✓	✓	✓	✓	✓	✓	✓					✓	✓	✓	11	1.7
118	Podai												✓					✓				2	0.3
119	Pordi							✓														1	0.2
120	Poroi buta												✓									1	0.2
121	Poyan	✓		✓									✓									3	0.5
122	Puruda	✓	✓	✓		✓	✓	✓	✓	✓	✓	✓	✓	✓				✓	✓	✓	✓	16	2.5
123	Puti karla							✓	✓	✓			✓									4	0.6
124	Ranbeli							✓					✓									2	0.3

Sl No	Names[1]	Homestead	Herbal garden	Farm land	Wet land	Rainfed	Shifting cultivation	Plantations					Protected forest	Sacred grove	Tank 1	Tank 2	Tank 3	Check dam	Streams			Total	
								S.forestry	Cashew nut	Eucalyptus	Silver oak	Road side							Kotra am jhola	Kudi kanda jhola	Boko sakadi	Number	Percentage
		(1)	(2)	(3)	(4)	(5)	(6)	(7)	(8)	(9)	(10)	(11)	(12)	(13)	(14)	(15)	(16)	(17)	(18)	(19)	(20)		
125	Randuli												✓									1	0.2
126	Reteli												✓									1	0.2
127	Rupni												✓									1	0.2
128	Sakra												✓									1	0.2
129	Sata bari							✓					✓									2	0.3
130	Siadi												✓									1	0.2
131	Sika ghas						✓	✓					✓									3	0.5
132	Simili			✓			✓	✓					✓									4	0.6
133	Sindi												✓									1	0.2
134	Sindur	✓						✓					✓	✓								4	0.6
135	Sitakuti							✓					✓									2	0.3
136	Solap			✓																		1	0.2
137	Sonari							✓					✓									2	0.3
138	Sorenda						✓	✓					✓									3	0.5

Sl No	Names[1]	Homestead	Herbal garden	Farm land	Wet land	Rainfed	Shifting cultivation	Plantations					Protected forest	Sacred grove	Tank 1	Tank 2	Tank 3	Check dam	Streams			Total	
								S.forestry	Cashew nut	Eucalyptus	Silver oak	Road side							Kotra am jhola	Kudi kanda jhola	Boko sakadi	Number	Percentage
		(1)	(2)	(3)	(4)	(5)	(6)	(7)	(8)	(9)	(10)	(11)	(12)	(13)	(14)	(15)	(16)	(17)	(18)	(19)	(20)		
139	Sua kanda												✓						✓	✓	✓	4	0.6
140	Tangiachina	✓						✓					✓									3	0.5
141	Targa						✓	✓	✓	✓	✓	✓	✓									7	1.1
142	Tendka kanda												✓									1	0.2
143	Tentuli	✓		✓		✓		✓					✓									5	0.8
144	Thakurani phulo												✓									1	0.2
145	Thalkudi	✓	✓	✓	✓	✓	✓	✓	✓	✓	✓	✓	✓	✓	✓	✓	✓	✓	✓	✓	✓	20	3.2
146	Tirimundi												✓									1	0.2
147	Tutkuli			✓																		1	0.2
148	Usku buta	✓	✓	✓		✓	✓	✓	✓	✓	✓	✓	✓	✓	✓	✓	✓	✓	✓	✓	✓	19	3.0
	Total	**35**	**7**	**25**	**7**	**23**	**43**	**83**	**26**	**27**	**22**	**17**	**134**	**23**	**12**	**8**	**9**	**15**	**37**	**37**	**40**	**630**	**100**

1=All the names are in Kuvi except for a few which are in Oriya; Chilli in serial. Number 35 above is not pepper.

Plate 4.2: Kirchi Plants in Puligunta.

Plate 4.3: Dumuri (baya) Plants in Kotra Ambo.

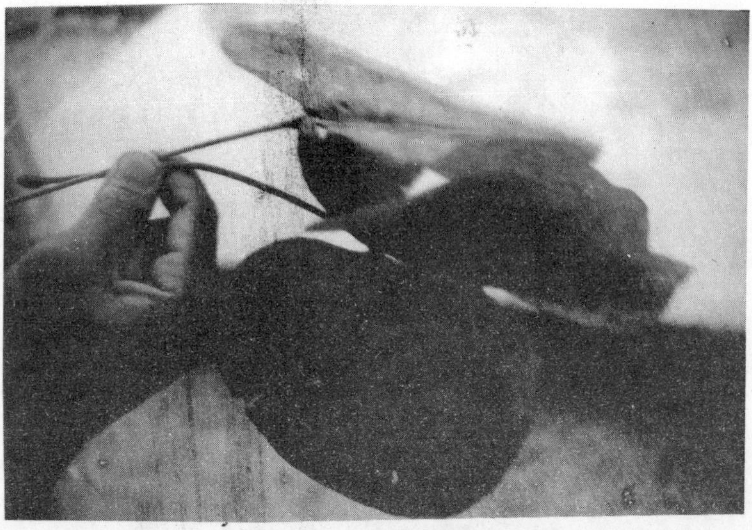

Plate 4.4: Siadi Leaves in Puligunta.

Plate 4.5: Purda Koli (Lantana) has Colonised Hills from Kupa Khal to Kudi Kanda.

Plate 4.6: Golaki (Livestock Treatment) Plant in Kupa Khal.

Plate 4.7: Ronvelli in Puligunta Forest.

Plate 4.8: Char Koli Found above Kotra Ambo Hill and Kupa Khal.

Variation in Number of Wild Plant Species Occurring in Different Land and Waterscape Elements

In Table 4.8 and Fig. 4.4 there are given the number of wild plant species occurring in different areas; arranged in descending order. As expected, maximum number of plants (134) occurred in protected forest area followed by social forestry area (83 plants), shifting cultivation (43 plants), etc. Only seven species occur in the herbal garden and wet lands.

From data presented in Table 4.9 and Fig. 4.5 it is observed:

- (i) that in seven areas (35 per cent), seven to 20 wild plant species occur;
- (ii) that in 10 areas (50 per cent) between 21-40 species occur;
- (iii) that in shifting cultivation areas 43 species occur; and
- (iv) that in protected forest and social forestry plantations more than 80 species have been found.

In summary; as expected in view of the existence of different land use practices prevailing in the village coupled with the nature of topography of the village and diversity of water bodies, there is an enormous inter-area variation in the occurrence of the numbers of wild plant species observed.

Table 4.8: Occurrence of Number of Wild Plant Species in Different Land and Waterscape Elements Arranged in Descending Order

Sl. No.	*Name of the Element*	*No. of Wild Plant Species*
1.	Protected area	134
2.	Social forestry	83
3.	Shifting cultivation	43
4.	Boko sakadi	40
5.	Kotra am jhola	37
6.	Kudi kanda jhola	37
7.	Homestead	35
8.	Eucalyptus plantation	27
9.	Cashew plantation	26
10.	Farm land	25
11.	Sacred grove	23
12.	Rainfed	23
13.	Silver oak	22
14.	Road side	17
15.	Check dam	15
16.	Tank-1	12
17.	Tank-3	9
18.	Tank-2	8
19.	Herbal garden	7
20.	Wet land	7

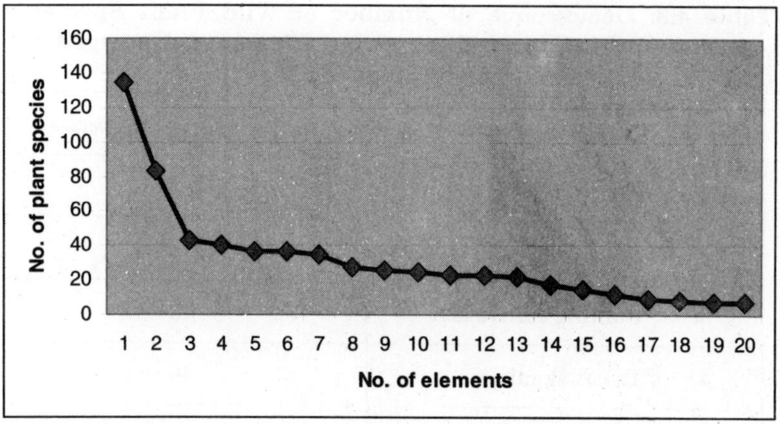

Fig. 4.4: Occurrence of Number of Wild Plant Species in Different Land and Waterscape Elements Arranged in Descending Order.

Table 4.9: Distribution of Number of Wild Plant Species in 20 Areas

No. of wild plant species	*No. of areas*	*Percentage*
1–20	7	35
21–40	10	50
41–60	1	5
>60	2	10
Total	**20**	**100**

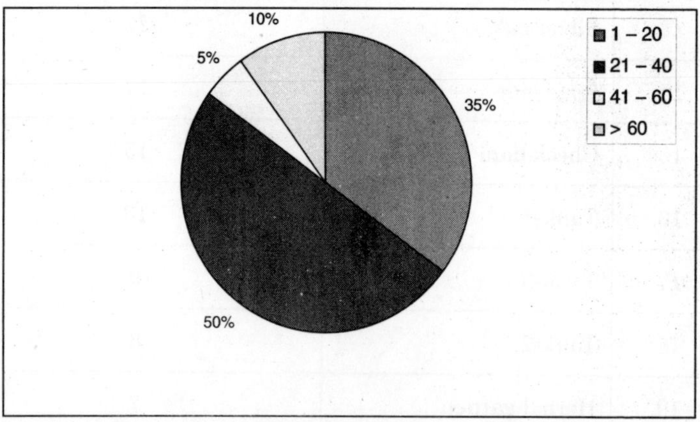

Fig. 4.5. Distribution of Percentage of Wild Plant Species in 20 Areas.

Inter-wild Plant Species Variation in 20 Land and Waterscape Areas

As expected, some wild plant species occur in several habitats while others occur in limited habitats. Data given in Table 4.10 and Fig. 4.6 supports this inference. From the table the following main features emerge:

(i) There are two species-Dubo ghas and Thalkudi (medicinal herbs) that occur in all the 20 areas;

(ii) There are 46 species that occur only in one of the 20 areas. For example Arjun, Bagonaki, Ban jhudongo, Baria kanda, Bislya karani, Harchand, Kosa kanda etc;

(iii) There are 17 species that occur in more than 50 per cent of the elements. For example Koi hirsa, Kukur languid, Lajokuli, Mirchinga, Thalkudi, Puruda etc; and

(iv) Nine most widely distributed species are Ghantia, Thalkudi, Usku buta, Puruda, Lajokuli, Kukur languid, Gereda, Ambo and Apama rongo; these are also socially and economically very relevant in the lives of the villagers.

Table 4.10: Inter-wild Plant Species Variation in 20 Land and Waterscape Areas

Sl. No.	*Name of the Elements*	*Occurrence of no. of plant species*	*Percentage*
1.	Protected area	46	31.1
2.	Social forestry	33	22.3
3.	Shifting cultivation	16	10.8
4.	Boko sakadi	13	8.8
5.	Kotra am jhola	8	5.4
6.	Kudi kanda jhola	4	2.7
7.	Homestead	5	3.4
8.	Eucalyptus plantation	4	2.7
9.	Cashew plantation	2	1.4
10.	Farm land	0	0
11.	Sacred grove	2	1.4
12.	Rainfed	2	1.4
13.	Silver oak	1	0.7
14.	Road side	1	0.7

Sl. No.	Name of the Elements	Occurrence of no. of plant species	Percentage
15.	Check-dam	2	1.4
16.	Tank-1	2	1.4
17.	Tank-3	0	0
18.	Tank-2	1	0.7
19.	Herbal garden	4	2.7
20.	Wet land	2	1.4
	Total	**148**	**100**

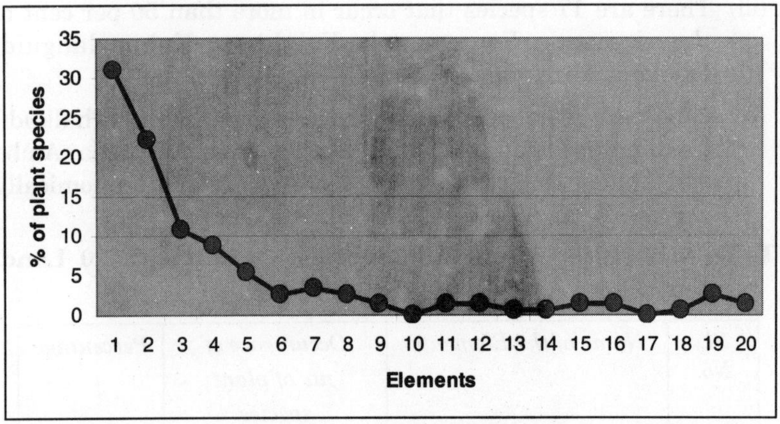

Fig. 4.6. Inter-wild Plant Species Variation in 20 Land and Waterscape Elements.

Wild Mushrooms Occurring in the Village

As seen from Table 4.11, nine types of wild mushrooms occur primarily in three types of landscape elements i.e. rainfed land, farm land and forests. All the mushroom types occur between July and October and only seven are edible.

Table 4.11: Wild Mushrooms Found in the Village

Sl. No.	Oriya Name	Kuvi Name	Availability	Occurrence in landscape elements	Edible / non-edible
1.	Bitok chotu	Menda kundu	July to October	Rainfed, farm land and forest land	Edible
2.	Piri chotu	Pitu kundu	July to October	Rainfed, farm land and forest land	Edible

Sl. No.	*Oriya Name*	*Kuvi Name*	*Availability*	*Occurrence in landscape elements*	*Edible/non-edible*
3.	Bhat chotu	Puchi puyu	July to October	Rainfed, farm land and forest land	Edible
4.	Bali chotu	Manji kutka	July to October	Rainfed, farm land and forest land	Edible
5.	Taku chotu	Taku kutka	July to October	Rainfed, farm land and forest land	Edible
6.	Khat chotu	Marli kutka	July to October	Rainfed, farm land and forest land	Edible
7.	Gobor chotu	Dapi kutka	July to October	Rainfed, farm land and forest land	Non-edible
8.	Busu kutka	Busu kutka	July to October	Rainfed, farm land and forest land	Edible
9.	Jam chotu	Jambu kutka	July to October	Rainfed, farm land and forest land	Non-edible

4.3. A Comparative Analysis of the Occurrence of Wild Animal Species in Different Land and Waterscape Elements

In Table 4.12 given is a list of the wild animals that have been sighted in different land and waterscape elements. At least 66 wild animals frequent the village. It may be noted here that compared to the wild plant species, this list is even more conservative. Also this list does not include aquatic wild animals. They have been described separately in section 4.5.

Variation in the Occurrence of Number of Wild Animal Species in Different Land and Waterscape Elements

In Tables 4.13 and 4.14 and Fig. 4.7 are given the numbers of wild animal species occurring in 20 areas. The following main features emerge from this table:

(i) A maximum number of 56 species (84.8 per cent) are sighted in homestead lands;

(ii) The least number of wild animals 25 species (37.9 per cent) are sighted in wet lands;

(iii) As expected, in protected forest area a large number of wild animals, i.e., 53 species (80.3 per cent) are sighted; and

(iv) It is interesting to note that there are 13 wild species that are not found in protected forest area instead they are sighted in other parts of the village. These species are: Ada gundicha, Baya chodhai, Bilei, Chopeda, Dhadka, Dhandia, Gharchatia, Gunduri, Kojolpati, Mankodo, Parja pati, Saru nago and Sungo poko.

Table 4.12: Wild Animal Species Occurring in Different Landscape and Waterscape Elements

Sl No	Name in Kuvi	Homestead	Herbal garden	Farm land	Wet land	Rainfed	Shifting cultivation	Plantations					Protected forest	Sacred grove	Tank 1	Tank 2	Tank 3	Check dam	Streams			Total	
								S.forestry	Cashew nut	Eucalyptus	Silver oak	Road side							Kotra am jhola	Kudi kanda jhola	Boko sakadi	No.	Percentage
		(1).	(2)	(3)	(4)	(5)	(6)	(7)	(8)	(9)	(10)	(11)	(12)	(13)	(14)	(15)	(16)	(17)	(18)	(19)	(20)		
1	Ada gundicha	✓		✓	✓										✓	✓	✓	✓			✓	8	0.9
2	Bon bilie	✓	✓	✓	✓	✓	✓	✓	✓	✓	✓	✓	✓	✓					✓	✓	✓	16	1.9
3	Budinia	✓	✓	✓	✓	✓	✓	✓	✓	✓	✓	✓	✓	✓				✓	✓	✓	✓	17	2.0
4	Badudi	✓		✓		✓	✓	✓		✓	✓	✓	✓									9	1.1
5	Bago	✓	✓	✓	✓	✓							✓		✓	✓	✓	✓			✓	11	1.3
6	Bohurupi anduo	✓	✓	✓		✓	✓	✓	✓	✓	✓	✓	✓	✓	✓	✓	✓					15	1.8
7	Ban kukuda					✓	✓	✓	✓	✓	✓		✓	✓					✓	✓	✓	11	1.3
8	Bani	✓	✓	✓		✓	✓	✓	✓	✓	✓	✓	✓	✓	✓	✓	✓	✓	✓	✓	✓	19	2.2
9	Baria						✓	✓	✓	✓	✓		✓	✓					✓	✓	✓	10	1.2
10	Baya chodhai	✓		✓																		2	0.2
11	Bengo	✓	✓	✓	✓	✓	✓	✓	✓	✓	✓	✓	✓	✓	✓	✓	✓	✓	✓	✓	✓	20	2.3
12	Bhalu	✓		✓		✓	✓	✓	✓	✓	✓	✓	✓	✓					✓	✓	✓	13	1.5
13	Bilei	✓		✓																		1	0.1

Sl No	Name in Kuvi	Homestead	Herbal garden	Farm land	Wet land	Rainfed	Shifting cultivation	Plantations					Protected forest	Sacred grove	Tank 1	Tank 2	Tank 3	Check dam	Streams			Total	
								S.forestry	Cashew nut	Eucalyptus	Silver oak	Road side							Kotra am jhola	Kudi kanda jhola	Boko sakadi	No.	Percentage
		(1).	(2)	(3)	(4)	(5)	(6)	(7)	(8)	(9)	(10)	(11)	(12)	(13)	(14)	(15)	(16)	(17)	(18)	(19)	(20)		
14	Chabara	✓	✓	✓		✓	✓	✓	✓	✓	✓	✓	✓	✓								**12**	**1.4**
15	Chanchana	✓	✓	✓	✓	✓	✓	✓	✓	✓	✓	✓	✓	✓					✓			**14**	**1.6**
16	Chia	✓	✓	✓	✓	✓	✓	✓	✓	✓	✓	✓	✓	✓	✓	✓	✓	✓	✓	✓	✓	**20**	**2.3**
17	Chita bagh	✓		✓		✓	✓	✓	✓	✓	✓	✓	✓	✓					✓	✓	✓	**13**	**1.5**
18	Chiti	✓					✓	✓	✓	✓	✓	✓	✓	✓								**9**	**1.1**
19	Chopeda	✓		✓		✓	✓	✓	✓	✓												**7**	**0.8**
20	Dhadka				✓	✓									✓	✓	✓				✓	**6**	**0.7**
21	Dhamana	✓	✓	✓		✓	✓	✓	✓	✓	✓	✓	✓					✓				**12**	**1.4**
22	Dhandia	✓			✓										✓	✓	✓		✓	✓	✓	**7**	**0.8**
23	Dhulia nago	✓	✓	✓		✓	✓	✓	✓	✓	✓	✓	✓	✓					✓	✓	✓	**15**	**1.8**
24	Dingiri	✓				✓	✓	✓	✓	✓	✓	✓	✓	✓								**9**	**1.1**
25	Dud boda	✓	✓	✓		✓	✓	✓	✓	✓	✓	✓	✓	✓								**12**	**1.4**
26	Endua	✓	✓	✓		✓	✓	✓	✓	✓	✓	✓	✓	✓	✓	✓	✓	✓	✓	✓		**18**	**2.1**
27	Gharchatia	✓		✓		✓						✓										**4**	**0.5**

Sl No	Name in Kuvi	*Homestead*	*Herbal garden*	*Farm land*	*Wet land*	*Rainfed*	*Shifting cultivation*	*Plantations*					*Protected forest*	*Sacred grove*	*Tank 1*	*Tank 2*	*Tank 3*	*Check dam*	*Streams*			*Total*	
								S.forestry	*Cashew nut*	*Eucalyptus*	*Silver oak*	*Road side*							*Kotra am jhola*	*Kudi kanda jhola*	*Boko sakadi*	*No.*	*Percentage*
		(1).	(2)	(3)	(4)	(5)	(6)	(7)	(8)	(9)	(10)	(11)	(12)	(13)	(14)	(15)	(16)	(17)	(18)	(19)	(20)		
28	Girna	✓	✓	✓		✓	✓	✓	✓	✓	✓	✓	✓	✓								**12**	**1.4**
29	Gobor poko	✓	✓	✓		✓	✓	✓	✓	✓	✓	✓	✓	✓					✓	✓	✓	**15**	**1.8**
30	Gunduchi	✓	✓	✓		✓	✓	✓	✓	✓	✓	✓	✓	✓					✓	✓	✓	**15**	**1.8**
31	Gunji	✓			✓										✓	✓	✓	✓	✓	✓	✓	**8**	**0.9**
32	Gunduri	✓				✓	✓	✓	✓	✓	✓	✓	✓						✓	✓	✓	**11**	**1.3**
33	Holdi basanta	✓	✓	✓		✓	✓	✓	✓	✓	✓	✓	✓	✓					✓	✓	✓	***15***	***1.8***
34	Jia	✓	✓	✓	✓	✓	✓	✓	✓	✓	✓	✓	✓	✓	✓	✓	✓	✓	✓	✓	✓	***20***	**2.3**
35	Jhiji pok	✓	✓	✓		✓	✓	✓	✓	✓	✓	✓	✓	✓								***12***	***1.4***
36	Jhitipiti	✓	✓	✓		✓	✓	✓	✓	✓	✓	✓	✓	✓	✓	✓	✓	✓	✓			***17***	***2.0***
37	Kala nag	✓	✓	✓		✓	✓	✓	✓	✓	✓	✓	✓	✓	✓	✓						***14***	***1.6***
38	Kalet	✓	✓	✓		✓	✓	✓	✓	✓	✓	✓	✓	✓	✓				✓			***14***	***1.6***
39	Kalia	✓	✓	✓	✓	✓	✓	✓	✓	✓	✓	✓	✓	✓	✓	✓	✓	✓	✓	✓	✓	***20***	***2.3***
40	Kankada bicha	✓	✓	✓	✓	✓	✓	✓	✓	✓	✓	✓	✓	✓	✓	✓	✓	✓	✓	✓	✓	***20***	***2.3***
41	Kapto	✓	✓	✓	✓	✓	✓	✓	✓	✓	✓	✓	✓	✓	✓	✓	✓	✓	✓	✓	✓	***20***	***2.3***

Sl No	Name in Kuvi	Homestead	Herbal garden	Farm land	Wet land	Rainfed	Shifting cultivation	Plantations					Protected forest	Sacred grove	Tank 1	Tank 2	Tank 3	Check dam	Streams			Total	
								S.forestry	Cashew nut	Eucalyptus	Silver oak	Road side							Kotra am jhola	Kudi kanda jhola	Boko sakadi	No.	Percentage
		(1).	(2)	(3)	(4)	(5)	(6)	(7)	(8)	(9)	(10)	(11)	(12)	(13)	(14)	(15)	(16)	(17)	(18)	(19)	(20)		
42	Kia chadei	✓	✓	✓	✓	✓	✓	✓	✓	✓	✓	✓	✓	✓	✓	✓	✓	✓	✓	✓	✓	**20**	**2.3**
43	Koili	✓	✓	✓		✓	✓	✓	✓	✓	✓	✓	✓	✓	✓	✓	✓	✓	✓	✓		**18**	**2.1**
44	Kosa nuheudi			✓		✓	✓	✓	✓	✓	✓	✓	✓	✓	✓	✓	✓	✓	✓	✓		**16**	**1.9**
45	Kojolpati	✓		✓																		**2**	**0.2**
46	Kua	✓	✓	✓		✓	✓	✓	✓	✓	✓	✓	✓	✓	✓	✓	✓	✓	✓	✓	✓	**19**	**2.2**
47	Kutra					✓	✓	✓	✓	✓	✓		✓	✓				✓	✓	✓	✓	**12**	**1.4**
48	Mankodo					✓	✓	✓	✓	✓	✓	✓	✓	✓	✓	✓	✓	✓	✓	✓	✓	**16**	**1.9**
49	Mayur	✓				✓	✓	✓	✓	✓	✓		✓	✓					✓	✓	✓	**11**	**1.3**
50	Machronka				✓										✓	✓	✓	✓			✓	**6**	**0.7**
51	Musa	✓	✓	✓	✓	✓	✓	✓	✓	✓	✓	✓	✓	✓	✓	✓	✓	✓	✓	✓	✓	**20**	**2.3**
52	Nago	✓	✓	✓	✓	✓	✓	✓	✓	✓	✓	✓	✓	✓	✓	✓	✓	✓	✓	✓	✓	**20**	**2.3**
53	Odho												✓		✓	✓	✓		✓	✓	✓	**7**	**0.8**
54	Parja pati	✓	✓	✓	✓	✓	✓	✓	✓	✓	✓	✓	✓	✓	✓	✓	✓	✓	✓	✓	✓	**20**	**2.3**
55	Pecha	✓	✓	✓	✓	✓	✓	✓	✓	✓	✓	✓	✓	✓	✓	✓						**15**	**1.8**

Sl No	Name in Kuvi	Homestead	Herbal garden	Farm land	Wet land	Rainfed	Shifting cultivation	Plantations					Protected forest	Sacred grove	Tank 1	Tank 2	Tank 3	Check dam	Streams			Total	
								S.forestry	Cashew nut	Eucalyptus	Silver oak	Road side							Kotra am jhola	Kudi kanda jhola	Boko sakadi	No.	Percentage
		(1).	(2)	(3)	(4)	(5)	(6)	(7)	(8)	(9)	(10)	(11)	(12)	(13)	(14)	(15)	(16)	(17)	(18)	(19)	(20)		
56	Pimpudi	✓	✓	✓		✓	✓	✓	✓	✓	✓	✓	✓	✓	✓	✓	✓	✓	✓	✓		*18*	*2.1*
57	Potra sap	✓	✓	✓		✓	✓	✓	✓	✓	✓	✓	✓	✓					✓	✓	✓	*15*	*1.8*
58	Sailm	✓	✓	✓	✓	✓	✓	✓	✓	✓	✓	✓	✓	✓	✓	✓	✓	✓	✓	✓	✓	*20*	*2.3*
59	Saru nago	✓	✓	✓	✓	✓	✓	✓	✓	✓	✓	✓	✓	✓	✓	✓	✓	✓	✓			*18*	*2.1*
60	Singoti				✓										✓	✓	✓	✓				*5*	*0.6*
61	Sua chadei		✓	✓	✓	✓	✓	✓	✓	✓	✓	✓	✓		✓	✓	✓	✓	✓	✓	✓	*19*	*2.2*
62	Sungo poko	✓	✓	✓	✓	✓	✓	✓	✓	✓	✓	✓	✓	✓	✓	✓	✓	✓	✓			*18*	*2.1*
63	Tekor	✓						✓	✓	✓	✓	✓	✓	✓								*7*	*0.8*
64	Thekua	✓				✓	✓	✓	✓	✓	✓	✓	✓									*8*	*0.9*
65	Rambi	✓																				*1*	*0.1*
66	Pandka	✓																				*1*	*0.1*
	Total	**56**	**38**	**48**	**25**	**52**	**51**	**52**	**51**	**52**	**51**	**48**	**53**	**46**	**34**	**33**	**31**	**30**	**41**	**36**	**36**	***855***	***100***

Note: While the data in this table were finalised with the list of 64 wild animals, the villagers provided names of two more wild animals listed in serial numbers 65 and 66. In Chapter 5, however in terms of various usages of the wild animals the analysis is based only on 64 wild animals.

Table 4.13: Occurrence of Number of Wild Animals in Different Landscape and Waterscape Elements

Sl. No.	*Name of the Elements*	*No. of Wild Animal Species*
1.	Homestead	56
2.	Protected area	53
3.	Rainfed	52
4.	Social forestry	52
5.	Eucalyptus plantation	52
6.	Shifting cultivation	51
7.	Cashew plantation	51
8.	Silver oak	51
9.	Road side	48
10.	Farm land	48
11.	Sacred grove	46
12.	Kotra am jhola	41
13.	Herbal garden	38
14.	Kudi kanda jhola	36
15.	Boko sakadi	36
16.	Tank-1	34
17.	Tank-2	33
18.	Tank-3	31
19.	Check-dam	30
20.	Wet land	25

Table 4.14: Distribution of Number of Wild Animal Species in 20 Areas

No. of Wild Animal Species	*No. of Areas*	*Percentage*
20–30	2	10
31–40	6	30
41–50	4	20
> 50	8	40
Total	**20**	**100**

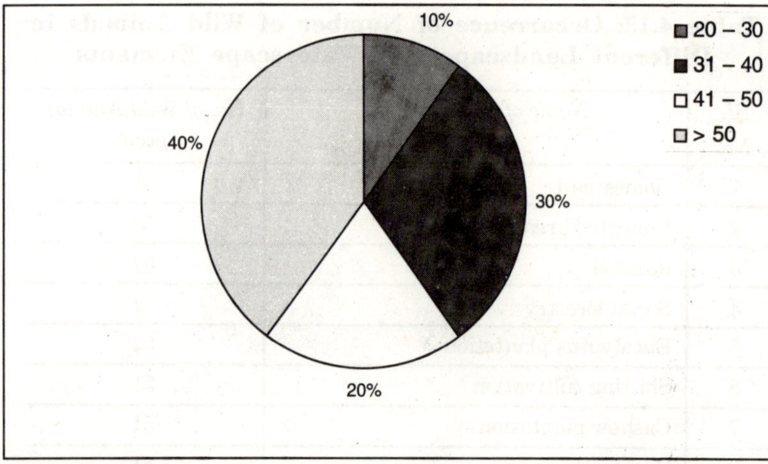

Fig. 4.7. Distribution of Number of Wild Animal Species in 20 Areas.

Inter-wild Animal Species Variation in 20 Land and Waterscape Areas

From Table 4.15 the following key observations emerge:

(i) There are 11 wild animal species that are found in all the 20 areas;

(ii) There are a large number of animals numbering 47 (71.2 per cent) that are sighted in more than 50 per cent of the areas; and

(iii) The 10 most often sighted animals in large number in the 20 elements are Bengo, Chia, Jia, Kalia, Kankada bicha, Kapto, Kia chadhei, Musa, Parjapati and Salim.

Table 4.15: Inter-wild Animal Species Variation in 20 Land and Waterscape Elements

No. of Elements	*No. of Animal Species*	*Percentage*
1.	3	4.5
2.	2	3.0
3.	0	0.0
4.	1	1.5
5.	1	1.5
6.	2	3.0
7.	4	6.1
8.	3	4.5

contd...

No. of Elements	*No. of Animal Species*	*Percentage*
9.	3	4.5
10.	1	1.5
11.	4	6.1
12.	6	9.1
13.	2	3.0
14.	3	4.5
15.	7	10.6
16.	3	4.5
17.	2	3.0
18.	5	7.6
19.	3	4.5
20.	11	16.7
Total	**66**	**100**

4.4 A Comparative Analysis of the Occurrence of Aquatic and Wild Animal Species in Different Waterscape Elements

Table 4.16 and Fig. 4.8 give a list of aquatic and wild animal species in different waterscape elements. The salient observations emerging from this Table are:

(i) there are three wild species of fishes Godsi, Karandi and Magur that are found in all the three tanks as well as in the check dam;

(ii) in none of the three streams of the village neither one of the above mentioned fishes are seen;

(iii) there are two wild animals which are seen in and around the waterscape areas. They are Bengo and Kankada which are seen around the three tanks, check-dam and the stream Boko sakadi; and

(iv) Pani sap (water snake) is seen only in tank No. 3 and check dam.

Table 4.16: Occurrence of Aquatic and Wild Animal Species in Different Waterscape Elements

Sl. No.	*Name of fishes*	*English name*	*Tank 1*	*Tank 2*	*Tank 3*	*Check dam*	*Streams*			*Total*	*Percentage*
							Kotra am jhola	*Kudi kanda jhola*	*Boko sakadi*		
1.	Godsi	Fish	✓	✓	✓	✓				4	19.0
2.	Karandi	Fish				✓				1	4.8
3.	Magur	Fish	✓	✓	✓	✓				4	19.0
	Wild animals found in the vicinity										
1.	Bengo	Frog	✓	✓	✓	✓			✓	5	23.8
2.	Kankda	Crab	✓	✓	✓	✓			✓	5	23.8
3.	Pani sap	Water snake			✓	✓				2	9.5
	Total		4	4	5	6	0	0	2	21	100

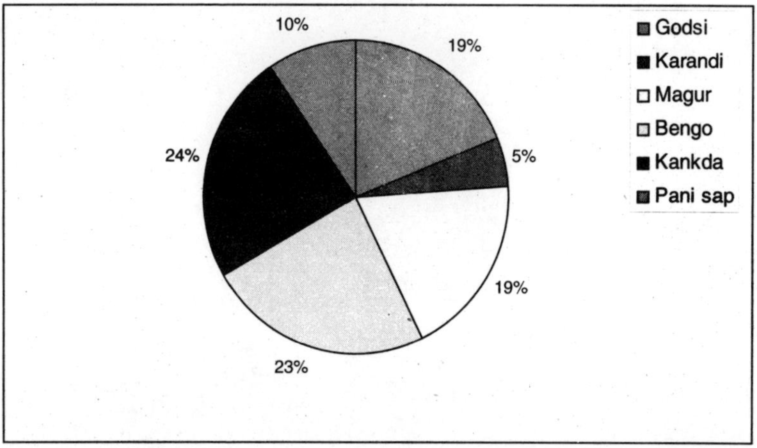

Fig. 4.8. Occurrence of Aquatic and Wild Animal Species in Different Waterscape Elements.

5

Biodiversity and Sustainable Livelihoods

In the preceeding Chapters 3 and 4, an analysis and description were presented with respect to, (a) the various cultivated plants found in different landscape elements in the village, (b) livestock holding pattern in the village, (c) names and distribution of various wild plants and animals in the delineated 20 land and waterscape elements, and (d) wild and introduced aquatic animals in waterscape elements. It was observed that an enormous variety of cultivated and wild plants are found in the village.

In this chapter it is described the various usages of cultivated and wild plants and animals. An attempt has also been made to demonstrate qualitatively, that both wild and cultivated biodiversity found in the village plays a very vital role in the livelihoods of the villagers.

The materials in this chapter have been organised and described under the following heads:

5.1. Cultivated crops, vegetables and trees and their usages

5.2. Wild plants and their usages,

5.3. Wild animals and their usages, and

5.4. Aquatic animals and their usages.

5.1. Cultivated Crops, Vegetables and Trees and Their Usages

Diversity of Usages

In Table 5.1 there are given a list of plants that are grown in the village together with their names in Kuvi, Oriya and English. This table also gives the habits of the plants grown. The usages of various plants are also given, together with the information of whether they are consumed at home and/or marketed. This list is derived by pulling data from all the individual landscape elements described earlier in Chapter 3 and 4. Data given in Table 5.1 reveals the following:

(i) Ninety five different plant species are grown in the village. Out of these 95 species, 37 species are represented by trees. The remaining 58 species (61 per cent) are annual in nature and mostly comprise of crops and vegetables-tubers, bulbs, climbers, creepers, etc.; and

(ii) These 95 plant species are used for a variety of purposes: food including edible oil, medicine, for making agricultural implements and musical instruments, for house construction, furniture, fuelwood, fodder, manure, mulching, fencing etc.

In Table 5.2 and Fig. 5.1 are given the number of cultivated plants that are used for seven selected purposes. A substantial number of plants 71 (74.7 per cent) are used as food, 15 plants are used as medicines, 24 provide fuelwood, 20 yield fodder for animals, 17 provide wood for house construction, making agricultural implements and furniture, and 10 plants are used as manure and for mulching and seven plants are used for live fencing.

Pattern of Consumption

In Table 5.3 and Fig. 5.2 the details of the cultivated biodiversity that is consumed at home and/or sold in the market are given. Products of 26 plants (27.4 per cent) are exclusively consumed at home. Only products of three plants (3.1 per cent) are exclusively sold in the market. An overwhelming number of products 66 plants (69.5 per cent) are both consumed at home and also sold in the market.

It is thus evident that the cultivated biodiversity fulfills a variety of subsistence needs of the people and also generates income to cater to the other needs such as education, health, clothing communication, festivals, etc.

Table 5.1: Cultivated Crops, Vegetables and Trees and their Usages

Sl. No.	*Name of the plants*				*Habit*	*Usages*	*Consumed at home*	*Mar-keted*
	Kuvi	*Oriya*	*English*	*Scientific*				
1.	Aalsi	Alsi	Niger	*Guizotia abbysinica*	Herb	Fodder, mulching, manure, edible oil		✓
2.	Alami	Ada	Ginger	*Zinziber officinale*	Herb	Medicine, food	✓	✓
3.	Amruti	Amrutbhanda	Papaya	*Carica papaya*	Tree	Food, medicine	✓	✓
4.	Arjun	Arjun	Arjun	*Terminalia arjuna*	Tree	Construction, implements	✓	
5.	Arka	Kangu	Finger millet	?	Herb	Food, fodder	✓	
6.	Bailo	Jhota	Indian bean	*Dolichos sp.?*	Climber	Food, fodder	✓	✓
7.	Bateri	Paluo	Arrowroot	?	Herb	Food, medicine	✓	✓
8.	Bendi	Bhendi	Lady's finger	*Abelmoschus esculantus*	Herb	Food	✓	✓
9.	Bhumi sana	China badam	Ground nut	*Arachis hypogea*	Herb	Food	✓	✓
10.	Bileikanta	Bada gacha	Lantana	*Lantana camara*	Shrub	Fencing, fuelwood	✓	
11.	Borokoli	Borkoli	Chinies date, Jujube	*Ziziphus jujuba*	Tree	Food	✓	
12.	Chakunda	Chakunda	Cassia Siamea	*Cassia siamea*	Tree	Fuelwood, construction	✓	
13.	Chandan	Chandan	Sandal wood	*Santalum album*	Tree	Fuelwood	✓	
14.	Chichoni	Janhi	Ridged gourd	*Luffa acutangula*	Climber	Food	✓	✓
15.	Chilor	Chilor	Acacia	*Acacia torta?*	Shrub	Fencing	✓	
16.	Citramurka	Chitramul	??	?	Creeper	Medicine		✓

Sl. No.	Name of the plants				Habit	Usages	Consumed at home	Mar-keted
	Kuvi	Oriya	English	Scientific				
17.	Danduli	Tutkoli	Melbury	?	Tree	Food,fodder,fuelwood	✓	
18.	Deru	Baunsa	Bamboo	*Dendrocalamus sp.*	Tree	Food, fencing, fodder, construction, implements, fuelwood	✓	✓
19.	Dhania	Dhania	Coriander	*Coriandrum sativum*	Herb	Food	✓	✓
20.	Doblauli	Rasuno	Garllic	*Allium sativum*	Herb	Food, medicine	✓	✓
21.	Dohi	Dimri	?	?	Tree	Food, fodder	✓	
22.	Dongar oding	Dongor rani	Green gram	?	Herb	Food, mulching	✓	✓
23.	Gajori	Gajor	Carrot	*Daucus carota*	Herb	Food	✓	✓
24.	Gati Kobi	Ganti kobi	Knolkhol	*Brassica coulorapa*	Herb	Food	✓	✓
25.	Gocha kanga	Buda beans	French beans	?	Climber	Food	✓	✓
26.	Guanr	Guanr	Cluster bean	*Cymopsis tetragonoloba*	Herb	Food	✓	✓
27.	Gumna	Gambhari	Gmelina	*Gmelina arborea*	Tree	Implements, furniture	✓	
28.	Harsu	Soriso	Mustard	*Brassica campestris var. glauca*	Herb	Food, edible oil, medicine,	✓	✓
29.	Heyan	Baigono	Brinjal	*Solanum melongena*	Herb	Food	✓	✓
30.	Hinga	Holdi	Turmeric	*Curcuma domestica*	Herb	Food, medicine	✓	✓
31.	Hopa	Saru	Arum	*Colocasia esculanta*	Herb	Food	✓	✓

Sl. No.	*Name of the plants*				*Habit*	*Usages*	*Consumed at home*	*Mar-keted*
	Kuvi	*Oriya*	*English*	*Scientific*				
32.	Hurwe	Simbo	Bean	*Dolichos sp.*	Climber	Food, fodder	✓	✓
33.	Jafra	Jafra	Annatto	*Bixa orellana*	Tree	Fodder		✓
34.	Jambo	Jamkoli	Black berry	*Syzigium cumini*	Tree	Food, fodder, construction, implements, fuelwood	✓	✓
35.	Jona	Makka	Maize	*Zea mays*	Herb	Food, fodder, mulching	✓	✓
36.	Kajuri	Khojuri	Date palm	*Phoenix sp.*	Tree	Food, construction	✓	✓
37.	Kala kanga	Jhudongo	Cow pea	*Vigna sp.*	Climber	Food, fodder	✓	✓
38.	Kamala	Kamala	Orange	*Citrus reticulata*	Tree	Food, fuelwood	✓	✓
39.	Karanji	Karanjo	Pongamia	*Pongamia pinnata*	Tree	Edible oil, medicine,manure, construction, implements, fuelwood	✓	✓
40.	Karla	Kolora	Bitter gourd	*Momordica charantia*	Climber	Food	✓	✓
41.	Kawa janna	Khed jonna	Sorghum	*Sorghum vulgare*	Herb	Food, fodder	✓	✓
42.	Keeni	Joda	Castor	*Ricinus communis*	Tree	Edible oil, medicine,	✓	✓
43.	Kodtang	Koloth	Horse gram	*Dolichos uniflorus*	Creeper	Food, fodder, medicine	✓	✓
44.	Kofi	Kafi	Coffee	*Coffea arabica*	Tree	Food		✓

Sl. No.	Name of the plants				Habit	Usages	Consumed at home	Mar-keted
	Kuvi	Oriya	English	Scientific				
45.	Kohoda	Suan	Finger millet	?	Herb	Food,fodder, mulching,manure	✓	
46.	Kopakucha	Borda	?	?	Tree	Food, fuelwood	✓	✓
47.	Krushna chuda	Krushna chuda	Gulmohar	*Delonix regia*	Tree	Fuelwood	✓	
48.	Kuliyan	Dhano	Paddy	*Oryza sativa*	Herb	Food,fodder,mulchin g,manure	✓	
49.	Kumuda	Boit alu	Pumpkin	*Cucurbita maxima*	Creeper	Food, fodder, mulching,	✓	✓
50.	Kunduru	Kunduri	Ivy gourd	*Coccinia sp.?*	Climber	Food	✓	✓
51.	Leka kuna	Similikonda	Tapioca	*Manihot esculanta*	Shrub	Food, fencing,	✓	✓
52.	Lekha	Simili	Indian cotton tree	*Bombax malabaricum*	Tree	Fuelwood, construction	✓	
53.	Lembu	Lembu	Lemon	*Citrus sp.*	Tree	Food, medicine	✓	✓
54.	Lobiya	Borboti	Cow pea	*Vigna unguiculata*	Climber	Food, fodder	✓	✓
55.	Mahaa	Ambo	Mango	*Mangifera indica*	Tree	Food, fuelwood, construction, implements	✓	✓
56.	Mahaa neem	Moha neem	Neem	*Melia azedirach*	Tree	Medicine, manure, fuelwood	✓	
57.	Mandar	Mandar	China rose	*Hibiscus rosa-sinensis*	Tree	Ornaments	✓	

Sl. No.	*Name of the plants*				*Habit*	*Usages*	*Consumed at home*	*Mar-keted*
	Kuvi	*Oriya*	*English*	*Scientific*				
58.	Mandia	Mandia	Ragi	*Elucine carnacea*	Herb	Food,fodder, mulching,manure	✓	
59.	Manji jambo	Pijuli	Guava	*Psidium guajava*	Tree	Food, medicine, construction, implements, fuelwood	✓	✓
60.	Marnu kanga	Kandul	Pigeon pea	*Cajanus cajan*	Tree	Food, fuelwood	✓	✓
61.	Matakucha	Khosla sago	?	?	Herb	Food	✓	✓
62.	Matakucha	Khada sago	?	?	Herb	Food	✓	✓
63.	Matakucha	Palongo sago	?	?	Herb	Food	✓	✓
64.	Mirlo	Mirlo	Squash	*Cucurbita moschata*	Climber	Food	✓	✓
65.	Mirsi	Maricho	Chilly	*Capsicum annuum*	Herb	Food	✓	✓
66.	Mula	Mula	Radish	*Raphanus sativus*	Herb	Food	✓	✓
67.	Mundra	Kakudi	Cucumber	*Cucumis sativus*	Creeper	Food	✓	✓
68.	Muninga	Sajana	Drumstick	*Moringa oleifera*	Tree	Food	✓	✓
69.	Murga/sinki	Murga	Sisal	*Agave americana*	Shrub	Fencing, implements,	✓	
70.	Nadeli	Nadia	Coconut	*Cocos nucifera*	Tree	Food	✓	✓
71.	Nangeli kuna	Khombo alu	Yam	?	Herb	Food	✓	✓

Sl. No.	Name of the plants				Habit	Usages	Consumed at home	Mar-keted
	Kuvi	Oriya	English	Scientific				
72.	Niligiri	Niligiri	Eucalyptus	*Eucalyptus globulus*	Tree	Medicine, fencing, construction, implements, fuelwood	✓	
73.	Panaha	Panasa	Jackfruit	*Artocarpus integrifolia*	Tree	Food, fodder ,construction, implements, fuelwood	✓	✓
74.	Peja(kajai)	Bilati Baigono	Tomato - large size	*Lycopersicum esculantum*	Herb	Food	✓	✓
75.	Peja(una)	Bhejiri	Tomato - small size	?	Herb	Food	✓	✓
76.	Puda kobi	Banda kobi	Cabbage	*Brassica oleracea var. capitata*	Herb	Food, fodder	✓	✓
77.	Pula	Tentuli	Tamarind	*Tamarindus indica*	Tree	Food, edible oil, medicine, fodder, construction, implements, fuelwood	✓	✓
78.	Puyu kobi	Phul kobi	Cauliflower	*Brassica oleracea var.botrytis*	Herb	Food	✓	✓
79.	Radhachuda	Radhachuda	Indian laburnun	*Cassia fistula*	Tree	Fencing, ornaments, construction, fuelwood	✓	
80.	Rani kuna	Mati konda	Sweet potato	*Ipomea batatas*	Herb	Food, fodder	✓	✓
81.	Ranja benisi	Malo beans	Beans	?	Climber	Food	✓	✓

Sl. No.	*Name of the plants*				*Habit*	*Usages*	*Consumed at home*	*Marketed*
	Kuvi	*Oriya*	*English*	*Scientific*				
82.	Rupa	Silver oak	Silver oak	*Grevillea robusta*	Tree	Fuelwood	✓	
83.	Sana	Motor channa	Green peas	*Pisum sativum*	Creeper	Food	✓	✓
84.	Sapta	Sapota	Sapota	*Achrus sapota*	Tree	Food	✓	✓
85.	Simarani	Kontagocho	Thorny Bush	?	Shrub	Fencing, fuelwood	✓	
86.	Sitaphol	Atta	Custard apple	*Annona squamosa*	Tree	Food, fuelwood	✓	✓
87.	Solop	Salab	Fishtail palm	*Caryota urens*	Tree	Construction	✓	✓
88.	Tadi	Kadali	Banana	*Musa paradisica*	Tree	Food, mulching, manure, fodder	✓	✓
89.	Tala bonda	Gendu phul	Mari gold	*Tagetes erecta*	Herb	Ornaments	✓	✓
90.	Tek	Saguan	Teak	*Tectona grandis*	Tree	Construction, implments, furniture	✓	
91.	Tini lau	Lau	Bottle gourd	*Lagenaria vulgaris*	Climber	Food	✓	✓
92.	Toba	Batapi	Grape fruit	*Citrus paradisica?*	Tree	Food ,fuelwood	✓	✓
93.	Tua	?	?	?	Tree	Food, fuelwood	✓	
94.	Ulli	Piajo	Onion	*Allium cepa*	Herb	Food, medicine	✓	✓
95.	Valia	Kaju	Cashew	*Anacardium occidentale*	Tree	Food, fuelwood	✓	✓

Note: (?) denotes that we could not ascertain name in English or scientific name.

Table 5.2: Number of Plant Species out of 95 used for a Select Seven Purposes

Sl. No.	*Purposes*	*No of Species*	*Percentage*
1.	Food	71	67.45
2.	Medicine	15	14.25
3.	Fuelwood	24	22.8
4.	Fodder	20	19
5.	Structural	17	16.15
6.	Manure, mulching	10	9.5
7.	Fencing	7	6.65

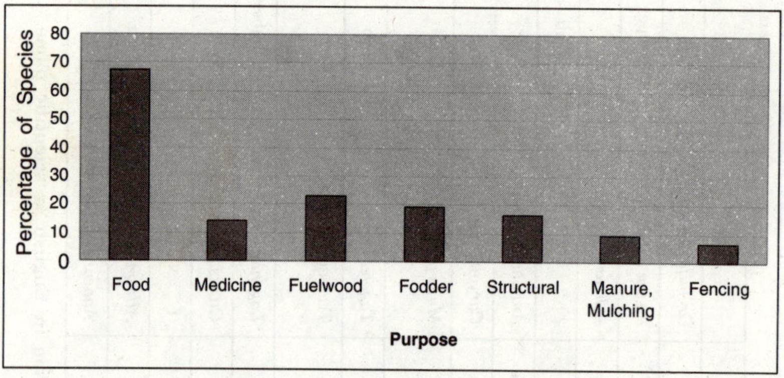

Fig. 5.1. Number of Plant Species out of 95 used for a Select Seven Purposes.

Table 5.3: Pattern of Use of the 95 Cultivated Plants

Sl. No.	*Use Pattern*	*No of Species*	*Percentage*
1.	Consumed at home	26	27.4
2.	Marketed	3	3.1
3.	Consumed at home and marketed	66	69.5
Total		**95**	**100**

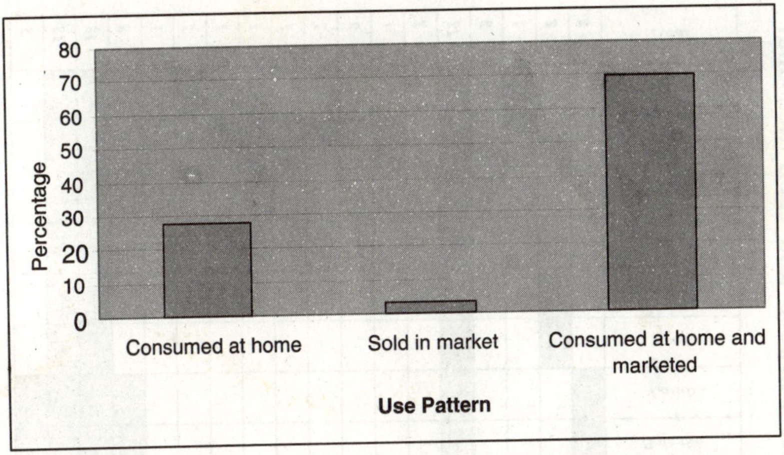

Fig. 5.2. Pattern of Use of the 95 Cultivated Plants.

5.2 Wild Plants and their Usages

As noted earlier in Chapter 4, a large number of wild plants numbering over 148 (Table 4.7) occur in different landscape elements of the village. In this section, we have described diversity of usages of various plants and seasonal availability of plant products. The material has been presented under the following three heads:

(i) Diversity of usages;

(ii) Seasonal availability of various wild plant products; and

(iii) Edible wild mushrooms.

(i) Diversity of Usages

Although as noted earlier, there are 148 wild plants in the village. However, presently 15 plants are not being used. Information of the nine plants with respect to their useage could not be collected. Thus the total number of plants available for the purpose of analysis of pattern of usages is 124. In Table 5.4 are given the names of the 124 wild plants, their parts used and the pattern of usage. The table also gives their seasonal availability. A large number of plants, i.e., 124 (83.8 per cent) out of 148 are used for a variety of purposes. Fifteen plants that are not used currently are listed in Table 5.5. The plants for which information in respect of their use could not be collected are: Bandona, Berongo, Chitini, Gorimenda, Kalikochandi, Renduli, Sakra, Sika ghas and Sua kanda.

Table 5.4: Names of the 124 Wild Plants, their Parts used with the Purpose and their Seasonal Availability

Plants	*Parts*	*Name in Oriya*	*Kuvi name*	*Plant parts*	*Usages*	*Pouso*	*Magh*	*Faguno*	*Chaito*	*Boisakh*	*Landi*	*Asad*	*Bondapon*	*Osa*	*Doshra*	*Diali*	*Pond*	*Total*
1	1	Ambo	Mahaaa	Fruit	Food					■	■							2
	2			Seed	Food							■	■					2
2	3	Amla	Jurha	Fruit	Medicine			■	■							■	■	4
3	4	Apama rongo	Duchabondru	Root	Medicine	■	■											2
4	5	Arjun	Arjun marnu	Wood	Fuelwood	■	■	■	■	■	■	■	■	■	■	■	■	12
	6			Stem	Housing	■	■	■										3
5	7	Bagonaki	Launikoti	Root	Medicine											■		1
6	8	Bahada	Trahu	Fruit	Medicine	■	■											2
7	9	Baidonko	Tudayan	Root	Medicine											■		1
	10			Seed	Medicine											■		1
8	11	Bajra mali	Melukukuti	Flower	Medicine											■		1
	12			Root	Medicine											■		1
9	13	Ban jhudongo	Jada kala kanga	Root	Medicine												■	1
10	14	Bansaru	Konja tahaodi	Tuber	Fodder	■												1
11	15	Baria kanda	Dkli kunaya	Tuber	Fodder	■				■	■							3
12	16	Baunso	Deru	Stem	Fencing	■	■	■	■	■	■	■	■	■	■	■	■	12
	17		Deru	Stem	Housing	■	■	■	■	■	■	■	■	■	■	■	■	12
13	18	Belo	Belo marnu	Fruit	Medicine					■	■							2

Plants	Parts	Name in Oriya	Kuvi name	Plant parts	Usages	Pouso	Magh	Faguno	Chaito	Boisakh	Landi	Asad	Bondapon	Osa	Doshra	Diali	Pond	Total
14	19	Bernga	Bernga	Bark	Shampoo	■	■	■	■	■	■				■	■	■	*9*
15	20	Bhaira bhuta	Motopatarimada	Leaf	Fodder					■						■		*2*
16	21	Bhalu dar	Jholajambu	Bark	Medicine											■		*1*
17	22	Bhalu jam	Oodijambu	Bark	Medicine		■									■		*2*
18	23	Bhui amla	Bumi juro	Plant	Medicine	■	■									■	■	*4*
19	24	Bichhauati	Karselimada	Root	Medicine											■		*1*
20	25	Bila	Tani marnu	Fruit	Medicine				■	■								*2*
21	26	Bileikanta	Bileikata	Seed	Medicine			■	■	■								*3*
	27			Plant	Fencing	■	■	■	■	■	■	■	■	■	■	■	■	*12*
22	28	Bisalya korani	Mitie jada	Leaf	Medicine	■	■	■	■	■	■	■	■	■	■	■	■	*12*
23	29	Bod tetenka	Darmel marnu	Plant	Fuelwood						■							*1*
24	30	Bodkokodi	Kaja kotikucha	Leaf	Food		■											*1*
25	31	Bojra mukhi	Koyu hirsa	Root	Medicine	■	■	■	■	■	■	■	■	■	■	■	■	*12*
26	32	Bon kodli	Jada tading	Stem	Food	■	■	■	■	■	■	■	■	■	■	■	■	*12*
27	33	Bondari	Kambli goacha	Root	Medicine		■											*1*
28	34	Bongordal	Loho dandi	Leaf	Fodder	■	■	■	■	■	■	■	■	■	■	■	■	*12*
29	35	Borkoli	Borkoli	Fruit	Food		■	■										*2*
30	36	Boruwa	Boruajada	Leaf	Fodder		■											*1*

Plants	*Parts*	*Name in Oriya*	*Kuvi name*	*Plant parts*	*Usages*	*Pouso*	*Magh*	*Faguno*	*Chaito*	*Boisakh*	*Landi*	*Asad*	*Bondapon*	*Osa*	*Doshra*	*Diali*	*Pond*	*Total*
31	37	Chandan	Chandan	Branch	Fuelwood	■	■	■	■	■	■	■	■	■	■	■	■	*12*
32	38	Chikni	Hirsa	Leaf	Fodder	■	■	■	■	■	■	■	■	■	■	■	■	*12*
33	39	Chilli	Siding	Seed	Shampoo		■	■										*2*
34	40	Dabpiri	Wika	Straw	Fodder		■	■										*2*
	41		Wika	Straw	Roofing		■	■										*2*
35	42	Dakli	Sorenda	Root	Food						■	■	■	■	■			*5*
36	43	Damon	Dameni	Stem	Agri.implement	■	■	■	■	■	■	■	■	■	■	■	■	*12*
37	44	Deruharja		Grass	Fodder						■	■	■	■	■	■	■	*7*
38	45	Dhopki	Dhopki	Bark	Medicine												■	*1*
39	46	Didendimada	Didendimada	Root	Medicine	■	■	■	■	■	■	■	■	■	■	■	■	*12*
40	47	Dondera	Dondro	Flower	Medicine						■	■						*2*
41	48	Dubo ghas	Garkijada	Grass	Medicine	■	■											*2*
42	49	Dudmal	Misimada	Root	Medicine					■								*1*
43	50	Dumri	Toya	Fruit	Food					■	■							*2*
44	51	Gadel	Grawee	Plant	Medicine	■	■	■	■	■	■	■	■	■	■	■	■	*12*
45	52	Gali morka	Gali morka	Tree	Timber	■	■	■	■	■	■	■	■	■	■	■	■	*12*
46	53	Gandi buta	Amorjoda	Tree	Fuelwood	■	■	■	■	■	■	■	■	■	■	■	■	*12*
47	54	Gandiri	Gandiri	Plant	Fuelwood	■	■	■	■	■	■	■	■	■	■	■	■	*12*

Plants	*Parts*	*Name in Oriya*	*Kuvi name*	*Plant parts*	*Usages*	*Pouso*	*Magh*	*Faguno*	*Chaito*	*Boisakh*	*Landi*	*Asad*	*Bondapon*	*Osa*	*Doshra*	*Diali*	*Pond*	*Total*
48	55	Gatamarka	Ghata morka	Plant	Fencing	■	■	■	■	■	■	■	■	■	■	■	■	*12*
49	56	Gereda	Potugarda	Leaf	Fodder		■											*1*
50	57	Ghantia	Ghantiajada	Grass	Fodder	■	■	■	■	■	■	■	■	■	■	■	■	*12*
51	58	Girli	Leda	Flower	Food	■	■											*2*
52	59	Gana mandia	Gana mandia	Leaf	Fodder	■	■	■	■	■	■	■	■	■	■	■	■	*12*
53	60	Golaki	Golaki	Root	Medicine										■	■		*2*
54	61	Gombari	Gumna	Bark	Medicine	■												*1*
	62			Seed	Marketed				■	■								*2*
55	63	Gorudo	Grawee marnu	Bark	Medicine										■	■		*2*
56	64	Gugunimal	Gugunimada	Root	Medicine											■		*1*
57	65	Gurdi sago	Gurudi kucha	Leaf	Food								■					*1*
58	66	Harchand	Hadchandan	Bark	Medicine											■		*1*
59	67	Hatimal	Podamada	Bark	Rope							■	■	■				*3*
	68			Tuber	Medicine												■	*1*
60	69	Hirsi	Hirsi	Leaf	Fodder	■	■	■	■	■	■	■	■	■	■	■	■	*12*
61	70	Horida	Tarhoo	Seed	Medicine	■					■							*2*
	71		Tarhoo	Seed	Marketed	■					■							*2*
62	72	Jamkoli	Manjijanbu	Fruit	Food						■							*1*

Plants	*Parts*	*Name in Oriya*	*Kuvi name*	*Plant parts*	*Usages*	*Pouso*	*Magh*	*Faguno*	*Chaito*	*Boisakh*	*Landi*	*Asad*	*Bondapon*	*Osa*	*Doshra*	*Diali*	*Pond*	*Total*
63	73	Kadruhirsa	Kadruhirsa	Plant	Fuelwood	■	■	■	■	■	■	■	■	■				*9*
64	74	Karakuta	Kadhakuta marnu	Trunk	Furniture										■	■		*2*
65	75	Karanjo	Karngi	Seed	Medicine				■	■								*2*
66	76	Kathi badni	Koliabadni	Plant	Broom	■											■	*2*
67	77	Keu kanda	Keukuna	Root	Medicine				■	■								*2*
	78		Keukuna	Root	Food						■							*1*
68	79	Khajuri niali	Kajuri	Fruit	Food				■	■								*2*
69	80	Kichi	Kisi	Fruit	Oil								■					*1*
70	81	Klia konda	Kaliakuna	Root	Food		■											*1*
71	82	Koi hirsa	Koyu hirsa	Seed	Medicine	■												*1*
72	83	Koicho	Gunjeri kanga	Seed	Medicine	■	■											*2*
73	84	Konior	Kundeli punga	Flower	Worship	■	■	■	■	■	■	■	■	■	■	■	■	*12*
74	85	Kontakoli	Andgo	Fruit	Food				■	■								*2*
75	86	Kosa kanda	Hemikuna	Tuber	Food	■	■	■	■	■								*5*
76	87	Kudupa	Kudupa	Fruit	Food								■					*1*
77	88	Kukudi sago	Kotikuca	Leaf	Food						■	■						*2*
78	89	Kukur langudi	Nehudileguni	Fruit	Food	■	■	■	■									*4*
79	90	Kuramal	Konjareoni	Root	Medicine											■	■	*2*

Plants	*Parts*	*Name in Oriya*	*Kuvi name*	*Plant parts*	*Usages*	*Pouso*	*Magh*	*Faguno*	*Chaito*	*Boisakh*	*Landi*	*Asad*	*Bondapon*	*Osa*	*Doshra*	*Diali*	*Pond*	*Total*
80	91	Lajokuli	Gorisaweli	Root	Medicine	■	■	■	■	■	■	■	■	■	■	■	■	*12*
81	92	Lohomada	Lohomada	Root	Medicine					■								*1*
82	93	Mankodo kendu	Potaduri	Tree	Fuelwood	■	■	■	■	■	■	■	■	■	■	■	■	*12*
83	94	Mirchinga	Kduan	Leaf	Spice	■	■	■	■	■	■	■	■	■	■	■	■	*12*
84	95	Modoi	Modoi	Plant	Fuelwood	■	■	■	■	■	■	■	■	■	■	■		*11*
85	96	Monjorsulia	?	Plant	Fuelwood	■	■	■	■	■	■	■	■	■	■	■		*11*
86	97	Mota ghas	Motojada	Grass	Fodder	■	■	■	■	■	■	■	■	■	■	■		*11*
87	98	Munch kondh	Muknipuyu	Flower	Medicine	■	■	■	■	■	■	■	■	■	■	■	■	*12*
88	99	Muniga	Munga muniga	Fruit	Food			■	■	■								*3*
89	100	Musa kani	?	Leaf	Fodder								■	■	■	■	■	*5*
90	101	Muturimala	Prashkamada	Plant	Medicine		■											*1*
91	102	Nilgiri	Niligiri	Leaf	Medicine	■	■	■	■	■	■	■	■	■	■	■	■	*12*
	103			Seed	Medicine	■	■	■	■	■	■	■	■	■	■	■	■	*12*
	104			Bark	Medicine	■	■	■	■	■	■	■	■	■	■	■	■	*12*
	105			Wood	Fuelwood	■	■	■	■	■	■	■	■	■	■	■	■	*12*
	106			Stem	Housing	■	■	■	■									*4*
92	107	Orka	Paji dohi	Tree	Fuelwood	■	■	■	■	■	■	■	■	■	■	■	■	*12*
93	108	Pakodimala	Pakodimala	Plant	Fuelwood	■	■	■	■	■	■	■	■	■	■			*10*

Plants	*Parts*	*Name in Oriya*	*Kuvi name*	*Plant parts*	*Usages*	*Pouso*	*Magh*	*Faguno*	*Chaito*	*Boisakh*	*Landi*	*Asad*	*Bondapon*	*Osa*	*Doshra*	*Diali*	*Pond*	*Total*
94	109	Panasa	Panha	Fruit	Food					■	■	■						*3*
95	110	Pardamal	Padadmada	Plant	Rope							■	■	■	■	■	■	*6*
96	111	Patal garudo	Pusihiru	Root	Medicine												■	*1*
97	112	Patro goja	Akugoja	Leaf	Medicine	■	■	■	■	■	■	■	■	■				*9*
98	113	Pengo	Pengomada	Seed	Oil	■	■	■	■	■	■	■	■	■				*9*
99	114	Phul jhadu	Hepori	Plant	Broom	■	■	■	■									*4*
100	115	Pijuli	Lakajambu	Fruit	Food					■	■	■	■					*4*
101	116	Pit konda	Hirukuna	Tuber	Food	■	■	■	■	■							■	*6*
102	117	Pita konda	Napa	Tuber	Food	■	■	■	■	■							■	*6*
103	118	Pitmari	Kambelikalapara	Plant	Tooth brush	■	■	■	■	■	■	■	■	■	■	■	■	*12*
104	119	Podai	Dohi	Fruit	Food							■	■					*2*
105	120	Poyan	Poyan	Seed	Medicine											■		*1*
106	121	Puti karla	Jadakarla	Fruit	Food								■	■				*2*
107	122	Ranbeli	Katri	Bark	Medicine	■	■	■	■	■	■	■	■	■	■	■	■	*12*
108	123	Sata bari	Penuhepori	Root	Medicine	■	■	■	■	■	■	■	■	■	■	■	■	*12*
109	124	Siadi	Paeri	Leaf	Marketed	■	■	■	■	■	■	■	■	■	■	■	■	*12*
	125			Seed	Food	■												*1*
110	126	Simili	Leko	Branch	Worship		■		■									*2*

Plants	Parts	Name in Oriya	Kuvi name	Plant parts	Usages	Pouso	Magh	Faguno	Chaito	Boisakh	Landi	Asad	Bondapon	Osa	Doshra	Diali	Pond	Total
111	127	Sindi	Sindi	Fruit	Food				■	■								2
112	128	Sindur	Hinduri	Fruit	Marketed					■								1
113	129	Sitakuti	Kuti pujeri	Root	Medicine		■									■		2
114	130	Solap	Marakadu marnu	Sap	Fermented drink	■	■	■	■	■	■	■	■	■	■	■	■	12
115	131	Sonari	Bundeni	Tree	Fuelwood	■	■	■	■	■	■	■	■	■	■	■	■	12
116	132	Sorenda	Huwa	Root	Food						■							1
117	133	Tangiachina	Kdalichinna	Bark	Medicine	■	■	■	■	■	■	■	■	■	■	■	■	12
118	134	Targa	Ro odi	Root	Food									■				1
119	135	Tendka kanda	Drogikuna	Root	Medicine	■	■	■	■	■	■	■	■	■	■	■	■	12
120	136	Tentuli	Pula	Fruit	Marketed			■	■	■								3
	137		Pula	Fruit	Food			■	■	■								3
121	138	Thakurani phulo	Malti	Flower	Worship								■	■	■			3
122	139	Thalkudi	Duakucha	Leaf	Medicine	■	■	■	■	■	■	■	■	■	■	■	■	12
123	140	Tirimundi	Mardimarnu	Plant	Fuelwood	■	■	■	■	■	■	■	■	■	■	■	■	12
124	141	Tutkuli	Danduli	Fruit	Food	■	■	■	■									4
		Total				**70**	**75**	**65**	**68**	**72**	**64**	**57**	**60**	**55**	**53**	**66**	**54**	**759**

Note: Names of the 12 months in this table are kuvi names. Broadly speaking, they correspond to the English months. pouso is the equivalent to January and pond corresponds with December. (?) denotes that we could not ascertain name in English or scientific name.

Table 5.5. The 15 Wild Plant Species that are not Used Currently

Sl. No.	*Oriya Name*	*Kuvi Name*
1.	Karseli	Karseli
2.	Koineteri	Koineteri
3.	Kurei	Manglajati
4.	Marda mala	Pdodomada
5.	Mendhamal	Gorimenda
6.	Pakua	Pakua jada
7.	Paldua	Dandi
8.	Palsi	Palsi
9.	Patpadandi	Patpadandi
10.	Pordi	Lduweli
11.	Poroi buta	Poroi buta
12.	Puruda	Simarani
13.	Reteli	Reteli
14.	Rupni	Taala
15.	Usku buta	Jetia buta

In Table 5.6 and Fig. 5.3 are given the diversity in usages of the wild plants. For many of the plants more than one part is used. Thus altogether the numbers of plant parts used are 141. From the table and the figure it is observed that:

(a) broadly speaking, the plant products are used for 11 different purposes;

(b) a large number of plant parts are used for food (22 per cent) and medicine (37.6 per cent);

(c) 9.9 per cent of the parts are used as fuelwood;

(d) five per cent of the parts are used as timber for furniture, agricultural implements, house construction etc;

(e) animal fodder is obtained from 9.9 per cent of the plant parts;

(f) there are 12 (8.5 per cent) plant products that are marketed and are used for a variety of purposes such as making brooms, ropes and leaf plates etc;

(g) parts of three plants are used for religious purpose; and

(h) while a majority of the plants yield products that are used for a single purpose, there are many plants that are used for more than a single purpose. For example,

- Dabpiri is used as fodder and as roofing material,
- Harida is used as medicine and also tanning material,
- Keu kanda is used as food and also medicine,
- Siadi is used as leaf plates and food (seeds),
- Tentuli is used as food (fruit) and also for extracting starch (seed).

Below are given further details with regard to the various usages mentioned above.

Table 5.6: Diversity of Usages of the Wild Plants

Sl. No.	*Usages*	*Number of plants*	*Total*	*Per-centage*
1.	Food	31	31	22.0
2.	Medicine	53	53	37.6
3.	Fuelwood	14	14	9.9
4.	Fodder	14	14	9.9
5.	**Structural**			
	(i) Furniture	1		
	(ii) Agriculture implements	1		
	(iii) Roofing and timber	5	7	5.0
6.	Fencing	3	3	2.1
7.	**Commercial use**			
	(i) Broom grass	2		
	(ii) Rope	2		
	(iii) Oil	2		
	(iv) Seeds and leaf	6	12	8.5
8.	Worship	3	3	2.1
9.	Tooth brush	1	1	0.7
10.	Shampoo	2	2	1.4
11.	Fermented drink	1	1	0.7
	Total	**141**	**141**	**100.0**

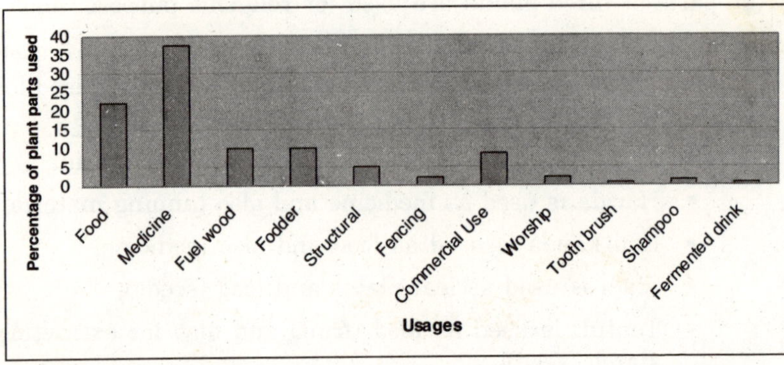

Fig. 5.3. Diversity of usages of the wild plant products.

Food Security

In Table 5.7 and Fig. 5.4 there is given the list of 31 plants, products that are used as food. Except for Ambo (Mango) of which both fruits and seeds are consumed, for the remaining thirty plants only one part is used. Therefore, the number of parts used exceeds by one compared to the number of trees. In Table 5.8 and Fig. 5.4 there are given the various parts of the plant that are consumed as food. It is observed that fruits of 51.6 per cent of the plant parts are used as food followed by roots (16.1 per cent), leaf and tubers (9.7 per cent each), seeds (6.5 per cent), and flowers and stem of only one plant each are used.

Table 5.7: Plants Consumed as Food

Sl. No.	*Oriya Name*	*Kuvi Name*	*Sl. No.*	*Plant Parts*
1.	Ambo	Mahaaa	1.	Fruit
			2.	Seed
2.	Bodkokodi	Kaja kotikucha	3.	Leaf
3.	Bon kodli	Jada tading	4.	Stem
4.	Borkoli	Borkoli	5.	Fruit
5.	Dakli	Sorenda	6.	Root
6.	Dumri	Toya	7.	Fruit
7.	Girli	Leda	8.	Flower
8.	Gurdi sago	Gurudi kucha	9.	Leaf
9.	Jamkoli	Manjijanbu	10.	Fruit
10.	Keu kanda	Keu kuna	11.	Root
11.	Khajuri niali	Kajuri	12.	Fruit

Sl. No.	*Oriya Name*	*Kuvi Name*	*Sl. No..*	*Plant Parts*
12.	Klia konda	Kaliakuna	13.	Root
13.	Kontakoli	Andgo	14.	Fruit
14.	Kosa kanda	Hemi kuna	15.	Tuber
15.	Kudupa	Kudupa	16.	Fruit
16.	Kukudi sago	Kotikuca	17.	Leaf
17.	Kukur langudi	Nehudileguni	18.	Fruit
18.	Muniga	Munga muniga	19.	Fruit
19.	Panasa	Panha	20.	Fruit
20.	Pijuli	Lakajambu	21.	Fruit
21.	Pit konda	Hiru kuna	22.	Tuber
22.	Pita konda	Napa	23.	Tuber
23.	Podai	Dohi	24.	Fruit
24.	Puti karla	Jada karla	25.	Fruit
25.	Siadi	Paeri	26.	Seed
26.	Sindi	Sindi	27.	Fruit
27.	Sorenda	Huwa	28.	Root
28.	Targa	Ro odi	29.	Root
29.	Tentuli	Pula	30.	Fruit
30.	Tutkuli	Danduli	31.	Fruit

Table 5.8: Plant Parts Consumed as Food

Sl. No.	*Parts*	*No.*	*Percentage*
1.	Flower	1	3.2
2.	Fruit	16	51.6
3.	Leaf	3	9.7
4.	Root	5	16.1
5.	Seeds	2	6.5
6.	Stem	1	3.2
7.	Tuber	3	9.7
	Total	**31**	**100**

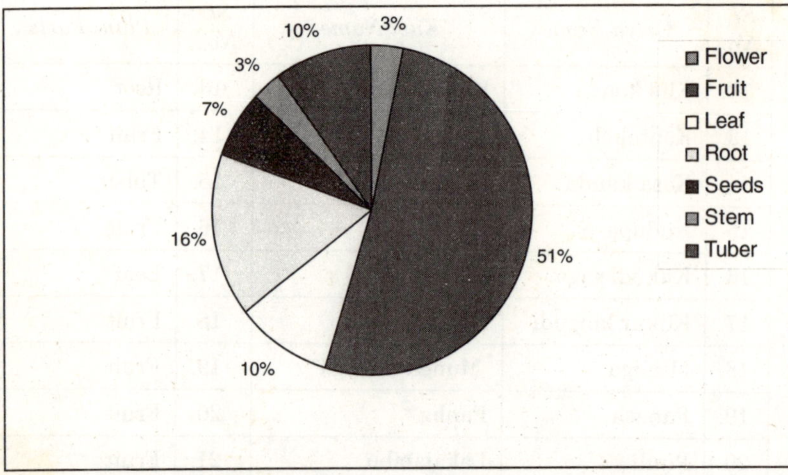

Fig. 5.4. Plant Parts Consumed as Food.

(a) **Health Care Security:** In Table 5.9 and Fig. 5.5 the names of plants and their parts used as medicines are given. Although the numbers of plants yielding medicines are 49 but the number of parts used are 53. In Table 5.10 and Fig. 5.5 there are given the frequency of distribution of various plant parts used as medicines. Roots of 37.7 per cent of the plants are used as medicine followed by the bark (17 per cent) and seeds (15.1 per cent). Plant parts such as flower, fruit, leaf, whole plant and tuber are used in small numbers not exceeding 10 per cent in each case.

Table 5.9: Plant Parts used as Medicine

Sl. No.	*Oriya Name*	*Kuvi Name*	*Sl. No.*	*Plant Parts*
1.	Amla	Jurha	1.	Fruit
2.	Apama rongo	Duchabondru	2.	Root
3.	Bagonaki	Launikoti	3.	Root
4.	Bahada	Trahu	4.	Fruit
5.	Baidonko	Tudayan	5.	Root
			6.	Seed
6.	Bajramali	Melukukuti	7.	Flower
			8.	Root
7.	Ban jhudongo	Jada Kala kanga	9.	Root

Sl. No.	*Oriya Name*	*Kuvi Name*	*Sl. No.*	*Plant Parts*
8.	Belo	Belo marnu	10.	Fruit
9.	Bhalu dar	Jholajambu	11.	Bark
10.	Bhalu jam	Oodijambu	12.	Bark
11.	Bhui amla	Bumi juro	13.	Plant
12.	Bichhauati	Karselimada	14.	Root
13.	Bila	Tani marnu	15.	Fruit
14.	Bileikanta	Bileikata	16.	Seed
15.	Bisalya korani	Mitie jada	17.	Leaf
16.	Bojra mukhi	Koyu hirsa	18.	Root
17.	Bondari	Kambli goacha	19.	Root
18.	Dhopki	Dhopki	20.	Bark
19.	Didendimada	Didendimada	21.	Root
20.	Dondera	Dondro	22.	Flower
21.	Dubo ghas	Garkijada	23.	Grass
22.	Dudmal	Misimada	24.	Root
23.	Gadel	Grawee	25.	Plant
24.	Golaki	Golaki	26.	Root
25.	Gombari	Gumna	27.	Bark
26.	Gorudo	Grawee marnu	28.	Bark
27.	Gugunimal	Gugunimada	29.	Root
28.	Harchand	Hadchandan	30.	Bark
29.	Hatimal	Podamada	31.	Tuber
30.	Horida	Tarhoo	32.	Seed
31.	Karanjo	Karngi	33.	Seed
32.	Keu kanda	Keu kuna	34.	Root
33.	Koi hirsa	Koyu hirsa	35.	Seed
34.	Koicho	Gunjerikanga	36.	Seed
35.	Kuramal	Konjareoni	37.	Root
36.	Lajokuli	Gorisaweli	38.	Root
37.	Lohomada	Lohomada	39.	Root
38.	Munch kondh	Muknipuyu	40.	Flower

Sl. No.	*Oriya Name*	*Kuvi Name*	*Sl. No.*	*Plant Parts*
39.	Muturimala	Prashkamada	41.	Plant
40.	Nilgiri	Niligiri	42.	Leaf
			43.	Seed
			44.	Bark
41.	Patal garudo	Pusihiru	45.	Root
42.	Patro goja	Akugoja	46.	Leaf
43.	Poyan	Poyan	47.	Seed
44.	Ranbeli	Katri	48.	Bark
45.	Sata bari	Penuhepori	49.	Root
46.	Sitakuti	Kuti pujeri	50.	Root
47.	Tangiachina	Kdalichinna	51.	Bark
48.	Tendka kanda	Drogi kuna	52.	Root
49.	Thalkudi	Duakucha	53.	Leaf

(b) **Dental care:** Tender branches of the tree Pitmari are used as toothbrushes and are available all around the year. Although we do not sell it but many people in our region regularly sell it in the weekly markets.

(c) **Head and hair care:** Seeds of plant Chilli (*Shikakai*) and the bark of Bernga are used for preparing a homemade shampoo for head and hair cleaning and conditioning. Both men and women, in particular women use this shampoo regularly.

Table 5.10: Plant Parts Consumed as Medicine

Sl. No.	*Parts*	*No.*	*Percentage*
1.	Root	20	37.7
2.	Bark	9	17.0
3.	Seed	8	15.1
4.	Fruit	4	7.5
5.	Leaf	4	7.5
6.	Flower	3	5.7
7.	Whole plant	3	5.7
8.	Grass	1	1.9
9.	Tuber	1	1.9
	Total	**53**	**100**

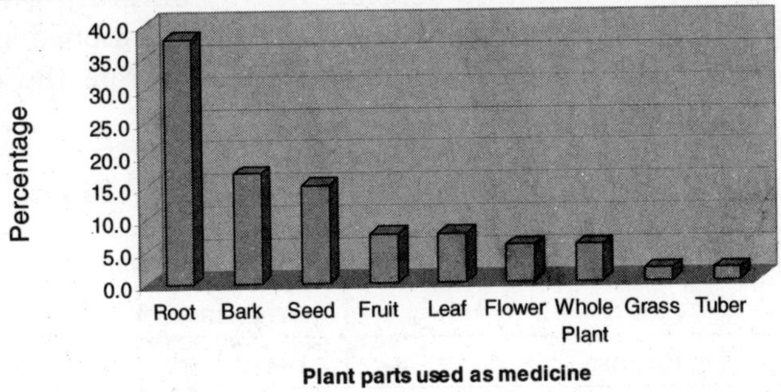

Fig. 5.5. Plant Parts Consumed as Medicine.

Energy Security: For energy the needs of the villagers are met by renewable biomass. As seen from Table 5.11, 14 plants provide fuelwood.

Table 5.11: Names of 14 Plants that Provide Fuelwood

Sl. No.	*Oriya Name*	*Kuvi Name*
1.	Arjun	Arjun marnu
2.	Bod tetenka	Darmel marnu
3.	Chandan	Chandan
4.	Gandi buta	Amorjoda
5.	Gandiri	Gandiri
6.	Kadruhirsa	Kadruhirsa
7.	Mankodo kendu	Potaduri
8.	Modoi	Modoi
9.	Monjorsulia	?
10.	Nilgiri	Niligiri
11.	Orka	Paji dohi
12.	Pakodimala	Pakodimala
13.	Sonari	Bundeni
14.	Tirimundi	Mardi marnu

Fodder Security: In Table 5.12, the names 14 fodder yielding plants are given. A large number of these plants are grasses and shrubs. In general there is no practice of stall feeding. The live stock in the village therefore depends heavily on grazing in the forest areas; atleast goats and ships that are mentioned in the village obtain their fodder requirements entirely from the forest landscape elements.

Table 5.12: Names of 14 Fodder Yielding Plants

Sl. No.	*Oriya Name*	*Kuvi Name*
1.	Arjun	Arjun marnu
2.	Baunso	Deru
4.	Damon	Dameni
5.	Gali morka	Gali morka
6.	Karakuta	Kadhakuta marnu
7.	Nilgiri	Niligiri

Timber: Names of the 7 plants of which timber is used for a variety of purposes such as house construction, furniture, for making agricultural, hunting implements and musical instruments etc. are given in Table 5.13.

Table 5.13: Names of the Seven Trees used as Timber

Sl. No.	*Oriya Name*	*Kuvi Name*
1.	Arjun	Arjun marnu
2.	Baunso	Deru
4.	Damon	Dameni
5.	Gali morka	Gali morka
6.	Karakuta	Kadhakuta marnu
7.	Nilgiri	Niligiri

Financial Security

(a) Products such as seeds, leaf, fruit, bark and the whole plant of the 12 plants are used commercially. The names of these plants are given in Table 5.14. It may be noted that for some of the products primary processing is carried out in the village like broom making, leaf plate making, rope making while other products are sold without any processing. The women's Self-Help Group in the village looks after both, processing as well as marketing of broom grasses.

Table 5.14: Names of the Twelve Trees and their Parts Used for Commercial Purposes

Sl. No.	*Oriya Name*	*Kuvi Name*	*Plant Parts*	*Use*
1.	Gombari	Gumna	Seed	Seed
2.	Hatimal	Podamada	Bark	Rope
3.	Horida	Tarhoo	Seed	Medicine
4.	Kathi badni	Kolia badni	Plant	Broom
5.	Kichi	Kisi	Fruit	Oil
6.	Mirchinga	Kduan	Leaf	Spice
7.	Pardamal	Padadmada	Plant	Rope
8.	Pengo	Pengomada	Seed	Oil
9.	Phul jhadu	Hepori	Plant	Broom
10.	Siadi	Paeri	Leaf	Leaf-plate
11.	Sindur	Hinduri	Fruit	Dye
12.	Tentuli	Pula	Fruit	Food and starch

(b) Sap of Solop tree: Solop trees are domesticated and also occur in the wild. The sap of this tree is used both at home, village functions and a part of it also marketed; for many households it contributes as a supplementary income to the mannual income.

Spiritual Security: Among other aspects, three plant species (Konior, Simili and Thakurani phula) are extensively used for various rituals in the village.

Social Bondage: Leaf of Siadi plant plays an important role in community functions in the village. On the occasion of community functions (marriage, death ceremony, festivals, etc.,) held in the village, members of the Self-Help Group and others go to the forest, collect the required number of Siadi leaves, stich them into plates and serve food to the community.

Plate 5.1. Timber Harvested from Puligunta and Pasiamba for Preparing Agricultural Implements.

Plate 5.2. Timber Harvested from Puligunta and Pasiamba for Preparing Agricultural Implements.

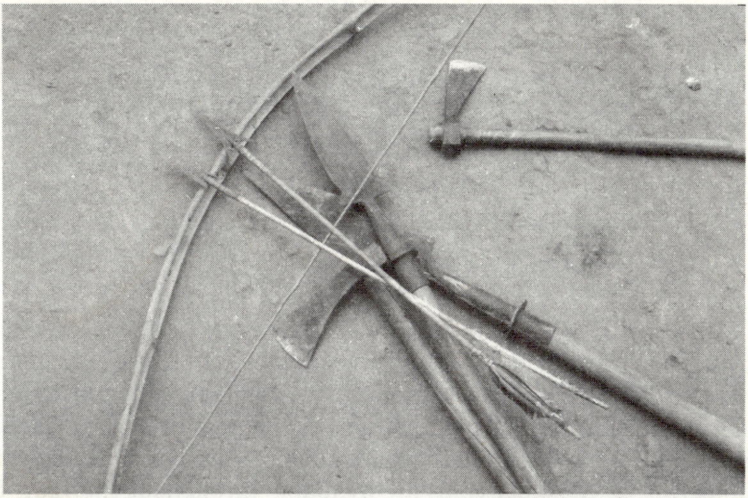

Plate 5.3. Wood from Puligunta and Bamboo from Farm Land Used for Making Hunting Implements.

Plate 5.4. Youth of Kondhpungar with Hunting Implements.

(ii) Seasonal Availability of Various Wild Plant Products

As it can be seen from Table 5.4 a large number of plant products used for a variety of purposes are available throughout the year. In Table 5.15 and Fig. 5.6 there are given the numbers of plant products that are available during each of the 12 months of the year. Altogether the plant parts that are used and is summed upto over 12 months comes to 759 parts. The numbers of products available in each month is out of 759 parts. The salient features of the seasonal availability of the plant products are:

(a) the availability of products varies from 53 in the month of Doshra to 75 in Magh; and

(b) in five months 50 to 60 products are available, in another five months 61 to 70 products are available whereas in Magh and Boisakh more than 70 products are available.

In Table 5.16 are given the frequency of number of plant products available in number of months. Out of the 141 plant products, 35 (24.8 per cent) products are available only during one month as well as for two months, zero to nine products are available between three to 11 months and a large number of products numbering 40 (28.4 per cent) are available throughout the year. In other words, the analysis of the data demonstrates that a number of wild plant products are available to the villagers throughout the year, fulfilling a variety of livelihood needs, as elaborated below.

Table 5.15: Number of Plant Products Available during Different Months

Sl. No.	*Month (Kuvi)*	*No. of Products*	*Percentage*
1.	Pouso	70	9.22
2.	Magh	75	9.88
3.	Faguno	65	8.56
4.	Chaito	68	8.96
5.	Boisakh	72	9.49
6.	Landi	64	8.43
7.	Asad	57	7.51
8.	Bondapon	60	7.91
9.	Osa	55	7.25
10.	Doshra	53	6.98
11.	Diali	66	8.70
12.	Pond	54	7.11
	Total	**759**	100

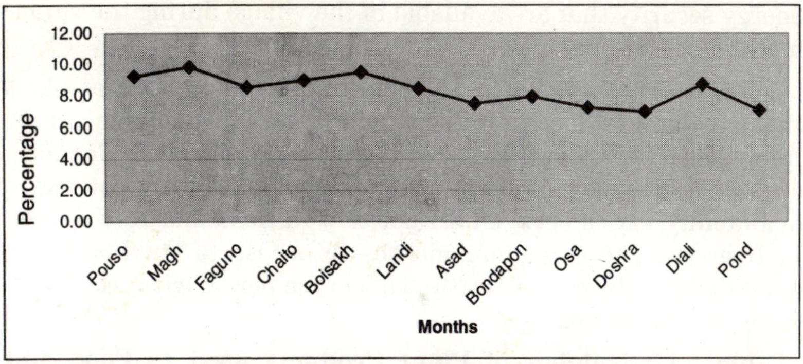

Fig. 5.6. Number of Plant Products Available during Different Months.

Table 5.16: Frequency of Availability of Number of Plant Products in Number of Months

No. of Months	*No. of Products*	*Percentage*
1.	35	24.8
2.	35	24.8
3.	9	6.4
4.	7	5.0
5.	3	2.1
6.	3	2.1
7.	1	0.7
8.	0	0.0
9.	4	2.8
10.	1	0.7
11.	3	2.1
12.	40	28.4
Total	**141**	100

Food, Health and Energy Security

Below is presented an analysis of three very important aspects of the livelihoods of the people of Kondhpungar. They are food security, health care security and energy security. The data presented above has been re-examined in terms of various plants and their parts used for food security, health care security and energy security that are available in the village during the various months of the year.

Food security: Table 5.17 and Fig. 5.7 reveales that plants that provide food for human consumption are available in varying frequencies through all the 12 months. During *Pouso* to *Bondapon* several food yielding plants are also available; the frequency of availability varies between 8.1 per cent in Asad and 15.1 per cent in Boisakh. There are four months from Osa to Pond when the availability reduces drastically. This is the period when the *Kharif* crops are harvested.

Table 5.17: Number of Plant Products used as Food and Medicines and their Seasonal Availability

Sl. No.	*Month (Kuvi)*	*No. of Plant Products*					
		Food Security		*Health Care Security*		*Energy Security*	
		No.	*Percent-age*	*No.*	*Percent-age*	*No.*	*Percent-age*
1.	Pouso	8	9.3	23	9.7	13	8.7
2.	Magh	10	11.6	24	10.1	13	8.7
3.	Faguno	9	10.5	17	7.1	13	8.7
4.	Chaito	11	12.8	20	8.4	13	8.7
5.	Boisakh	13	15.1	22	9.2	13	8.7
6.	Landi	10	11.6	18	7.6	14	9.3
7.	Asad	7	8.1	16	6.7	13	8.7
8.	Bondapon	8	9.3	15	6.3	13	8.7
9.	Osa	4	4.7	15	6.3	13	8.7
10.	Doshra	2	2.3	16	6.7	12	8.0
11.	Diali	1	1.2	31	13.0	11	7.3
12.	Pond	3	3.5	21	8.8	9	6.0
	Total	**86**	**100**	**238**	**100**	**150**	**100**

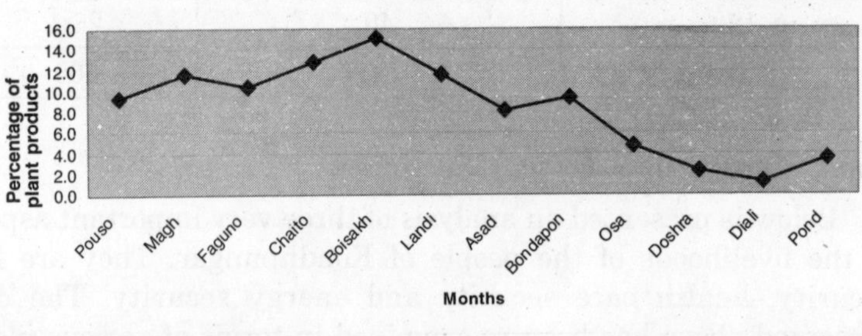

Fig. 5.7. Seasonal Availability of Plant Products used as Food.

Availability of food from cultivated plants from May (*Boisakh*) to August (*Bondapon*) is very low, the crops being standing in the field. During this lean period it is highly note worthy that there is abundance availability of food from the wild plants.

Health care security: From data given in Table 5.17 and Fig. 5.8, it is evident that medicinal plant products are available in

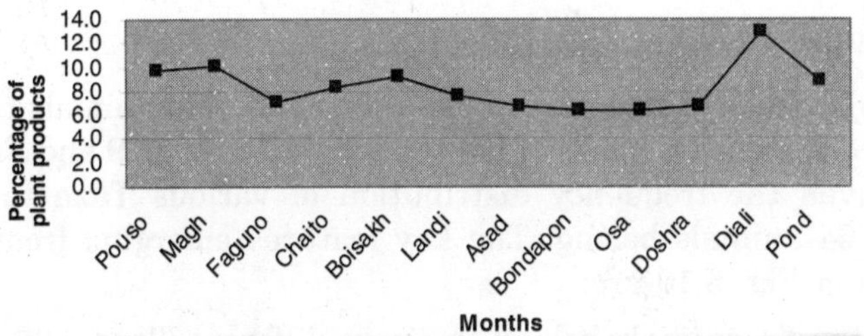

Fig. 5.8. Seasonal Availability of Plant Products used as Medicine.

fairly large numbers throughout the year. It is noteworthy that during the month of Diali (October-November) maximum number of medicinal products becomes available. The least numbers are seen during the months of Bondapon and Osa (August-September).

Energy security: From Table 5.17 and Fig. 5.9 it is evident that at least nine fuelwood yielding plants are available throughout

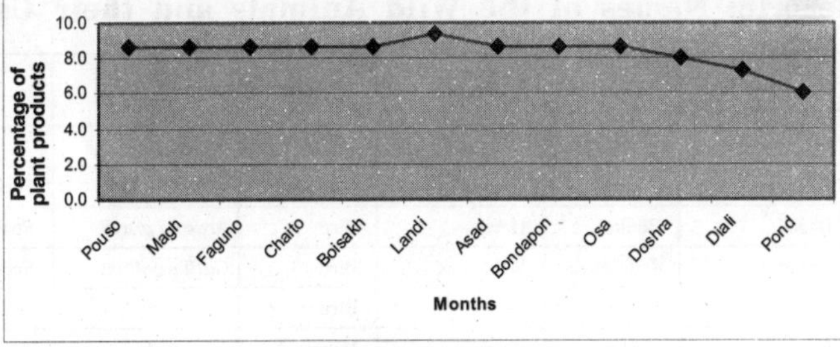

Fig. 5.9. Seasonal Availability of Plant Products used as Fuelwood.

the year. This shows that the villagers have a reasonable range of diversity for fuelwood yielding plants available to them throughout the year. It is appropriate to mention that the only source of fuel in the village is fuelwood. Biomass from various landscape elements in particular the protected forest, social forestry areas, jhum fields, etc; fulfill the annual requirements of fuelwood of the entire village. The village therefore is self-sufficient for energy requirements.

iii. Edible Wild Mushrooms

Edible wild mushrooms are mostly found in rainfed land, farm land and forest lands between July and October. Nine different types of mushrooms are found in the village. Of these only seven are edible. Thus, the food yielding numbers of wild plant parts taking together the data presented in Table 5.8 (n=31) and the seven edible mushrooms increases to 38.

5.3. Wild Animals and their Usages

In Table 5.18 there are given a list of 64 wild animals that are sighted in different parts of the village. In Table 5.19 and Fig. 5.10 are given the frequency distribution of various Taxa to which these 64 animals belong. The key features emerging from Table 5.19 and Fig. 5.10 are:

(a) the 64 animals belong to seven different Taxa;

(b) the largest number of animals belong to the Taxa of birds, 21 (32.8 per cent);

(c) a significant number of animals are reptiles, 15 (23.4 per cent);

(d) mammals also constitute a significant number of animals being 14 (21.9 per cent); and

(e) in the remaining Taxa amphibians, arachnids, insects and invertebrates occurs in small numbers.

Table 5.18: Names of the Wild Animals and their Usages

Sl. No.	*Oriya*	*Kuvi*	*English*	*Taxa*	*Scientific Name*	*Use*
1.	Azogor	Adagunsa	Python	Reptile	*Python morulus*	
2.	Badudi	Padudi	Bat	Mammal		Food
3.	Bago	Bonko	Heron	Bird	*Ardeola grayii*	Food
4.	Ban kukuda	Jada koyu	Wild cook	Bird	*Gallus gallus?*	Food
5.	Bani	Rambi		Bird		Pet
6.	Baria	Barhan	Wild boar	Mammal	*Sus scrofa*	Food
7.	Baya chodhai	Khorlia		Bird		Rain forecasting
8.	Bengo	Pana	Frog	Amphibian		
9.	Bhalu	Oodi	Bear	Mammal	*Melursus ursinus*	
10.	Bharubi anduo	Gogodrogi	Lizard	Reptile	*Varanus versicolor*	
11.	Bilua	Kolia	Jackal	Mammal	*Canis aureus*	
12.	Biradi	Bilei	Cat	Mammal	*Felis sp.*	Good omen
13.	Bono bilei	Joda bilei	Wild cat	Mammal	*Felis chaus*	
14.	Budiani	Kochoti	Spider	Insect		

Sl. No.	*Oriya*	*Kuvi*	*English*	*Taxa*	*ScientificName*	*Use*
15.	Chabara	Sima	Ant	Insect		
16.	Chanchana	Dega	Eagle	Bird		
17.	Chia chadei	Chia pota		Bird	*Prinia sp*	Bad omen
18.	Chita bagh	Tiring rengna	Leopard	Mammal	*Panthera pardus*	
19.	Chiti	Siti rachu		Reptile		
20.	Chopeda	Miriyanka	Red ant	Insect		Food
21.	Dhadka	Dhadka rachu	Snake	Reptile		
22.	Dhamana	Damna	Snake	Reptile		Food
23.	Dhandia	Dhandia	Snake	Reptile		
24.	Dhulia nago	Palu naga	Snake	Reptile		
25.	Dingiri	Dingiri pota		Bird		Food
26.	Dud boda	Palu jhupuni	Snake	Reptile		
27.	Endua	Drogi	Garden lizard	Reptile	*Calotes sp?*	
28.	Gharchatia	Jeta pota		Bird		Medicine
29.	Girna	Kidska droki	Lizard	Reptile		
30.	Gobor poko	Gurunda		Insect		
31.	Gunduchi	Tilli	Squirrel	Mammal	*Funambulus pennanti*	Food
32.	Gunduri	Tumba	Quail	Bird	*Perdicula asiatica*	Food
33.	Gunji	Gunji		Bird		
34.	Holdi basanta	Gumeti		Bird	*Oriolus xanthornus*	Food
35.	Jhiji pok	Saura koyu		Insect		Rain forecasting
36.	Jhitipiti	Kadha kota		Insect		
37.	Jia	Kechsua	Earth-worm	Invertebrate		
38.	Kala nag	Kala rachu	Snake	Reptile		
39.	Kalet	Kala rachu	Snake	Reptile		
40.	Kankada bicha	Kacha kupi	Scorpion	Arachnids		
41.	Kapto	Kuguri	Dove	Bird	*Streptopelia chinensis*	Food
42.	Kia chadei	Chia pota		Bird		Food
43.	Koili	Kdisker	Earth-worm	Invertebrate		
44.	Kojolpati	Dingiri	Cuckoo	Bird	*Eudynamys scolopacea*	Food
45.	Kua	Kawa	Crow	Bird	*Corvus spendens*	Forecasting the arrival of guest
46.	Kutra	Kurhu	More	Mammal	*Muntiacus muntjak*	Food
47.	Macho ranka	Banda gnoti	Kingfisher	Bird	*Halcyon smyrnensis*	Food
48.	Mankodo	Muhun	Monkey	Mammal	*Macaca radiate*	

Sl. No.	*Oriya*	*Kuvi*	*English*	*Taxa*	*ScientificName*	*Use*
49.	Mayur	Melu	Peacock	Bird	*Pavo cristatus*	Food, rain forecasting
50.	Musa	Orli	Rat	Mammal	*Rattus sp.*	Food
51.	Nago	Naga rachu	Cobra	Reptile		Rain forecasting
52.	Odho	Maraa	Mongoose	Mammal	*Herpestes edwardsi*	Food
53.	Parja pati	Pubuli	Butterfly	Insect		
54.	Pecha	Korkoti	Owl	Bird	*Athene brama*	Good omen
55.	Pimpudi	Sima	Ant	Insect		Rain' forecasting
56.	Potra sap	Gocha rachu	Leaf snake	Reptile		
57.	Sailm	Sahin	Porcupine	Mammal	*Hystrix indica*	Food
58.	Saru nago	Una nag	Cobra	Reptile	*Naja naja*	
59.	Singoti	Aci koyu		Bird		Food
60.	Sua chadei	Keta kura	Parrot	Bird	*Psitticula krameri*	Pet
61.	Sungo poko	Dendi		Insect		
62.	Tekor	Tekeri	Bee	Insect		Food
63.	Thekua	Kadha	Rabbit	Mammal	*Lepus nigricollis nigricollis*	Food, good omen
64.	Valia kukuro	Kosa nuhudi	Wild dog	Mammal	*Cuon alpinus?*	

Plate 5.5. Chutia Chorni Snake in Pasiamba Hills.

Plate 5.6. Chutia chorni snake in Pasiamba hills; Scorpion (Kacha kupi) trying to kill the snake by attacking its tail with its venom. The snake may die. The dead snake will be eaten by the scorpion.

Plate 5.7. Hare found in Plenty in Several Places in the Village.

Plate 5.8. Caged Tumba (Quil).

Plate 5.9. Habitat for Porcupine.

Plate 5.10. Habitat for Porcuopine.

Plate 5.11. Nest with Eggs of Chiapota Bird.

Plate 5.12. Crabs found in Plenty Wetlands and around Diki Banda.

Table 5.19: Frequency Distribution of Different Taxa of Wild Animals

Sl. No.	*Taxa*	*No.*	*Percentage*
1.	Amphibian	1	1.6
2.	Arachnids	1	1.6
3.	Birds	21	32.8
4.	Insect	10	15.6
5.	Mammal	14	21.9
6.	Reptile	15	23.4
7.	Invertebrate	2	3.1
	Total	**64**	**100**

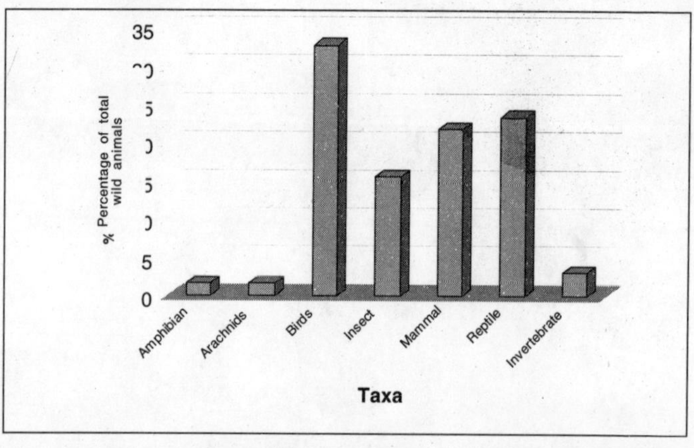

Fig. 5.10. Frequency Distribution of Different Taxa of Wild Animals.

Type of Usages of the Wild Animals

Out of the 64 animals, 33 animals are used for a variety of purposes. While 32 animals are used for only one purpose, there are two animals Mayur and Thekua that are used for more than one purpose. Therefore, the number of usages becomes 35. From Table 5.20 and Fig. 5.11 the following main features emerge:

Table 5.20 Types of Usages

Sl. No.	*Usages*	*No.*	*Percentage*
1.	Bad omen	1	2.9
2.	Food	22	62.9
3.	Good omen	3	8.6
4.	Rain forecasting	5	14.3
5.	Guest arrival	1	2.9
6.	Medicine	1	2.9
7.	Pet	2	5.7
	Total	**35**	**100**

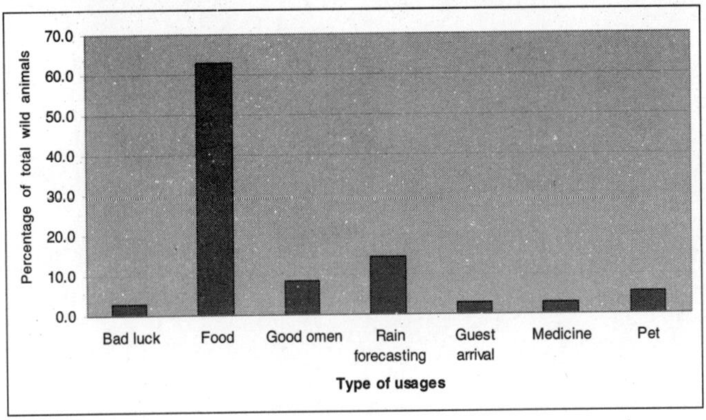

Fig. 5.11. Frequency Distribution of Type of Usages.

(a) the wild animals are used for seven different purposes;

(b) the largest number, i.e., 22 animals (62.9 per cent) are consumed as food;

(c) there is only one animal i.e., Gharchatia, a bird, used for medicinal purposes;

(d) thus altogether 23 animals are used for the purpose of consumption; and

(e) there are five different non-consumptive uses for which 12 wild animals are used. The non-consumptive usages are for signaling bad and good omen, forecasting of rain and arrival of guests. There are two animals Bani and Sua chadei (parrot), both birds that are used as pets.

5.4. Use of Wild Aquatic Animals

As noted in Chapter 4, there are five wild aquatic animals that are found in and around the water bodies. They are Godsi, Karandi, Magur (all fishes), Kankada (crab) and Bengo (frog). Of these five, all the three fishes and Kankada are consumed as food.

6

History of Change in Landscape and Waterscape Elements

In the preceeding Chapters 3 to 5 there was given a description and analysis of the domesticated and wild biodiversity that exists in 20 different landscape and waterscape elements in the village. It was also observed that an overwhelming array of domesticated and wild fauna and flora are present in the village. The rich biodiversity supported the various aspects-social, cultural, spiritual and economic lives of the people in the village.

In this chapter an attempt is being made to give an account of the major changes-positive and negative-that have occurred during the last 10 years or so in all the land and waterscape elements. The changes that have occurred have been considered from the following aspects:

(i) Whether the area under each of the elements has changed in terms of size;

(ii) Whether the useage pattern of these elements has changed in terms of crops and tree species grown;

(iii) Whether the frequency of cropping seasons have changed;

(iv) Whether the soil fertility has increased or decreased as well as how the productivity levels of crops have been impacted;

(v) Changes in number and type of livestock holdings;

(vi) Changes in levels of degradation/restoration of forest; and

(vii) Changes in abundance of wild animals.

6.1 Description of Changes in Land and Waterscape Elements

Homestead Gardens (Badas)

- Although the area under homestead garden has remained more or less the same over the years, the intensity of its useage has enormously increased:

(i) There is a significant increase in the number of vegetables grown and the number of fruits and other trees planted;

(ii) Cultivation of a few traditional varieties of crops have been discontinued; such as Desi kakudi (due to excess water), Jhota (moved to farm lands and shifting cultivation areas), Char kumuda—a variety of gourd and Jelinga a leafy vegetable.

(iii) The fertility of soils in these gardens has significantly improved due to the application of organic manures-compost, green manure, vermin-compost;

(iv) The protection mechanisms of these gardens show lots of improvement as most of the Badas are fenced with live fencing;

(v) A lot more water is now available for irrigating the Badas than before through improved irrigation system; and

(vi) Biomass produced in these gardens has significantly improved the livelihood status of the households.

The number of wild animal species and their frequency in Badas has considerably increased:

(i) The visits of Bhalu, Baria and Salim have increased. This is largely because of the introduction of trees such as Banana, Jackfruit, Papaya and tubers such as Tapioca; and

(ii) The visits have resulted in increased damage to the crops. Earlier, the villagers used to chase these animals but for the last two years they have stopped chasing because chasing resulted in more damage to the crops.

There is no change in the ownership pattern of Badas; they continue to be owned and managed by individual households.

Herbal Garden

- A herbal garden measuring to 0.1 ha was established in the village in 2005.

- Twentyone species were planted in the garden out of which 15 occured in the wild.
- The regeneration status has been satisfactory; out of 21 species, six have died.

However, according to the owner of the garden the purpose for which the garden was introduced has not been served its purpose as for most of the plants planted were for its ready availability of wild in the vicinity of the village.

Farm land: There have been a lot of significant changes in the farm lands in the village:

(i) A number of land development activities were initiated in 2002. This included levelling of the land and strengthening of soil and water conservation measures.

(ii) The area under cultivation has substantially increased due to enhanced irrigation facilities installed.

(iii) In some patches of farm lands where irrigation is available, three crops are grown in three seasons; during *Kharif* and *Rabi* a variety of crops and vegetables are grown while in summer season mostly vegetables are grown.

(iv) A significant change has occurred in the land use pattern; a number of fruit bearing trees have been planted on farm lands within the framework of agro-forestry models.

(v) Some noteworthy changes have occurred in the farm lands in terms of the crops grown due to various aspects mentioned above. Earlier more emphasis was given on growing subsistence crops such as Ragi, Paddy, Ginger, Turmeric, Cluster Beans, Maize, Pumpkin, Cowpea, Creeper Beans and Cucumber. However, presently in addition to the subsistence crops grown earlier, a number of new vegetable crops such as Tomato, Cabbage, Cauliflower, Carrot, Garlic, Onion, Chilly, Knol khol, Guanr, French beans, Beans, Pigeon pea, Bitter gourd, three types of leafy vegetables, Tapioca, Mustard, Bottle gourd, Buta beans, Sweet potatos, Yam etc have also been cultivated.

(vi) It may however be noted that the area under Maize and Cowpea which was very extensive in the past has been drastically reduced.

(vii) A number of fruit bearing trees such as Papaya, Orange, Banana, Lemon, Guava, Moringa, Mango, Pomegranate, Sitaphal etc. have also been planted on the farm lands, and

(viii) Two plant species Gliricidia used as green manure and Chillor used for fencing have been introduced in a large scale.

It is thus evident from above that the domesticated biodiversity on farm lands has increased enormously. This has not only provided additional sources for subsistence needs but also products that are marketed for cash. This change has positively impacted the economic status of a majority of the households in the village.

Wet Lands

Although the area under wet land has remained the same but some significant changes have also occurred:

(i) As earlier, only one crop during *kharif* season is grown presently;

(ii) In some patches of wet lands Sweet potatos during *Rabi* season are grown;

(iii) A significant change has occurred in terms of the paddy varieties that were grown in the past compared to the present. In Table 6.1 are given the names of the nine varieties of paddy that were grown in wet lands. However, cultivation of four verities, e.g., Karandi, Kandul Kati, Kola dhan and Nili dhan have been discontinued. The main reasons for the discontinuity of these varieties have been low productivity. In addition, in the case of Karandi its tastelessness also contributed in it being discontinued. In the case of Kola dhan and Nili dhan problem of securing seeds became a major handicap, and

(iv) Three new varieties of paddy that are now grown besides the five traditional ones are Lalat, Jajati and Khandagiri.

In short, it is noteworthy that while four traditional paddy varieties have been discontinued, three high yielding varieties have been introduced. Thus, the number of paddy varieties grown in the past was nine and at present it is eight. The discontinuation of the traditional varieties began 30 years back; the first one to go was Nili dhan 30 years ago followed by Kola dhan 20 years back and Karandi and Kandul kati have been discontinued since the last five years.

Table 6.1: Traditional Paddy Varieties Grown in Wet Lands

Sl. No.	*Paddy Varieties*	*Whether presently grown*	*If No, year of discont-inuation*	*If No, reasons thereof*
1.	Lochoi	Yes		
2.	Sopur lochoi	Yes		
3.	Bhata dhan	Yes		
4.	Amo dhan	Yes		
5.	Gorda lochoi	Yes		
6.	Karandi	No	5	Low productivity, not tasty
7.	Kandul kati	No	5	Low productivity, difficulties in thrashing
8.	Kola dhan	No	20	Low productivity, lack of seeds
9.	Nili dhan	No	30	Non-availability of seeds

Rainfed Land

- Since 2001 a number of land development activities that included stone bunding, land leveling and stone clearing were under taken on raifed lands.
- Due to the availability of irrigation a substantial amount of the land which was used earlier as rainfed is now used as farm land. Therefore, the crops grown in the farm lands have also been introduced in these lands.
- The above activities have enhanced the productivity of the crops that are grown.
- A small number of trees of three species such as Ambo, Panasa and Karanjo have been planted along the bunds of rainfed lands.

On rainfed lands, traditionally the villagers have grown three crop varieties, namely paddy, ragi and suan. Below are described the changes that have occurred in these three varieties of crops.

Paddy Varieties

Traditionally the villagers have been growing seven varieties of paddy as shown in Table 6.2 on rainfed lands. Of these, three have been discontinued beginning from 20 years back. The first to be discontinued was Kola dhan 20 years back followed by Baigonoi and Kandul kati about five years back. The reasons for discontinuation are low productivity, difficulty in thrashing and difficulty in obtaining seeds.

Table 6.2: Traditional Paddy Varieties Grown in Rainfed Lands

Sl.No.	*Paddy Varieties*	*Whether presently grown*	*If No, year of discon-tinuation*	*If No, reasons thereof*
1.	Lochoi	Yes		
2.	Sopur lochoi	Yes		
3.	Bhata dhan	Yes		
4.	Poda lochoi	Yes		
5.	Kandul kati	No	5	Low productivity, difficulties in thrashing
6.	Kola dhan	No	20	Non-availability of seeds, low productivity
7.	Baigonoi	No	5	Low productivity

Ragi Varieties

- In the past, the villagers cultivated 12 varieties of ragi as given in Table 6.3.
- Presently, however, six varieties have been discontinued. The six varieties being continued are Sonadei mandia, Bodeli, Dasra bodeli, Boddu, Majhia mandia, and Majhia bodeli.
- Of the six varieties that have been discontinued, three (Karanga, Modei mandia, Telenga mandia) have been discontinued for the last 20 years. The other three varieties (Chilli mandia, Marda mandia, Biri mandia) were discontinued over 10 years back.

- The reasons for discontinuation have been primarily low productivity, fungus attack and lack of availability of seeds.

Table 6.3 Traditional Ragi Varieties Grown in Rainfed Lands

Sl. No.	*Ragi Varieties*	*Whether presently Grown*	*If No, year of discon-tinuation*	*If No, reasons thereof*
1.	Sonadei mandia	Yes		
2.	Bodeli	Yes		
3.	Dasra bodeli	Yes		
4.	Baddu	Yes		
5.	Majhia mandia	Yes		
6.	Majhia bodeli	Yes		
7.	Marda mandia	No	10	Low-productivity, fungus infection
8.	Chilli mandia	No	15	Low-productivity, requires more water
9.	Telenga mandia	No	20	Low-productivity
10.	Karanga	No	25	Non-availability of seeds
11.	Biri mandia	No	10	Non-availability of seeds
12.	Modei mandia	No	25	Non-availability of seeds

Suan Varities

- In Table 6.4 are given the names of seven varieties of suan that have been grown traditionally in the village.
- Three varieties of suan, namely laiseri, mami suan and mathili suan have been discontinued. Mathili suan was

discontinued 20 years back while laiseri and mami suan have been discontinued during the last decade. The primary reasons have been non availability of the seeds and low productivity.

Table 6.4: Traditional Suan Varieties grown in Rainfed Lands

Sl. No.	*Suan Varieties*	*Whether presently grown*	*If No, year of discon-tinuation*	*If No, reasons thereof*
1.	Bod suan	Yes		
2.	Kola suan	Yes		
3.	Jinjiri suan	Yes		
4.	Jurua jetili	Yes		
5.	Laiseri	No	7	Non-availability of seeds
6.	Mami suan	No	10	Low productivity
7.	Mathili suan	No	20	Non-availability of seeds

Shifting Cultivation

- The area under shifting cultivation in the village has been reduced substantially.
- There is a significant reduction in the number of crops that were grown earlier. Earlier 20 different varieties of crops were grown (see Table 3.25). However, presently six varieties of crops have been abandoned during the past decade. These crops are Jona (Maize), Horu kulian (Paddy), Sweet potato, Saru (Arum), Joda (Castor) and Bhaji sag (leafy vegetable).
- The fallow period has drastically reduced from 10 years to two to three years at present.
- The productivity of different crops has also reduced significantly.

- Because of the shortened fallow period, the pattern of cultivation of crops during the first and second year has also changed.
- Lantana has invaded many shifing cultivation fields.

Social Forestry Plantation

- During 1994-1995 in about 24.28 ha of totally barren revenue land the villagers under took social forestry plantation.
- Due to rigorous protection measures followed by the villagers, the plantation area is now full of grown trees.
- From 2006 the villagers have started pruning the trees. The branches obtained from pruning were sold for a sum of Rs 7000. This amount is deposited in the bank account of women's SHG and will be used for the village development activities.
- The plantation also provides fuelwood to the villagers. This has partially reduced the dependence of the villagers for fuelwood from the protected forest area.

Cashew Nut Plantation

- Cashew plantation was undertaken about 7.28 ha in 1999-2000 and gap filling was carried out during 2003.
- The plantation has already started yielding cashew nuts; in 2007 about five kg have been harvested.
- The villagers decided not to sell the cashew nuts, instead have used these as seeds for plantation in a small area called Kupa khal adjacent to Pasiamba.
- For the next couple of years the cashew nuts harvested from the plantation will be used as seeds for raising plantation in Lelisira and Kotra ambo areas.
- Since the plantation is still young, grasing is strictly prohibited.

Eucalyptus Plantation

- Eucalyptus plantation was undertaken in several landscape elements like upper reaches of Pasiamba below Balipata, Kotra amba, Lelisira, Bariamba and Kotra kari during 1988–1990.
- Area under eucalyptus plantation has considerably reduced. From areas like Pasiamba, Kotra amba and Lelisira almost all the plants have been harvested.

- From Bariamba and Kotra kari also a lot of trees have been harvested. However, a small number of eucalyptus plants scattered in these areas are still available.
- The wood harvested from eucalyptus has been used for various purposes not only by the villagers but on occasions it has also been given to neighbouring villages on request in lieu of token or cash payment; this money has primarily been used for festive occassions in the village and/or organising community feasts.

Silver Oak Plantation

- Silver oak plantation was undertaken in 1998 in a limited area below Bariamba and Kotra kari. The plants have grown up luxuriently. As of now the villagers have not harvestd any biomass from this plantation. The villagers however plan to extract timber in future when the eucalyptus plants will no longer be available in the village.

Protected Forest

- Protected forest in hill ranges of Balipata, Puligunta and Kudi Kanda were earlier used entirely for shifting cultivation purposes
- During 1995 the village experienced unusual heavy rains that resulted in massive land slides. These interns damaged the cultivated fields. In response to this the villagers decided to restrict shifting cultivation area in Balipata and leave the rest of the area for regeneration of forest. Since then, the villagers have accorded complete protection to these patches. The protection has resulted presently in to a fairly well-wooded forest.
- The forest provides a wide range of products that fulfills the subsistence needs of the villagers (see Table 5.4).
- All the wood requirements for various purposes such as house construction, agricultural implements, musical instruments and hunting implements, etc., of all households in the village are met from the forest and plantation areas; no timber is purchased from the market.
- Since 1995 a lot of changes have occurred in the management of protected forests.
  - (i) Protection measures have been strengthened in terms of patrolling.

(ii) Strict rules have been framed for harvesting of fuelwood. Households are permitted to harvest fuelwood only three times in a year during the months of October, February and March. Fuelwood is collected by the women folk. They among themselves decide a given day or days during the three months mentioned above and collectively go to the forest and gather fuelwood. They are permitted by the People's Organisation in the village to collect only dry and fallen dead wood and branches. Cutting of standing live trees is totally prohibited. The youth of the village as well as some women rigidly monitor the fuelwood extraction that is being brought home. Till date no woman has violated this rule.

(iii) Matters pertaining to harvesting of fuelwood and other NTFPs are regularly discussed by SHG.

(iv) In view of the lack of grasing area in the village, the villagers have to graze their animals freely in forest areas.

(v) The number of species of wild animals and their numbers have substantially increased since 1995.

Thus, two institutions, namely, People's Organisation and SHG, and village youth with well defined reponsibilities jointly manage the use of forest resources.

Sacred Grove

- No major changes have been observed during the past 10 years in the sacred grove. People respect and follow the traditional rules of use of this space and the existing biodiversity.

Tank 1

- Bali banda tank although existed in the village but in 2001 it has been further developed and augmented.
- Some fishes were introduced in the tank but they did not survive.

Tank 2

- This tank was newly constructed in 2001 for irrigation purpose.
- Since then a lot of farm land is being irrigated from the water of this tank.

- The irrigation facility has helped not only enhanced productivity levels of the crops but has also provided opportunities for introducing a number of new crops requiring water, in particular, vegetables.
- On the bunds of this tank a few fruit bearing trees have been planted.

Tank 3

- In the year 2005 this tank was made on the western side of the farm lands.
- This was constructed primarily for introducing fisheries.
- Since then a number of wild species of fishes and other animals have also colonised the tank and its surrounding areas.
- A few fishes have also been introduced in the tank.
- On the bunds of the tank a number of plant species have been planted.

Check Dam

- The existing check dam in the village was repaired in 2004. A small channel was added to divert water to the farm lands.
- Because of the availability of the irrigation water in the check dam some rainfed land has been converted into farm lands. This change has resulted in increased productivity levels as well as choices of planting other crops and trees.
- Water from the check dam has not only ensured growing crops in Rabi season on some farm lands but has also provided opportunities for cultivating vegetables during summer season. Thus, on some patches of rainfed lands now instead of one crop two crops are grown and in some patches even three crops are grown.
- Not only the domesticated animals of the village now get ensured drinking water from the check dam throughout the year but also people of the neighbouring villages also often use this for their animals.
- Many wild animals also use this water source.
- Some wild fishes as well as other animals are now found in and around the check dam.
- Wild plant diversity has also increased in the vicinity of the check dam.

Streams

- No noticeable changes have been observed in two streams Kotra am jhola and Kudi kanda jhola.
- On the stream Boko sakadi in the year 2005 under UNDP project a small check dam was built which comes under the jurisdiction of the neighboring village Porjapungar.
- The water in the stream has decreased over the years.
- Water from this stream is used for irrigating a small patch of rainfed land in the village.
- The aquatic animal diversity remains almost unchanged.

Road Side Plantation

- Road side plantation was under taken during the year 1994.
- A number of trees have not survived and thus there are visible empty patches along the road.
- This road side plantation provided an opportunity for several other wild plants to colonize the area.
- Because of the trees, the number of sighting of wild animals along the road side has also increased.

6.2 Domesticated Animals

- The type and number of livestock in the village in the past ten years has substantially decreased.
- Numbers of cows and bullocks have significantly decreased.
- Earlier, a majority of the households in the village maintained pigs. However, currently except for one household, the remaining have discontinued keeping pigs. The reason for this change is because of the damage to the crops caused by the pigs and also it was posing health problems.
- There were a large number of goats in the village some 15 years back (about 200) but over years this number has steadily decreased largely due to diseases and damage by leopards.
- Sheep in the village was introduced for the first time in 1995. Since then the number is steadily increasing.

6.3 Changes in the Abundance of Wild Animals

In Table 6.5 are presented the assessment of changes in the abundance of the 64 wild animals often sighted in the village. The data presented in the Table 6.5 was generated through group discussions, individual interviews with knowledgeable persons as well as by visits to different biodiversity bearing areas in the village. The responses are therefore qualitative in nature.

From the table the following main observations emerge in respect of the abundance of wild animals:

(i) 29 wild animals (45.3 per cent) belonging to various Taxa showing increase in their abundance;

(ii) A substantial number of animals (37.5 per cent) according to villagers show a decline in abundance;

(iii) 11 (17.2 per cent) animals do not reveal any trend in change in their abundance; and

(iv) Of the 64 wild animals, 13 are often hunted and used for food and/or medicine.

The methodology that has been used for the collection of the data presented in Table 6.5 did not permit finding various reasons for the observed pattern of temporal changes in abundance of the wild animals. For a more comprehensive understanding of the temporal changes, long term ecological studies are required. Such an approach was out of the scope of the present study.

Table 6.5: Changes in the Abundance of Wild Animals

Sl. No.	*Name in Oriya*	*Increase*	*Decrease*	*Same*	*Hunted*
1.	Azgor	✓			
2.	Badudi		✓		✓
3.	Bago	✓			
4.	Ban kukuda	✓			
5.	Bani			✓	
6.	Baria	✓			
7.	Baya chodhai	✓			
8.	Bengo		✓		
9.	Bhalu		✓		
10.	Bilua			✓	
11.	Bohurupi anduo	✓			
12.	Bono bilie			✓	✓

Sl. No.	*Name in Oriya*	*Increase*	*Decrease*	*Same*	*Hunted*
13.	Budiani		✓		✓
14.	Chabara	✓			
15.	Chadei			✓	
16.	Chanchana	✓			
17.	Chita bagh	✓			
18.	Chiti		✓		
19.	Chopeda		✓		
20.	Dhadka	✓			✓
21.	Dhamana	✓			
22.	Dhandia		✓		✓
23.	Dhulia nago	✓			
24.	Dingiri		✓		
25.	Dud boda	✓			
26.	Endua			✓	
27.	Gharchatia	✓			
28.	Girna		✓		
29.	Gobor poko	✓			
30.	Gunduchi	✓			
31.	Gunduri		✓		
32.	Gunji		✓		
33.	Holdi basanta		✓		
34.	Jhiji pok	✓			
35.	Jhitipiti		✓		
36.	Jia			✓	
37.	Kala nag	✓			
38.	Kalet		✓		
39.	Kankada bicha	✓			
40.	Kapto	✓			✓
41.	Kia chadei	✓			✓
42.	Koili		✓		

Sl. No.	*Name in Oriya*	*Increase*	*Decrease*	*Same*	*Hunted*
43.	Kojolpati		✓		
44.	Kosa nuheudi	✓			
45.	Kua		✓		✓
46.	Kutra			✓	✓
47.	Macho ranka	✓			
48.	Mankodo		✓		
49.	Mayur	✓			✓
50.	Musa			✓	
51.	Nago	✓			
52.	Odho		✓		
53.	Parja pati			✓	
54.	Pecha	✓			
55.	Pimpudi	✓			
56.	Potra sap			✓	✓
57.	Sailm			✓	
58.	Saru nago		✓		✓
59.	Singoti		✓		
60.	Sua chadei		✓		
61.	Sungo poko		✓		✓
62.	Tekor	✓			
63.	Thekua		✓		
64.	Valia kukuro	✓			
	Total	**29**	**24**	**11**	**13**
	Percentage	**45.3**	**37.5**	**17.2**	

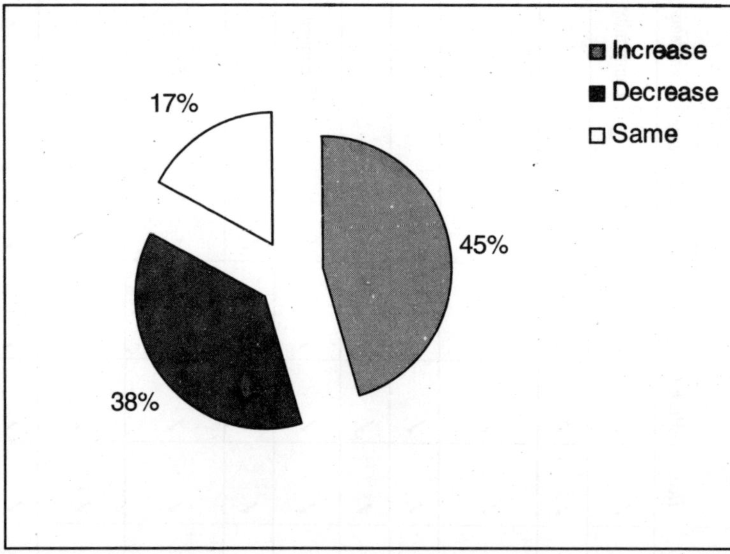

Fig. 6.1. Changes in the Abundance of Wild Animals.

6.4 Changes in the Abundance of 12 Socially Preferred Wild Plants

The villagers were encouraged to deliberate among themselves for identifying plant species which they considered are most important in their lives. After a series of meetings, in which youth, men and women participated vigorously, the villagers identified 12 such plant species. In Table 6.6 are given the names of the plants, places they are found in the village, parts of the plant used and the pattern of usage including whether the products are consumed at home and/or marketed, temporal changes in their abundance and pattern of ownership. The key findings from the table are:

(i) Of the 12 plants, three have two varieties each. The names of the plants are Mango, Jackfruit and Black berry;

(ii) These 12 plants are found in six different areas in the village- Puligunta, Bariamba, Kupa khal, Balipata and Lelisira (for details see Fig. 3.1);

(iii) Many parts of these plants such as bark, branch, fruit, gum, leaf, root, seed, stem and thorn are used for a variety of purposes;

(iv) The various purposes for which parts of these plants are used are for agricultural implements, fencing, food, fuelwood,

Table 6.6: Changes in the Abundance of 12 Socially Prefered wild Plants

Sl No	Name of the plant				Area in which found	Plant parts	Usage	Home	Market	Change			Ownership
	Kuvi	Variety	Oriya	Variety						Increase	Decrease	Same	
1	Mahaaa	1. Jurdi	Ambo	Sano ambo	Puligunta , Bariamba	Seed	Food	✓	✓	✓	✓		Community
						Fruit	Food	✓	✓	✓	✓		
		2. Tota	Ambo	Tota		Stem	Fuelwood, furniture	✓	✓	✓	✓		
						Bark	Medicine	✓	✓	✓	✓		
						Leaf	Manure	✓	✓	✓	✓		
2	Panha	1. Khoja	Panasa	Khoja	Puligunta , Bariamba	Seed	Food	✓	✓	✓	✓		Community
						Fruit	Food	✓	✓	✓	✓		
		2. Lalia		Lalia	Kupa khal	Stem	Fuelwood, furniture	✓	✓	✓	✓		
						Leaf	Manure, medicine	✓	✓	✓	✓		
						Gum	Bird trapping	✓	✓	✓	✓		

Sl No	Name of the plant				Area in which found	Plant parts	Usage	Home	Market	Change			Ownership
	Kuvi	Variety	Oriya	Variety						Increase	Decrease	Same	
3	Jambo	1. Manji jambo	Jamkoli		Bariamba, Puligunta	Fruit	Food	✓	✓	✓			Community
						Stem	House construction	✓	✓	✓	✓		Private
		2. Kaja jambo				Bark	Medicine	✓	✓	✓	✓		
						Leaf	Manure	✓	✓	✓	✓		
4	Paermal		Siadi		Puligunta	Fruit	Food	✓	✓	✓	✓		Community
						Leaf	Leaf plate	✓	✓	✓	✓		
							Chatudi (umbrella)	✓	✓	✓	✓		
							Puda (cup) tarla (basket)	✓	✓	✓	✓		
						Bark	Rope	✓	✓	✓	✓		
5	Andgo		Konta koli		Puligunta, Balipata	Fruit	Food	✓	✓	✓	✓		Community
						Leaf	Medicine	✓	✓	✓	✓		
						Bark	Medicine	✓	✓	✓	✓		
						Stem	Fuelwood	✓	✓	✓	✓		
						Branch	Fencing	✓	✓	✓	✓		

Sl No	Name of the plant				Area in which found	Plant parts	Usage	Home	Market	Change			Ownership
	Kuvi	Variety	Oriya	Variety						Increase	Decrease	Same	
6	Trahau		Harida		Balipata, Puligunta	Fruit	Medicine	✓	✓	✓	✓	3	Community
						Seed	Medicine	✓	✓	✓	✓		
						Bark	Medicine	✓	✓	✓	✓		
						Leaf	Worship	✓	✓	✓	✓		
						Stem	Agri. implements	✓	✓	✓	✓		
7	Tandi		Bahada		Balipata, Puligunta	Fruit	Food, medicine	✓	✓	✓	✓		Community
						Bark	Medicine	✓	✓	✓	✓		
						Stem	House construction	✓	✓	✓	✓		
						Leaf	Medicine	✓	✓	✓	✓		
8	Juro marnu		Amla		Balipata, Puligunta	Fruit	Food, medicine	✓	✓	✓	✓		Community
						Seed	Medicine	✓	✓	✓	✓		
						Leaf	Medicine	✓	✓	✓	✓		
						Bark	Medicine	✓	✓	✓	✓		
						Stem	House construction	✓	✓	✓	✓		

Sl No	Name of the plant				Area in which found	Plant parts	Usage	Home	Market	Change			Ownership
	Kuvi	Variety	Oriya	Variety						Increase	Decrease	Same	
9	Lekha marnu		Simili		Puligunta , Kup amba	Fruit	Medicine	✓		✓	✓		Community
						Seed	Medicine	✓		✓	✓		
						Thorn	Worship	✓		✓	✓		
						Stem	Worship, house construction	✓		✓	✓		
10	Gumna marnu		Gom bari		Bariamba, Puligunta, Balipata	Stem	House construction	✓	✓	✓	✓		Community
						Leaf	Medicine	✓	✓	✓	✓		
						Bark	Medicine	✓	✓	✓	✓		
						Fruit	Medicine	✓	✓	✓	✓		
						Leaf	Medicine	✓		✓	✓		
						Stem	Fuelwood, house construction	✓		✓	✓		
						Root	Medicine	✓		✓	✓		

Sl No	Name of the plant				Area in which found	Plant parts	Usage	Home	Market	Change			Ownership
	Kuvi	Variety	Oriya	Variety						Increase	Decrease	Same	
11	Pula		Tentuli		Lelisira	Stem	Fuelwood, house construction	✓	✓	✓	✓		Community
						Fruit	Food	✓	✓	✓	✓		
						Seed	Food	✓	✓	✓	✓		
						Leaf	Food	✓	✓	✓	✓		
12	Karanji marnu		Karanjo		Lelisira, Kup amba	Seed	Oil, medicine	✓	✓	✓	✓		Community, private
						Stem	House construction	✓	✓	✓	✓		
						Leaf	House construction, fuelwood, medicine	✓	✓	✓	✓		
						Bark	Medicine	✓	✓	✓	✓		

furniture, hunting, housing, leaf plate, medicine, manure, oil, rope, worship etc;

(v) There are altogether 54 plant parts of these 12 plants are either used at home and/or marketed. Thirty-six items are exclusively used at home, three are only marketed whereas 16 are used at home as well as marketed;

(vi) Out of 12 plants, nine plants have shown an increase in their abundance Mango, Jackfruit, Jambo (Black berry), Kantakoli (Berry), Bahada, Amla, Gambhari, Tamarind and Pongamia, the population of two plants have decreased (Siadi and Simili) and no changes in abundance was observed in the case of Harida; and

(vii) In terms of ownership of these plants, a variety called Kaja jambo is owned privately, Pongamia is owned either privately or by the community and the remaining 10 plants are owned by the community.

6.5 Plants Important as Source of Food for Wild Animals

As noted above, a large number of wild animals are often sighted in the village. It was also noted earlier that a large variety of both domesticated and wild plants are found in the village. The villagers identified an illustrative list of plants that provide food to some of the wild animals. The details about this are presented in Table 6.7. There are seven plants of which Jackfruit and Cashew are planted while the remaining five occur in the wild. Fruits, seeds and tubers of these plants are consumed as food by the wild animals such as Bear, Wild boar, Porcupine and Birds. The Bear has the widest base of food as it consumes fruits of seven plants.

Table 6.7: Plants Important as Source of Food for Wild Animals

Sl. No.	*Plants*	*Parts*	*Animals*
1.	Ambo (mango)	1. Fruit 2. Seed	Bear Wild boar Porcupine
2.	Andgo	Fruit	Bear, birds
3.	Cashew	Fruit	Bear
4.	Mirchinga (curry pata)	Fruit	Bear
5.	Pansa (jackfruit)	1. Fruit 2. Seed	Bear Porcupine
6.	Pitmari	Fruit	Bear, birds
7.	Sonari	1.Tuber 2. Fruit	Porcupine Bear

6.6 Assissted Natural Regeneration of Wild Mango in Kondhpungar

In the past, the natural forest of the village use to harbour hundreds of mature wild mango trees which was an important source of food for the wild animals (Wild boar and Bear) and the people of Kondhpungar and the neighbouring villages. However, steadily the number of mango trees declined due to the ageing process as well as by illegal cutting.

Earlier people used to bring ripe mangos to their homes or eat pulp in the forest and bring seeds for further use as food. In course of time, people realised that since there are no seeds left in forest, mango trees are not regenerating and if such a scenario continues the wild mango will vanish from the forest area. This realisation motivated the people to take appropriate methods which required only little effort and no technical and financial inputs. For the last nine years people are promoting planned and scientific regeneration practices. Ripe mangoes are collected and eaten in the forest or at the time of returning to village. While returning they eat mangoes and throw the seeds in the forest. Some seeds are put into the pits so that they are protected from anthropogenic disturbances and Porcupines and Bear. People never cut or damage mango seedlings or saplings.

Case Study

The Indian Institute of Forest Management (IIFM), Bhopal in collaboration with the people of Kondhpungar and IRDWSI undertook a study to document the impact of the above innovative practice introduced by the people of Kondhpungar to enhance regeneration of wild mangoes. The villagers shared the fact that the mango trees were not distributed in the entire forest area of the village, instead they were spread in three forest patches namely, Kotra am jhola forest area (five acres), Kudi kanda forest area (two acres) and Pasiamba forest patch (two acres). Therefore, the study was conducted only in these three forest areas.

A total four quadrates were laid (three in Kotra am jhola forest area and one in Kudi Kanda forest area) for the study. A seven members group which included four villagers and three researchers gathered the data. In case of mature mango trees, data pertaining to their number, girth at breast height (gbh), estimated age, crown size and health (hollowness, condition of the crown, gum, exudation were gathered). In case of mango recruits, seedlings and saplings their number, height and age were noted.

Preliminary results of the ongoing study showed that atleast over 1000 plants of wild mango have regenerated in the village. It is therefore safe to conclude that the impact of the practice initiated by the villagers described above has contributed enormously in regenerating wild mango trees.

6.7 Spiritually Empowered Seeds

In this section, a brief description about the unique practice followed by the villagers has been given that has a lot of implications in the biodiversity conservation of domesticated plants. This is based on a study jointly carried out by IIFM, people of Kondhpunagr and IRDWSI.

Chaitra Parab a festival celebrated during the April-May months constitutes a series of events. *Bihu Puja* (seed worship) is an important event in the celebration of *Chaitra Parab*. *Bihu Puja* is carried out either prior to the ritual hunt or after completion of the hunting event. This however, varies from village to village and community to community.

Empowering the seeds spiritually consists of two stages. First stage consists of performance of *Bihu Puja* in Jakhari (sacred grove) and the second stage comprises of the distribution of seeds to the people of the village.

Prior to *Bihu Puja*, a fistful of seeds of all important crops cultivated by the community in the preceding year are collected. Each household contributes to this collection. This collection of seeds is then taken to Jakhari where a puja is offered. Usually Disari assisted by Jani performs the puja. The seeds collected in a small bamboo basket is placed under a small pendal (tent) decorated with mango leaves and the flowers available in the village. Jakhari Debta (deity in the sacred grove) and the debtas (deities) in all directions are prayed and appealed to put into it the divine powers. Water used for this *puja* is customarily collected from the perennial stream of the village. To propotiate the deities, a black chicken and a goat are sacrificed. Women of the community are not allowed to attend this *puja*. Later the gathering enjoys a community feast prepared out of the sacrificed animals in the Jakhari itself. After the community feast the spiritually empowered seeds collected are taken back to the village. The *puja* in Jakhari is usually carried out during the day time. On the evening of the same day the spiritually empowered seeds are distributed among the community.

The entire village assembles at the Sadar (meeting place located at the centre usually under a banyan or peepal tree). Disari and Jani place the spiritually empowered seeds and the water (collected in the earthen pot in the morning from the perennial stream) at the Sadar. A small puja that also includes sacrificing a black chicken is offered to the Sadar debta (deity). Later Jani pours the water in the earthen pot on Disari and at the end releases the pot on the ground for free fall so that it breaks into pieces. Making sure that earthen pot is broken, the drenched Disari throws the seeds towards the community gathered at Sadar. While Disari is scattering the seeds, the villagers try their best to collect as many seeds as possible. During the entire process of scattering of seeds, the Disari does not face the people. He continues to chant *mantras* and throws the seeds towards the gathering with an over head action. The community members later mix the spiritually empowered seeds with their stored seeds to be planted in the current year.

6.8 Grain Bank

A grain bank was established in the village in 1995. In 2003 under UNDP-Women in Agriculture programme three large size metal containers were provided for proper storage of the grains. The grain bank is being managed by the People's Organisation. The facilities provided by this bank are being used very regularly by the villagers. The quantities are steadily increasing in the bank. The main practice followed by the villagers is that the borrower of the grains has to return to the bank four kgs in lieu of three kgs borrowed. As of 2007 the quantities of the grains available in the bank were: Ragi 500 kgs, Paddy 300 kgs and Rice 500 kgs.

7

Aspirations and Future Vision

In this chapter, we have given the future aspirations and visions of the people of Kondhpungar in terms of how they plan to manage their biodiversity and sustainable livelihoods. To appreciate this it is appropriate that we briefly recap salient features emerging from the preceding chapters.

In the preceding chapters of this document the following points were given:

(i) an account of the biodiversity bearing landscape and waterscape elements in the village;

(ii) documentation of the nature and extent of domesticated and wild fauna and flora occurring in various biodiversity bearing areas;

(iii) an analysis of the various usages of the documented biodiversity;

(iv) an analysis of the contributions made by the biodiversity in the livelihoods of the people;

(v) contributions made by the biodiversity to the subsistence needs of the people like fuelwood, grassing, medicine, food etc;

(vi) a description of the present status of the various landscape and waterscape elements in the village;

(vii) an analysis of the physical changes that have occurred in various landscape and waterscape elements in the village during the last two decades;

(viii) detailed description of changes that have occurred in domesticated and wild biodiversity in the village in different land and waterscape elements;

(ix) provided an account of the significant changes that have occurred in the governance system of the village; and

(x) gave an account of the linkages that the villagers of Kondhpungar have developed with civil society organisations and different government line departments.

7.1 Significant Observations

From the description and analysis presented in the preceeding chapters, the following salient features having future implications in biodiversity conservation and sustainable livelihoods of the people of Kondhpungar are given:

- Kondhpungar is a small remote and backward village with a population of 98 persons in Semiliguda block of Koraput district, Orissa.
- The main sources of livelihood of a majority of the people in the village are:
    - Agriculture,
    - Livestock,
    - Forest, and
    - Wage labour.
- A survey carried out by IRDWSI in 2004 revealed that the food produced in the village showed significant shortages. The total food grains produced by the people were 8547 kg whereas the requirement was 24660 kg.
- Vast variation existed among the households in the total annual income; it varies from Rs 6,400 to Rs 22,800 with an average of Rs 14,510.
- Agriculture is the main source of livelihood in the village and it contributes to Rs 1,88,650, i.e., 86.7 per cent to the total revenue, i.e., Rs 2,17,650 generated by all the households in the village. The other source of income that contributes significantly is income generated from wage labour, it contributes 8.65 per cent. Livestock contributes only 3.65 per cent. It is highly noteworthy that the income from forest products is only a dismal 1.03 per cent.
- Except for the month of June, it is highly noteworthy that atleast one festival related to biodiversity is celebrated in the remaining eleven months by the villagers.

- The village has a strong traditional governance structure. The affairs of the village are managed by headman called Nayak, supported by Challan (messenger), priest (*Pujari*), Gunia and Disari.
- Three new institutions in the village have been crafted: People's Organisation; Self-Help Group; and Rural Health and Environmental Programme.
- People of Kondhpungar have developed long and sustained partnerships with a local NGO, IRDWSI and other civil society organisations as well as various line departments of the Government of Orissa.
- The glimpses of Kondhpungar's journey demonstrated that if people wish, significant changes can be achieved even in a remote and backward village. It is remarkable that during the last two decades Kondhpungar has improved enormously the quality of life and economic status of its people. The village has now cemented concrete road, drinking water, durable housing, community centre, drainage, toilets, solar lights etc. In short the economic status as well as the quality of life of the people of Kondhpungar has improved remarkably.
- The undulating topography of the village has provided diverse habitats and therefore the village is extremely rich in having different landscape and waterscape biodiversity bearing areas: altogether 20 such elements are present in the village.
- Ninty-five plants are cultivated in different landscape and waterscape biodiversity areas in the village.
- Sixty-six wild animals are often sighted in the village.
- The village is also rich in aquatic biodiversity
- There are 148 wild plants in the village. However, presently 15 plants are not used. In addition for nine plants information with respect to their useage could not be gathered. A large number of plants i.e., 124 (83.8 per cent) out of 148 are used for a variety of purposes. Broadly speaking, the plant products are used for 11 different purposes:
  - 22 per cent of plants parts are used for food and 37.6 per cent for medicine;
  - 9.9 per cent of the parts are used as fuelwood;
  - five per cent of the parts are used as timber for furniture,

agricultural implements, house construction etc;

- Animal fodder is obtained from 9.9 per cent of the plant parts;
- 12 (8.5 per cent) plant products are used for making brooms, ropes and leaf plates etc. Some of these are also marketed;
- Parts of three plants are used for religious purpose; and
- While a majority of the plants yield products that are used for a single purpose, there are many plants that are used for more than single purpose. For example,

- Dabpiri is used as fodder and roofing material,
- Horida is used as medicine and tanning material,
- Keu kanda is used as food and medicine,
- Siadi leaves are used as leaf plate and seeds as food,
- Tentuli is used as food (fruit) and for extracting startch (seed).
- In short, the wild plants provide:
    - Food security,
    - Health care security,
    - Dental care,
    - Head hair care,
    - Energy security,
    - Fodder security,
    - Timber supplies,
    - Financial security,
    - Spiritual security, and
    - Social bondage.
- Sixty-fourwild animals that are sighted belong to the following seven Taxas:
    - the largest number of animals 21 (32.8 per cent) belong to the Taxa birds;
    - a significant number of animals 15 (23.4 per cent) are reptiles;
    - mammals also constitute a significant number being 14 (21.9 per cent), and

- the remaining Taxa are amphibian, arachnids, insect and invertebrate occurring in small numbers.

- Of the 64 animals 33 animals are used for seven different purposes:
  - the largest number i.e., 22 animals (62.9 per cent) are consumed as food;
  - there is only one animal i.e., Gharchatia, a bird, used for medicinal purposes;
  - thus altogether 23 animals are used for consumptive purposes, and
  - there are five different non-consumptive uses for which 12 wild animals are used. They are to signal bad and good omen, forecasting of rain and arrival of guests. There are two animals Bani and Sua chadei (parrot), both birds are used as pets.
- There are five wild aquatic animals that are found in and around the water bodies. They are Godsi, Karandi, Magur (all fishes), Kankada (crab) and Bengo (frog). Of these five, all the three fishes and Kankada are consumed as food.
- From Chapter 6 that described history of changes in landscape and waterscape elements the following salient features are noteworthy:
  - There is a significant increase in number of vegetables grown and the number of fruit and other trees planted in home gardens.
  - However, cultivation of a few traditional varieties of crops such as Desi kakudi (due to excess water), Jhota (moved to farm lands and shifting cultivation areas), Char kumuda-a variety of gourd and Jelinga a leafy vegetable, have been discontinued.
  - The fertility of the soils in these gardens has significantly improved due to the application of organic manures-compost, green manure, vermi-compost.
  - A lot more water is now available for irrigating Badas than before through improved irrigation system.
  - The number of wild animal species and their frequency in Badas has enormously increased.
  - The purpose for which the herbal garden was introduced has not served its purpose as most of the plants planted are readily available in wild in the vicinity of the village.
  - A number of land development activities were initiated in 2002. The area under cultivation has substantially increased due to enhanced irrigation.

- In some patches of farm lands where irrigation is available, three crops are grown in three seasons; during Kharif and Rabi a variety of crops and vegetables are grown while in summer season mostly vegetables are grown.
- A significant change has occurred in the land use pattern; a number of fruit bearing trees have been planted on farm lands within the framework of agro-forestry models.
- Some noteworthy changes have occurred in the farm lands. Earlier more emphasis was given on growing subsistence crops such as Ragi, Paddy, Ginger, Turmeric, Cluster beans, Maize, Pumpkin, Cowpea, Creeper Beans and Cucumber. Presently, in addition to the subsistence crops grown earlier, a number of new vegetable crops are also cultivated.
- A number of fruit bearing trees such as Papaya, Orange, Banana, Lemon, Gouva, Drumstick, Mango, Pomegranate, Custard apple, etc., have also been planted on the farm lands.
- A significant change has occurred in the paddy varieties that were grown in the past. Earlier nine varieties of paddy were grown. Cultivation of four varieties, e.g., Karandi, Kandul kati, Kola dhan and Nili dhan has been discontinued.
- Three new varieties of paddy Lalat, Jajati and Khandagiri are now grown besides the five traditional ones.
- Since 2001 a number of land development activities that included stone bunding, land leveling and stone clearing were under taken on rainfed lands.
- Due to the availability of irrigation, a substantial amount of the land which was used earlier as rainfed is now used as farm land. Therefore, the crops grown in the farm lands have also been introduced in these lands.
- The above activities have enhanced the productivity of the crops that are grown.
- A small number of trees of three species such as Mango, Jack fruit and Karanjo have been planted along the bunds of rainfed lands.

- There are a number of varieties of paddy, ragi and suan grown in the village.
- There is a significant reduction in the number of crops that were grown earlier in shifting cultivation areas. Earlier 20 different varieties of crops were grown. However, presently six varieties of crops have been abandoned during the past decade.
- The fallow period has drastically reduced from 10 years to two to three years presently.
- The productivity of different crops has also reduced significantly.
- Due to rigorous protection measures followed by the villagers, the plantations undertaken during 1994-1995 are now full of grown trees.
- From 2006 the villagers have started pruning the trees. The branches obtained from pruning were sold for a sum of Rs 7000.
- The plantation also provides fuelwood to the villagers. This has partially reduced the dependence of the villagers for fuelwood from the protected forest area.
- Cashew plantation was undertaken on about 7.28 ha in year 1999-2000. Further, gap filling was carried out during 2003.
- The plantation has already started yielding cashew nuts; last year (2007) about 5 kg has been harvested.
- The villagers have planned for next couple of years that the cashew nuts harvested from the plantation will be used as seeds for raising plantation in Lelisira and Kotra ambo areas.
- Protected forest in hill ranges of Balipata, Puligunta and Kudi Khanda were earlier used entirely for shifting cultivation purposes.
- During 1995 the village experienced unusual heavy rains that resulted in massive land slides. These interns damaged the cultivated fields. In response to this the villagers decided to restrict shifting cultivation area in Balipata and leave the rest of the area for regeneration of forest. Since then, the villagers have accorded complete protection to these patches. The protection has resulted presently into a fairly well wooded forest.

- Since 1995 a lot of changes have occurred in the management of protected forests.
- Protection measures have been strengthened in terms of patrolling.
- Strict rules have been framed for harvesting fuelwood.
- In view of the lack of grasing area in the village, the villagers have been grasing their animals freely in forest areas.
- The number of species of wild animals and their numbers have substantially increased since 1995.
- Because of the availability of the irrigation water in the check dam some rainfed land has been converted in to farm lands. This change has resulted in increased productivity levels as well as choices of planting other crops and trees.
- Water from the check dam has also ensured growing crops in Rabi season on some farm lands but also has provided opportunities for cultivating vegetables during summer season. Thus, on some patches of rainfed lands now instead of one crop two crops are grown and in some patches even three crops are grown.
- Not only the domesticated animals of the village now get ensured drinking water from the check dam throughout the year but also people of the neighbouring villages often use this for their animals.
- Many wild animals also use this water source.
- Some wild fishes as well as other animals are now found in and around the check dam.
- Wild plant diversity has also increased in the vicinity of the check dam.
- The villagers have identified fourteen socially most important wild plants.
- Eight plants have been identified by the villagers that are critical for the survival of a number of wild animals.
- The Indian Institute of Forest Management, Bhopal in collaboration with the people of Kondhpungar and IRDWSI undertook a study to document the impact of the above innovative practice introduced by the people of Kondhpungar.

- To enhance regeneration of wild mangoes the people of Kondhpungar for the last nine years are promoting planned and scientific regeneration practice. Ripe wild mangoes are collected and eaten at the spot or at the time of returning to village. While returning they eat mangoes and throw the seeds on both side of the forest. Some seeds are put into the pits so that it is protected from anthropogenic disturbances and Porcupines and Bear. People never cut or damage mango seedlings or saplings. Over 1000 plants of wild mango have regenerated in the village.
- During *Chait Parabo* a festival celebrated usually during April an important ceremony is performed to spiritually empower seeds of cultivated plants in the village.
- A grain bank was established in the year 1995 managed by the People's Organisation.

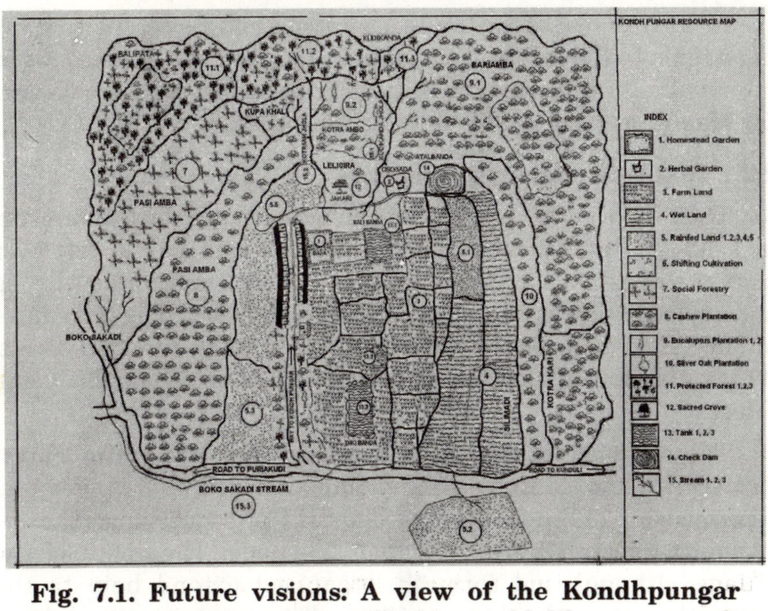

Fig. 7.1. Future visions: A view of the Kondhpungar village, the people of the village would like to see after ten years (Planned), Biodiversity areas.

7.2 Future Vision

Summing up this section, it is absolutely clear that the future well-being of the people, as in the past and present, will almost entirely depend on the health of the 20 landscapes and waterscape elements of the village. Therefore, the main focus of the future plans of the villagers are to ensure that the capabilities of the various biodiversity bearing areas are enhanced to support a wide range of domestic and wild biodiversity. It may be mentioned that the People's Organisations has various other plans to be pursued to enhance the quality of the life of the people. These plans however have not being included in the present study.

In Fig. 3.1 of the Chapter 3, the present status of the 20 biodiversity bearing elements in the village has been presented. The future vision of the people of Kondhpungar envisages a scenario of the village after ten years is as shown in Fig. 7.1.

The villagers in collaboration with Indian Institute of Forest Management, Bhopal and IRDWSI have prepared a micro-plan for the management of forests in the village. The plan incorporates time bound activities to be undertaken in the forests during the coming ten years.

In order to realise the future aspirations and vision, the villagers in addition to the micro-plan mentioned above have planned major interventions in two key areas: (i) Institutional arrangements, and (ii) Management of biodiversity bearing areas.

7.2.1 Institutional Arrangements

The People's Organisation which has been primarily interested in looking after the management of forest and has in fact ever since it was established has been at the centre stage for developing and implementing forest management practices including procedures of harvesting fuelwood, timber and other NTFPs from the forest: it has also formulated rules for grasing of the animals in the forest.

The organisation has formed a sub-committee called Forest Protection and Management Committee (FPMC) under the chairmanship of Singru Hontal. The SHG provides support to the committee especially in protection functions. The youth of the village although not formally organised extend help to the committee as and when required. The committee has been empowered to negotiate with the State Forest Department as well as other agencies to realise its objectives.

The People's Organisation has also established another sub-committee which looks after the management of landscape and waterscape elements other than the forest. Like FPMC, this committee has also developed a village development plan that not only includes the biodiversity concernes but addresses the overall well-being of the people of the village including livelihoods based on non forest and non farm sectors.

7.2.2 Management of biodiversity bearing areas

The work plans in different micro-plans specifically were developed keeping in view the details presented in Chapters 5 and 6 summerised above in Section 7.1. Although the detailed year wise breakdown of the activities are given in the micro-plans which are readily available on request from the people of Kondhpungar, IIFM and IRDWSI, here are given some of the significant activities to be undertaken related to different landscape and waterscape elements in the village. Wherever, relevant the two committees mentioned above will work in unison.

(a) Homestead garden: The main strategy in homestead gardens in the village to be implemented is:

- Gradually replace seasonal crops to perennial crops and trees. The proposed crops to be introduced are Ivy gourd, bitter gourd, papaya, drumstick, lemon. These will not only provide nutritional security to the village but will also reduce problems of labour and damage to crops by the wild life.
- Use of vermi compost will be enhanced to increase crop productivity.

Plate 7.1. Vermi-composting: Demonstration Unit Installed by IRDWSI.

(b) Herbal Garden

- Locally available important herbal plants needed by the traditional healers which are not available presently in the garden will be planted. This will ensure livelihood of the traditional health practitioners in the area as well as health security of the village.

(c) Farm Land

- The agro-forestry model introduced on a pilot scale among five families in the village by IIFM, Bhopal has yielded highly positive results in generating enhanced income. This model will be adopted by all the families and extended to all the farm lands in the village. This will reduce labour problem as well as will enhance biomass productivity and provide food security to the villagers.
- Gliricidia as green manure and improved composting methods will be introduced in all the house holds of the village.
- Water from Silimadi stream will be diverted to farm lands lying on the western end in the vicinity of Diki banda: the village has already prepared a proposal and submitted to the Panchayat under the provision of National Rural Employment Guarantee Scheme (NREGA).

(d) Wet Land

- Attempts will be made to reintroduce in small way some of the paddy varieties like karandi, kandul kati, kola dhan and nili dhan that have been discontinued in the village.

(e) Rainfed Land

- The rainfed lands are extremely important as a future source of food security in the village. Lots of efforts and investments will be made for the purpose of clearing of stone, land levelling, stone bunding and live fencing in rainfed lands. The village has already prepared a proposal and submitted to the Panchayat under the provision of National Rural Employment Guarantee Scheme (NREGA).
- Rainfed lands in Pasiamba hills adjacent to the left side of the road (landscape elements number eight in Fig. 7.1) will be converted into silver oak plantation as these lands are not suitable for cultivation of crops. However, gradually these lands wherever feasible will be leveled as terraces and used for growing crops and trees.

(f) Shifting Cultivation

- FPMC, SHG and the youth of the village have already decided that shifting cultivation will be totally discontinued in the village. The patches where shifting cultivation is being practiced presently in Bariamba and Kotra kari hills will be converted into cashew nut plantation. The patch in Balipata hills will be left for natural regeneration of wild vegetation.

(g) Social Forestry Plantation

- Protection measures will be strengthened, gap filling will be undertaken and procedures for harvesting of biomass and its sale will be streamlined.

(h) Cashew Nut Plantation

- Presently the cashew nut plantation is found in two hill ranges, Pasiamba and Kotra ambo. Gradually, the plantation will be extended to Balipata, Bariamba and Kotra kari.

(i) Eucalyptus Plantation

- Eucalyptus plantation in the village will be gradually totally replaced by cashew nut plantation.

(j) Silver Oak Plantation

- Silver oak plantation has now matured and harvesting of timber in a sustainable manner will be undertaken from 2008. Elaborate rules for sustainable harvesting are being developed.

(k) Protected Forest

- Protected forest exists in three patches of the village in the hill ranges of Balipata, Puligunta and Kudi kanda. Protection measures have been enhanced in respect of illegal felling and forest fires; harvesting of biomass has been regulated; grassing will be regulated in future and the patch in Balipata used currently as shifting cultivation will be gradually replaced by natural regeneration.
- Assisted natural regeneration of wild mangoes will be further extended: a similar process will be initiated for several other wild plant species.
- Long-term measures have been proposed in the micro-plan including a scientific study to be undertaken by IIFM and IRDWSI to increase populations and regulate the use of

twelve socially most important wild plants identified by the villagers.

- Seven plants that have been identified by the villagers that are critical for the survival of a number of wild animals; will be accorded protection, their populations increased and harvesting regulated: IIFM and IRDWSI have been entrusted to undertake a detailed study of the levels of dependence including the seasons of the wild life on these plant resources.

(l) Sacred grove

- Presently the area under sacred grove is rather small. Provisions in the micro-plan have been made to increase the area of the grove.

(m) Tanks

- The construction of the two tanks in the village will be strengthened, embankment fortified with soil work and plantation, annual disiltation will be taken and fisheries and duckery will be introduced.

(n) Check dam

- Plantation and stone-bunding at the hill slope of up side of the dam will be undertaken to protect it from land slides and to reduce siltation load from the stream.

(o) Livestock

- Gradually more milch animals will be introduced. Grassing specially in the forest areas will be regulated. Village youth will be trained to take health care needs of the domesticated animals.

The glimpses of Kondhpungar's journey demonstrated that if people wish, significant changes can be achieved even in a remote and backward village. It is remarkable that during the last two decades Kondhpungar has improved enormously the quality of life and economic status of the people. The aspirations and future vision plans envisaged by the villagers will undoubtedly further enhance the health of the biodiversity and livelihoods of the people.

7.3 Knowledgeable Persons in the Village

There are a number of persons in the village with special knowledge. An illustrative list of such people is presented in 7.1. These persons will provide guidance and support to FPMC, SHG and the youth of the village for the effective implementation of the various provisions contained in the Future Vision—micro-plan of the village.

Plate 7.2. Gunia: Native Traditional Healer.

Table 7.1 Knowledgeable Persons in the Village

Sl. No.	*Name*	*Sex*	*Age*	*Areas of Expertise*
1.	Sapura Hontal	M	46	Snake bite treatment and wild plant identification
2.	Hari Hontal	M	48	Fits treatment and astrology
3.	Sambru Hontal	M	48	Agro-forestry
4.	Singru Hontal	M	28	Plant identification

Appendices

Appendix 1: Genealogy of the Hontal Clan 1 in Kondhpungar

Gene-ration	*Index No.*	*Name*	*Age*	*Gene-ration*	*Index No.*	*Name*	*Age*
I	1	Bodu Hontal	N.A.	VII	63	Ratnu Hontal	15
	1A	N.A.	N.A.		64	Sumitra Hontal	12
II	2	Bitu Hontal	N.A.		65	Besa Hontal	10
	2A	N.A.	N.A.		66	Raju Hontal	8
	3	Linga Hontal	N.A.		67	Mini Hontal	4
	3A	N.A.	N.A.		34	Chandra Hontal	25
III	4	Ranju Hontal	N.A.		34A	Kousalya Hontal	23
	4A	N.A.	N.A.		35	Dinamani Hontal	23
	5	Hari Hontal	N.A.		36	Mahendra Hontal	20
	5A	Butuli Hontal	N.A.		36A	Sabita Hontal	18
	6	N.A.	N.A.		37	Lachma Hontal	16
IV	7	Laxmi Hontal	95		38	Krushna Hontal	14
	7A	N.A.	90		39	Champa Hontal	10
	8	Linga Hontal	70		40	Singru Hontal	30
	8A	Sambari Hontal	80		40A	Tikmo Hontal	28
V	9	Sarbu Hontal	90		41	Sapai Hontal	26
	9A	Sulai Hontal	60		42	Site Hontal	24
	10	Mulia Hontal	65		43	Kishore Hontal	22
	10A	Pilko Hontal	100		43A	Kosai Hontal	21
	11	Singana Hontal	70		44	Domni Hontal	20
	11A	Sinde Hontal	50		45	Biswanath Hontal	18

Generation	*Index No.*	*Name*	*Age*	*Generation*	*Index No.*	*Name*	*Age*
VI	12	Sambru Hontal	52		45A	Phulmati Hontal	17
	12A	Rupai Hontal	50		46	Panchulata Hontal	23
	13	Bali Hontal	45		47	Bijaya Hontal	20
	13A	Julai Hontal	42		47A	Jurme Hontal	18
	14	Muti Hontal	34		48	Sanjaya Hontal	18
	15	Laxmi Hontal	37		48A	Sushila Hontal	17
	15A	Gunduli Hontal	35		49	Luku Hontal	15
	16	Hari Hontal	55		50	Sunita Hontal	13
	16A	Jimlo Hontal	53		51	Tuni Hontal	10
	17	Sapura Hontal	50		52	Banguru Hontal	25
	17A	Nila Hontal	48		52A	Butuli Hontal	22
	18	Ramachandra Hontal	45		53	Beturu Hontal	20
	18A	Rajmani Hontal	43		54	Katko Hontal	15
	19	Tubri Hontal	33		55	Phulmani Hontal	13
	20	Kamlu Hontal	42		56	Lingaraj Hontal	10
	20A	Ratai Hontal	40		57	Dalimo Hontal	8
	21	Nawe Hontal	30		58	Namita Hontal	4
VII	22	Keshu Hontal	28	**VIII**	59	Ratnamani Hontal	13
	22A	Walsi Hontal	27		60	Rashmi Hontal	10
	23	Limbe Hontal	25		61	Pana Hontal	6
	24	Upendra Hontal	21		62	Achmi Hontal	3
	24A	Jirmo Hontal	19		68	Jimai Hontal	10
	25	Kamli Hontal	18		69	Ani Hontal	4
	26	Suno Hontal	17		70	Niranjan Hontal	1
	27	Male Hontal	14		71	Surendra Hontal	10
	28	Bimla Hontal	19		72	Ramesh Hontal	7
	29	Alme Hontal	17		73	Kitu Hontal	5
	30	Asto Hontal	14		74	Sunil Hontal	3
	31	Sane Hontal	12		75	Binod Hontal	4
	32	Sitme Hontal	7		76	Manoj Hontal	2
	33	Sineya Hontal	3				

Genealogy of Hontal Clan 1 in Kondhpungar

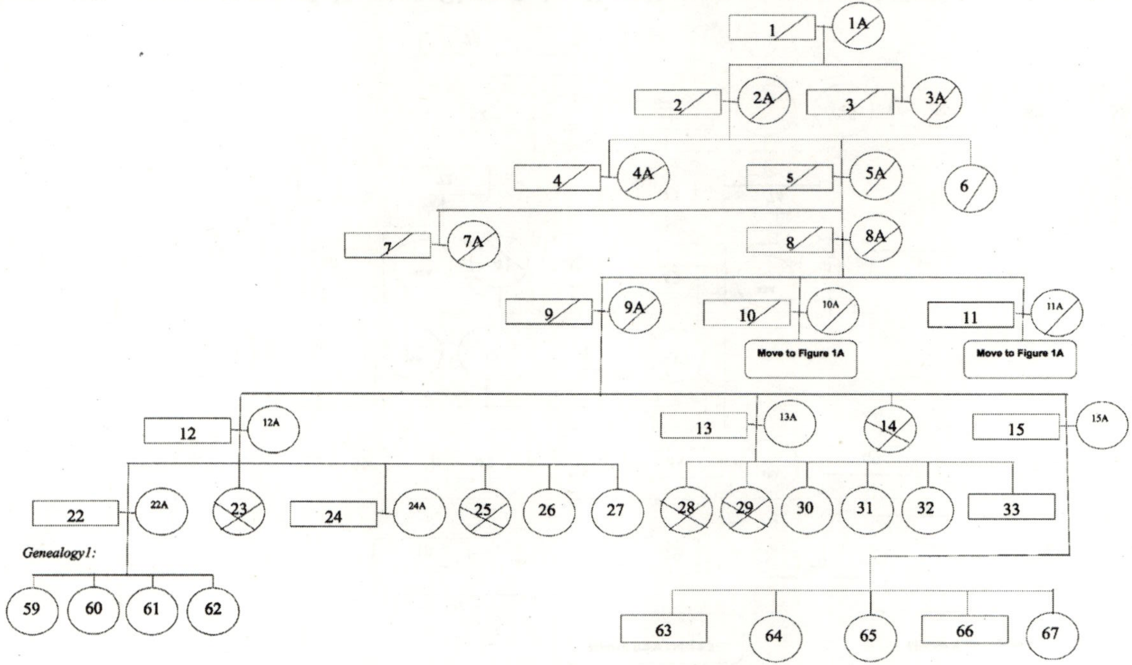

Genealogy 1: Genealogy of Hontal Clan 1 in Kondhpungar (explanation for symbols used in the figure are given in Genealogy 4).

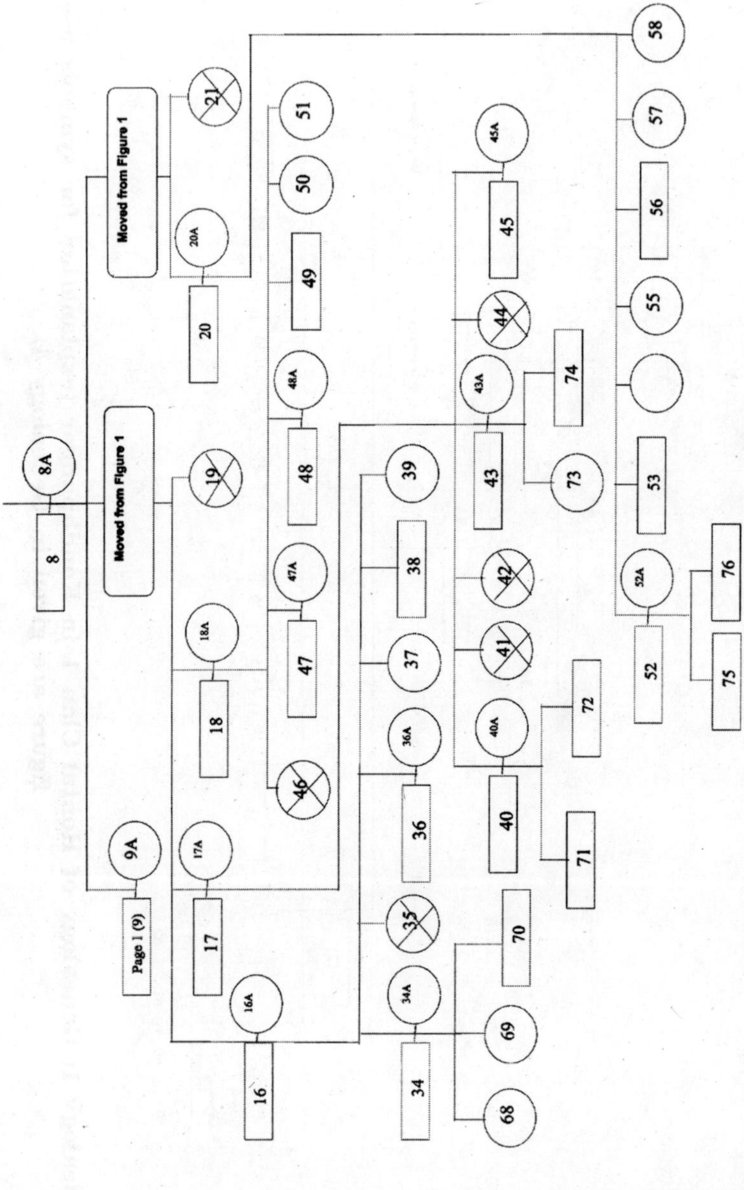

Genealogy 1A: Genealogy of Hontal Clan 1 in Kondhpungar (contd.) (explanation for symbols used in the figure are given in Genealogy 4).

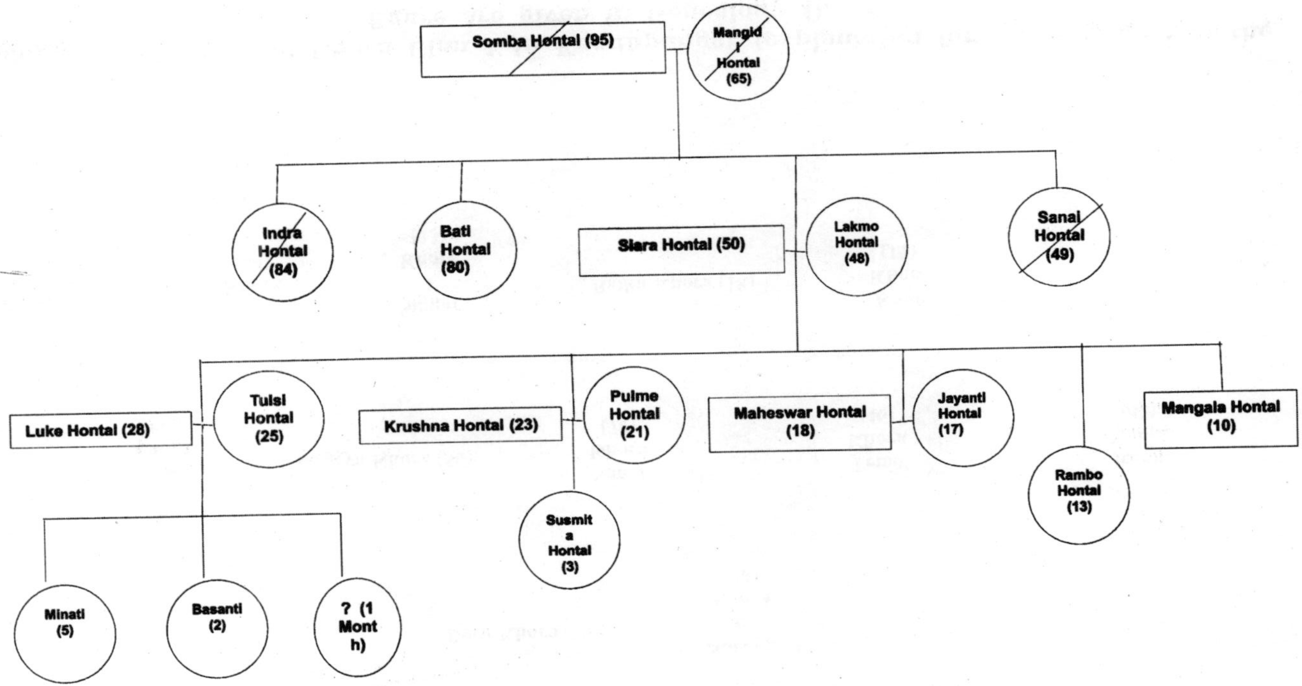

Genealogy 2: Genealogy of Hontal Clan 2 in Kondhpungar (explanation for symbols used in the figure are given in Genealogy 4).

Genealogy of Khora Clan 1 in Kondhpungar

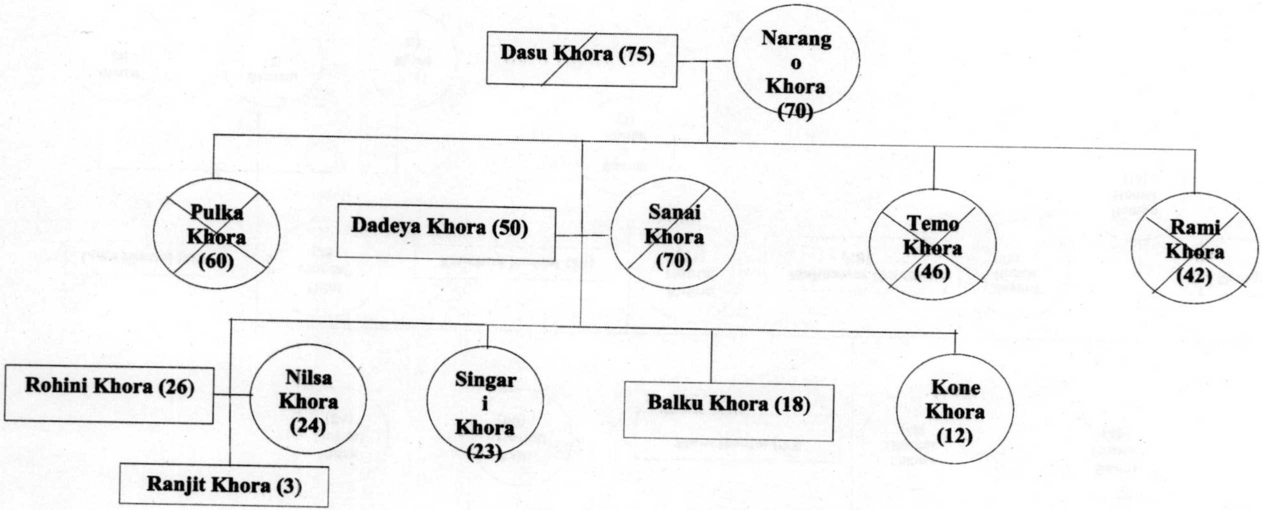

Genealogy 3: Genealogy of Khora Clan 1 in Kondhpungar (explanation for symbols used in the figure are given in Genealogy 4).

Genealogy of Khora Clan 2 in Kondhpungar

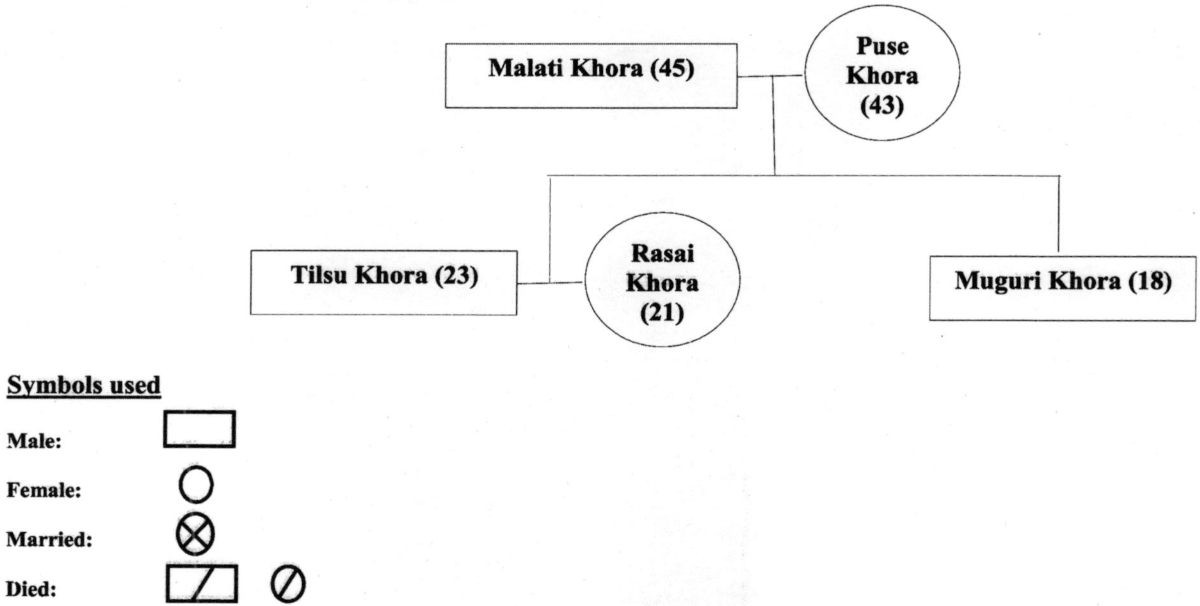

Genealogy 4: Genealogy of Khora Clan 2 in Kondhpungar.

Appendix 2: Names of Cultivated Crops, Vegetables and Trees grown in Kondhpungar for the Year 2007

Sl. No.	Name of the Plants				Habit
	Kuvi	Oriya	English	Scientific	
1.	Aalsi	Alsi	Niger	*Guizotia abbysinica*	Herb
2.	Alami	Ada	Ginger	*Zinziber officinale*	Herb
3.	Amruti	Amrutbhanda	Papaya	*Carica papaya*	Tree
4.	Arjun	Arjun	Arjun	*Terminalia arjuna*	Tree
5.	Arka	Kangu	Finger millet		Herb
6.	Bailo	Jhota	Indian bean	*Dolichos sp.?*	Climber
7.	Bateri	Paluo	Arrowroot		Herb
8.	Bendi	Bhendi	Lady's finger	*Abelmoschus esculantus*	Herb
9.	Bhumi sana	China badam	Ground nut	*Arachis hypogea*	Herb
10.	Bileikanta	Bada gacha	Lantana	*Lantana camara*	Shrub
11.	Borokoli	Borkoli	Chinies date, Jujube	*Ziziphus jujuba*	Tree
12.	Chakunda	Chakunda	Cassia Siamea	*Cassia siamea*	Tree
13.	Chandan	Chandan	Sandal wood	*Santalum album*	Tree
14.	Chichoni	Janhi	Ridged gourd	*Luffa acutangula*	Climber
15.	Chilor	Chilor	Acacia	*Acacia torta?*	Shrub
16.	Citramurka	Chitramul	?	?	Creeper
17.	Danduli	Tutkoli	Mulberry	?	Tree

Sl. No.	*Name of the Plants*				*Habit*
	Kuvi	*Oriya*	*English*	*Scientific*	
18.	Deru	Baunsa	Bamboo	*Dendrocalamus sp.*	Tree
19.	Dhania	Dhania	Coriander	*Coriandrum sativum*	Herb
20.	Doblauli	Rasuno	Garllic	*Allium sativum*	Herb
21.	Dohi	Dimri	?		Tree
22.	Dongar oding	Dongor rani	Green gram		Herb
23.	Gajori	Gajor	Carrot	*Daucus carota*	Herb
24.	Gati Kobi	Ganti kobi	Knolkhol	*Brassica coulorapa*	Herb
25.	Gocha kanga	Buda beans	French beans		Climber
26.	Guanr	Guanr	Cluster bean	*Cymopsis tetragonoloba*	Herb
27.	Gumna	Gambhari	Gmelina	*Gmelina arborea*	Tree
28.	Harsu	Soriso	Mustard	*Brassica campestris var. glauca*	Herb
29.	Heyan	Baigono	Brinjal	*Solanum melongena*	Herb
30.	Hinga	Holdi	Turmeric	*Curcuma domestica*	Herb
31.	Hopa	Saru	Arum	*Colocasia esculanta*	Herb
32.	Hurwe	Simbo	Bean	*Dolichos sp.?*	Climber
33.	Jafra	Jafra	Annatto	*Bixa orellana*	Tree
34.	Jambo	Jamkoli	Black berry	*Syzigium cumini*	Tree
35.	Jona	Makka	Maize	*Zea mays*	Herb
36.	Kajuri	Khojuri	Date palm	*Phoenix sp.*	Tree
37.	Kala kanga	Jhudongo	Cow pea	*Vigna sp.*	Climber
38.	Kamala	Kamala	Orange	*Citrus reticulata*	Tree
39.	Karanji	Karanjo	Pongamia	*Pongamia pinnata*	Tree
40.	Karla	Kolora	Bitter gourd	*Momordica charantia*	Climber
41.	Kawa janna	Khed jonna	Sorghum	*Sorghum vulgare*	Herb
42.	Keeni	Joda	Castor	*Ricinus communis*	Tree
43.	Kodtang	Koloth	Horse gram	*Dolichos uniflorus*	Creeper

Sl. No.	*Name of the Plants*				*Habit*
	Kuvi	*Oriya*	*English*	*Scientific*	
44.	Kofi	Kafi	Coffee	*Coffea arabica*	Tree
45.	Kohoda	Suan	Finger millet	?	Herb
46.	Kopakucha	Borda	?	?	Tree
47.	Krushna chuda	Krushna chuda	Gulmohar	*Delonix regia*	Tree
48.	Kuliyan	Dhano	Paddy	*Oryza sativa*	Herb
49.	Kumuda	Boit alu	Pumpkin	*Cucurbita maxima*	Creeper
50.	Kunduru	Kunduri	Ivy gourd	*Coccinia sp.?*	Climber
51.	Leka kuna	Similikonda	Tapioca	*Manihot esculanta*	Shrub
52.	Lekha	Simili	Indian cotton tree	*Bombax malabaricum*	Tree
53.	Lembu	Lembu	Lemon	*Citrus sp.*	Tree
54.	Lobiya	Borboti	Cow pea	*Vigna unguiculata*	Climber
55.	Mahaa	Ambo	Mango	*Mangifera indica*	Tree
56.	Mahaa neem	Moha neem	Neem	*Melia azedirach*	Tree
57.	Mandar	Mandar	China rose	*Hibiscus rosa-sinensis*	Tree
58.	Mandia	Mandia	Ragi	*Elucine carnacea*	Herb
59.	Manji jambo	Pijuli	Guava	*Psidium guajava*	Tree
60.	Marnu kanga	Kandul	Pigeon pea	*Cajanus cajan*	Tree
61.	Matakucha	Khosla sago	?	?	Herb
62.	Matakucha	Khada sago	?	?	Herb
63.	Matakucha	Palongo sago	?	?	Herb
64.	Mirlo	Mirlo	Squash	*Cucurbita moschata*	Climber
65.	Mirsi	Maricho	Chilly	*Capsicum annuum*	Herb
66.	Mula	Mula	Radish	*Raphanus sativus*	Herb
67.	Mundra	Kakudi	Cucumber	*Cucumis sativus*	Creeper
68.	Muninga	Sajana	Drumstick	*Moringa oleifera*	Tree
69.	Murga/sinki	Murga	Sisal	*Agave americana*	Shrub
70.	Nadeli	Nadia	Coconut	*Cocos nucıfera*	Tree
71.	Nangeli kuna	Khombo alu	Yam	?	Herb

Sl. No.	*Name of the Plants*				*Habit*
	Kuvi	*Oriya*	*English*	*Scientific*	
72.	Niligiri	Niligiri	Eucalyptus	*Eucalyptus globulus*	Tree
73.	Panaha	Panasa	Jackfruit	*Artocarpus integrifolia*	Tree
74.	Peja(kajai)	Bilati Baigono	Tomato-large size	*Lycopersicum esculantum*	Herb
75.	Peja(una)	Bhejiri	Tomato-small size	?	Herb
76.	Puda kobi	Banda kobi	Cabbage	*Brassica oleracea var. capitata*	Herb
77.	Pula	Tentuli	Tamarind	*Tamarindus indica*	Tree
78.	Puyu kobi	Phul kobi	Cauliflower	*Brassica oleracea var.botrytis*	Herb
79.	Radhachuda	Radhachuda	Indian laburnun	*Cassia fistula*	Tree
80.	Rani kuna	Mati konda	Sweet potato	*Ipomea batatas*	Herb
81.	Ranja benisi	Malo beans	Beans	?	Climber
82.	Rupa	Silver oak	Silver oak	*Grevillea robusta*	Tree
83.	Sana	Motor channa	Green peas	*Pisum sativum*	Creeper
84.	Sapta	Sapota	Sapota	*Achrus sapota*	Tree
85.	Simarani	Kontagocho	Thorny Bush	?	Shrub
86.	Sitaphol	Atta	Custard apple	*Annona squamosa*	Tree
87.	Solop	Salab	Fishtail palm	*Caryota urens*	Tree
88.	Tadi	Kadali	Banana	*Musa paradisica*	Tree
89.	Tala bonda	Gendu phul	Mari gold	*Tagetes erecta*	Herb
90.	Tek	Saguan	Teak	*Tectona grandis*	Tree
91.	Tini lau	Lau	Bottle gourd	*Lagenaria vulgaris*	Climber
92.	Toba	Batapi	Grape fruit	*Citrus paradisica?*	Tree
93.	Tua	?	?	?	Tree
94.	Ulli	Piajo	Onion	*Allium cepa*	Herb
95.	Valia	Kaju	Cashew	*Anacardium occidentale*	Tree

Note: (?) denotes that we could not ascertain name in English or Scientific name.

Appendix 3: Names of 124 Wild Plants, their Parts used with Purpose

Plants	Parts	Name	Kuvi name	Plant parts	Use
1.	1.	Ambo	Mahaaa	Fruit	Food
	2.			Seed	Food
2.	3.	Amla	Jurha	Fruit	Medicine
3.	4.	Apama rongo	Duchabondru	Root	Medicine
4.	5.	Arjun	Arjun marnu	Wood	Fuelwood
	6.			Stem	Housing
5.	7.	Bagonaki	Launikoti	Root	Medicine
6.	8.	Bahada	Trahu	Fruit	Medicine
7.	9.	Baidonko	Tudayan	Root	Medicine
	10.			Seed	Medicine
8.	11.	Bajramali	Melukukuti	Flower	Medicine
	12.			Root	Medicine
9.	13.	Ban jhudongo	Jada Kala kanga	Root	Medicine
10.	14.	Bansaru	Konja tahaodi	Tuber	Fodder
11.	15.	Baria kanda	Dkli kunaya	Tuber	Fodder
12.	16.	Baunso	Deru	Stem	Fencing
	17.		Deru	Stem	Housing
13.	18.	Belo	Belo marnu	Fruit	Medicine
14.	19.	Bernga	Bernga	Bark	Shampoo

Plants	*Parts*	*Name*	*Kuvi name*	*Plant parts*	*Use*
15.	20.	Bhaira bhuta	Motopatarimada	Leaf	Fodder
16.	21.	Bhalu dar	Jholajambu	Bark	Medicine
17.	22.	Bhalu jam	Oodijambu	Bark	Medicine
18.	23.	Bhui amla	Bumi juro	Plant	Medicine
19.	24.	Bichhauati	Karselimada	Root	Medicine
20.	25.	Bila	Tani marnu	Fruit	Medicine
21.	26.	Bileikanta	Bileikata	Seed	Medicine
	27.			Plant	Fencing
22.	28.	Bisalya korani	Mitie jada	Leaf	Medicine
23.	29.	Bod tetenka	Darmel marnu	Plant	Fuelwood
24.	30.	Bodkokodi	Kaja kotikucha	Leaf	Food
25.	31.	Bojra mukhi	Koyu hirsa	Root	Medicine
26.	32.	Bon kodli	Jada tading	Stem	Food
27.	33.	Bondari	Kambli goacha	Root	Medicine
28.	34.	Bongordal	Loho dandi	Leaf	Fodder
29.	35.	Borkoli	Borkoli	Fruit	Food
30.	36.	Boruwa	Boruajada	Leaf	Fodder
31.	37.	Chandan	Chandan	Branch	Fuelwood
32.	38.	Chikni	Hirsa	Leaf	Fodder
33.	39.	Chilli	Siding	Seed	Shampoo
34.	40.	Dabpiri	Wika	Straw	Fodder
	41.		Wika	Straw	Roofing
35.	42.	Dakli	Sorenda	Root	Food
36.	43.	Damon	Dameni	Stem	Agri. implement
37.	44.	Deruharja		Grass	Fodder
38.	45.	Dhopki	Dhopki	Bark	Medicine
39.	46.	Didendimada	Didendimada	Root	Medicine
40.	47.	Dondera	Dondro	Flower	Medicine
41.	48.	Dubo ghas	Garkijada	Grass	Medicine
42.	49.	Dudmal	Misimada	Root	Medicine
43.	50.	Dumri	Toya	Fruit	Food
44.	51.	Gadel	Grawee	Plant	Medicine
45.	52.	Gali morka	Gali morka	Tree	Timber

Plants	*Parts*	*Name*	*Kuvi name*	*Plant parts*	*Use*
46.	53.	Gandi buta	Amorjoda	Tree	Fuelwood
47.	54.	Gandiri	Gandiri	Plant	Fuelwood
48.	55.	Gatamarka	Ghata morka	Plant	Fencing
49.	56.	Gereda	Potugarda	Leaf	Fodder
50.	57.	Ghantia	Ghantiajada	Grass	Fodder
51.	58.	Girli	Leda	Flower	Food
52.	59.	Gna mandia	Ganamandia	Leaf	Fodder
53.	60.	Golaki	Golaki	Root	Medicine
54.	61.	Gombari	Gumna	Bark	Medicine
	62.			Seed	NTFP
55.	63.	Gorudo	Grawee marnu	Bark	Medicine
56.	64.	Gugunimal	Gugunimada	Root	Medicine
57.	65.	Gurdi sago	Gurudi kucha	Leaf	Food
58.	66.	Harchand	Hadchandan	Bark	Medicine
59.	67.	Hatimal	Podamada	Bark	Rope
	68.			Tuber	Medicine
60.	69.	Hirsi	Hirsi	Leaf	Fodder
61.	70.	Horida	Tarhoo	Seed	Medicine
	71.		Tarhoo	Seed	NTFP
62.	72.	Jamkoli	Manjijanbu	Fruit	Food
63.	73.	Kadruhirsa	Kadruhirsa	Plant	Fuelwood
64.	74.	Karakuta	Kadhakutamarnu	Trunk	Furniture
65.	75.	Karanjo	Karngi	Seed	Medicine
66.	76.	Kathi badni	Koliabadni	Plant	Broom
67.	77.	Keu kanda	Keukuna	Root	Medicine
	78.		Keukuna	Root	Food
68.	79.	Khajuri niali	Kajuri	Fruit	Food
69.	80.	Kichi	Kisi	Fruit	Oil
70.	81	Klia konda	Kaliakuna	Root	Food
71.	82.	Koi hirsa	Koyu hirsa	Seed	Medicine
72.	83.	Koicho	Gunjerikanga	Seed	Medicine
73.	84.	Konior	Kundeli punga	Flower	Worship
74.	85.	Kontakoli	Andgo	Fruit	Food
75.	86.	Kosa kanda	Hemikuna	Tuber	Food

Plants	*Parts*	*Name*	*Kuvi name*	*Plant parts*	*Use*
76.	87.	Kudupa	Kudupa	Fruit	Food
77.	88.	Kukudi sago	Kotikuca	Leaf	Food
78.	89.	Kukur langudi	Nehudileguni	Fruit	Food
79.	90.	Kuramal	Konjareoni	Root	Medicine
80.	91.	Lajokuli	Gorisaweli	Root	Medicine
81.	92.	Lohomada	Lohomada	Root	Medicine
82.	93.	Mankodo kendu	Potaduri	Tree	Fuelwood
83.	94.	Mirchinga	Kduan	Leaf	Curry leaf
84.	95.	Modoi	Modoi	Plant	Fuelwood
85.	96.	Monjorsulia	?	Plant	Fuelwood
86.	97.	Mota ghas	Motojada	Grass	Fodder
87.	98.	Munch kondh	Muknipuyu	Flower	Medicine
88.	99.	Muniga	Munga muniga	Fruit	Food
89.	100.	Musa kani	?	Leaf	Fodder
90.	101.	Muturimala	Prashkamada	Plant	Medicine
91.	102.	Nilgiri	Niligiri	Leaf	Medicine
	103.			Seed	Medicine
	104.			Bark	Medicine
	105.			Wood	Fuelwood
	106.			Stem	Housing
92.	107.	Orka	Paji dohi	Tree	Fuelwood
93.	108.	Pakodimala	Pakodimala	Creeper	Fuelwood
94.	109.	Panasa	Panha	Fruit	Food
95.	110.	Pardamal	Padadmada	Plant	Rope
96.	111.	Patal garudo	Pusihiru	Root	Medicine
97.	112.	Patro goja	Akugoja	Leaf	Medicine
98.	113.	Pengo	Pengomada	Seed	Oil
99.	114.	Phul jhadu	Hepori	Plant	Broom
100.	115.	Pijuli	Lakajambu	Fruit	Food
101.	116.	Pit konda	Hirukuna	Tuber	Food
102.	117.	Pita konda	Napa	Tuber	Food
103.	118.	Pitmari	Kambelikalapara	Plant	Tooth brush
104.	119.	Podai	Dohi	Fruit	Food
105.	120.	Poyan	Poyan	Seed	Medicine

Plants	Parts	Name	Kuvi name	Plant parts	Use
106.	121.	Puti karla	Jadakarla	Fruit	Food
107.	122.	Ranbeli	Katri	Bark	Medicine
108.	123.	Sata bari	Penuhepori	Root	Medicine
109.	124.	Siadi	Paeri	Leaf	NTFP
	125.			Seed	Food
110.	126.	Simili	Leko	Branch	Worship
111.	127.	Sindi	Sindi	Fruit	Food
112.	128.	Sindur	Hinduri	Fruit	NTFP
113.	129.	Sitakuti	Kuti Pujeri	Root	Medicine
114.	130.	Solap	Marakadu marnu	Sap	Fermented drink
115.	131.	Sonari	Bundeni	Tree	Fuelwood
116.	132.	Sorenda	Huwa	Root	Food
117.	133.	Tangiachina	Kdalichinna	Bark	Medicine
118.	134.	Targa	Ro odi	Root	Food
119.	135.	Tendka kanda	Drogikuna	Root	Medicine
120.	136.	Tentuli	Pula	Fruit	NTFP
	137.		Pula	Fruit	Food
121.	138.	Thakurani phulo	Malti	Flower	Worship
122.	139.	Thalkudi	Duakucha	Leaf	Medicine
123.	140.	Tirimundi	Mardimarnu	Plant	Fuelwood
124.	141.	Tutkuli	Danduli	Fruit	Food

Note: (?) denotes that we could not ascertain name in English or scientific name.

Appendix 4: Names of 148 Wild Plants found in Kondhpungar

Sl. No.	Name	Scientific name
1.	Ambo	*Mangifera indica*
2.	Amla	*Emblica officianalis*
3.	Apama rongo	
4.	Arjun	*Terminalia arjuna*
5.	Bagonaki	
6.	Bahada	*Terminalia belerica*
7.	Baidonko	
8.	Bajramali	
9.	Ban jhudongo	
10.	Bandona	
11.	Bansaru	
12.	Baria kanda	
13.	Baunso	*Dendrocalamus strictus*
14.	Belo	*Aegle marmelos*
15.	Bernga	
16.	Berongo	
17.	Bhaira bhuta	
18.	Bhalu dar	
19.	Bhalu jam	
20.	Bhui amla	*Phyllantuhs sp.*

Sl. No.	*Name*	*Scientific name*
21.	Bichhauati	
22.	Bila	
23.	Bileikanta	
24.	Bisalya korani	
25.	Bod tetenka	
26.	Bodkokodi	
27.	Bojra mukhi	
28.	Bon kodli	*Musa sp.*
29.	Bondari	*Chlorodendron sp.*
30.	Bongordal	
31.	Borkoli	*Ziziphus jujuba*
32.	Boruwa	
33.	Chandan	*Santalum album*
34.	Chikni	
35.	Chilli	
36.	Chitini	
37.	Dabpiri	
38.	Dakli	*Dioscorea pentaphylla*
39.	Damon	*Grewia tilifolia*
40.	Deruharja	
41.	Dhopki	
42.	Didendimada	*Cyclea peltata*
43.	Dondera	
44.	Dubo ghas	*Cynodon dactyolon*
45.	Dudmal	
46.	Dumri	
47.	Gadel	
48.	Gali morka	
49.	Gandi buta	
50.	Gandiri	
51.	Gatamarka	
52.	Gereda	

Sl. No.	Name	Scientific name
53.	Ghantia	
54.	Girli	
55.	Gna mandia	
56.	Golaki	
57.	Gombari	*Gmelina arborea*
58.	Gorimenda	
59.	Gorudo	
60.	Gugunimal	
61.	Gurdi sago	
62.	Harchand	
63.	Hatimal	
64.	Hirsi	*Lucaena leucocephala*
65.	Horida	*Terminalia chebula*
66.	Jamkoli	*Syzigium cumini*
67.	Kadruhirsa	
68.	Kalikochandi	
69.	Karakuta	
70.	Karanjo	*Pongamia pinnata*
71.	Karseli	*Girardinia diversifolia?*
72.	Kathi badni	
73.	Keu kanda	*Costus speciosus*
74.	Khajuri niali	
75.	Kichi	
76.	Klia konda	
77.	Koi hirsa	
78.	Koicho	
79.	Koineteri	
80.	Kcnior	
81.	Kontakoli	*Ziziphus rugosa*
82.	Kosa kanda	
83.	Kudei	

Sl. No.	*Name*	*Scientific name*
84.	Kudupa	
85.	Kukudi sago	
86.	Kukur langudi	
87.	Kuramal	
88.	Lajokuli	*Combretum ovalifolium*
89.	Lohomada	*Cryptolepis buchnani*
90.	Mankodo kendu	*Diospyros montana*
91.	Marda mala	*Terminalia sp.*
92.	Mendha mal	
93.	Mirchinga	
94.	Modoi	*Lannea coramadelica*
95.	Monjorsulia	
96.	Mota ghas	
97.	Munch kondh	*Pterospermum acerifolium*
98.	Muniga	
99.	Musa kani	
100.	Muturimala	
101.	Nilgiri	*Eucalyptus globulus*
102.	Orka	
103.	Pakodimala	
104.	Pakua	
105.	Paldua	
106.	Palsi	
107.	Panasa	*Artocarpus integrifolia*
108.	Pardamal	
109.	Patal garudo	*Rauwolfia serpentina*
110.	Patpadandi	
111.	Patro goja	
112.	Pengo	*Celastrus paniculata*
113.	Phul jhadu	
114.	Pijuli	*Psidium guajava*
115.	Pit konda	

Sl.No.	*Name*	*Scientific name*
116.	Pita konda	
117.	Pitmari	
118.	Podai	
119.	Pordi	
120.	Poroi buta	
121.	Poyan	
122.	Puruda	
123.	Puti karla	
124.	Ranbeli	
125.	Randuli	
126.	Reteli	
127.	Rupni	
128.	Sakra	
129.	Sata bari	*Asparagus racemosus*
130.	Siadi	*Bauhinia sp.*
131.	Sika ghas	
132.	Simili	*Bombax malabaricum*
133.	Sindi	
134.	Sindur	*Mallotus philipinensis*
135.	Sitakuti	
136.	Solap	*Caryota urens*
137.	Sonari	
138.	Sorenda	
139.	Sua kanda	
140.	Tangiachina	
141.	Targa	
142.	Tendka kanda	
143.	Tentuli	*Tamarindus indica*
144.	Thakurani phulo	
145.	Thalkudi	
146.	Tirimundi	
147.	Tutkuli	*Morus alba*
148.	Usku buta	

Note: Blank under column scientific name denotes that we could not ascertain scientific name.

Appendix 5: Wild Animals Sighted in Kondhpungar

Sl.. No.	*Oriya*	*Kuvi*	*English*	*Taxa*	*Scientific name*
1.	Azogor	Adagunsa	Python	Reptile	*Python morulus*
2.	Badudi	Padudi	Bat	Mammal	
3.	Bago	Bonko	Heron	Bird	*Ardeola grayii*
4.	Ban kukuda	Jada koyu	Wild cook	Bird	*Gallus gallus?*
5.	Bani	Rambi		Bird	
6.	Baria	Barhan	Wild boar	Mammal	*Sus scrofa*
7.	Baya chodhai	Khorlia		Bird	
8.	Bengo	Pana	Frog	Amphibian	
9.	Bhalu	Oodi	Bear	Mammal	*Melursus ursinus*
10.	Bharubi anduo	Gogodrogi	Lizard	Reptile	*Varanus versicolor*
11.	Bilua	Kolia	Jackal	Mammal	*Canis aureus*
12.	Biradi	Bilei	Cat	Mammal	*Felis sp.*
13.	Bono bilei	Joda bilei	Wild cat	Mammal	*Felis chaus*
14.	Budiani	Kochoti	Spider	Insect	
15.	Chabara	Sima	Ant	Insect	
16.	Chanchana	Dega	Eagle	Bird	
17.	Chia chadei	Chia pota		Bird	*Prinia sp*
18.	Chita bagh	Tiring rengna	Leopard	Mammal	*Panthera pardus*
19.	Chiti	Siti rachu		Reptile	
20.	Chopeda	Miriyanka	Red ant	Insect	

Sl. No.	*Oriya*	*Kuvi*	*English*	*Taxa*	*Scientific Name*
21.	Dhadka	Dhadka rachu	Snake	Reptile	
22.	Dhamana	Damna	Snake	Reptile	
23.	Dhandia	Dhandia	Snake	Reptile	
24.	Dhulia nago	Palu naga	Snake	Reptile	
25.	Dingiri	Dingiri pota		Bird	
26.	Dud boda	Palu jhupuni	Snake	Reptile	
27.	Endua	Drogi	Garden lizard	Reptile	*Calotes sp?*
28.	Gharchatia	Jeta pota		Bird	
29.	Girna	Kidska droki	Lizard	Reptile	
30.	Gobor poko	Gurunda		Insect	
31.	Gunduchi	Tilli	Squirrel	Mammal	*Funambulus pennanti*
32.	Gunduri	Tumba	Quail	Bird	*Perdicula asiatica*
33.	Gunji	Gunji		Bird	
34.	Holdi basanta	Gumeti		Bird	*Oriolus xanthornus*
35.	Jhiji pok	Saura koyu		Insect	
36.	Jhitipiti	Kadha kota		Insect	
37.	Jia	Kechsua	Earthworm	Invertebrate	
38.	Kala nag	Kala rachu	Snake	Reptile	
39.	Kalet	Kala rachu	Snake	Reptile	
40.	Kankada bicha	Kacha kupi	Scorpion	Arachnids	
41.	Kapto	Kuguri	Dove	Bird	*Streptopelia chinensis*
42.	Kia chadei	Chia pota		Bird	
43.	Koili	Kdisker	Earthworm	Invertebrate	
44.	Kojolpati	Dingiri	Cuckoo	Bird	*Eudynamys scolopacea*
45.	Kua	Kawa	Crow	Bird	*Corvus spendens*
46.	Kutra	Kurhu	More	Mammal	*Muntiacus muntjak*
47.	Macho ranka	Banda gnoti	Kingfisher	Bird	*Halcyon smyrnensis*

Sl. No.	*Oriya*	*Kuvi*	*English*	*Taxa*	*Scientific Name*
48.	Mankodo	Muhun	Monkey	Mammal	*Macaca radiate*
49.	Mayur	Melu	Peacock	Bird	*Pavo cristatus*
50.	Musa	Orli	Rat	Mammal	*Rattus sp.*
51.	Nago	Naga rachu	Cobra	Reptile	
52.	Odho	Maraa	Mongoose	Mammal	*Herpestes edwardsi*
53.	Parja pati	Pubuli	Butterfly	Insect	
54.	Pecha	Korkoti	Owl	Bird	*Athene brama*
55.	Pimpudi	Sima	Ant	Insect	
56.	Potra sap	Gocha rachu	Leaf snake	Reptile	
57.	Sailm	Sahin	Porcupine	Mammal	*Hystrix indica*
58.	Saru nago	Una nag	Cobra	Reptile	*Naja naja*
59.	Singoti	Aci koyu		Bird	
60.	Sua chadei	Keta kura	Parrot	Bird	*Psitticula krameri*
61.	Sungo poko	Dendi		Insect	
62.	Tekor	Tekeri	Bee	Insect	
63.	Thekua	Kadha	Rabbit	Mammal	*Lepus nigricollis nigricollis*
64.	Valia kukuro	Kosa nuhudi	Wild dog	Mammal	*Cuon alpinus?*

Note: Blank under column scientific name denotes that we could not ascertain scientific name.

Index

A

Adult Marriage, 41
Agricultural Implements, 330
Agro-Forestry, 338
Aquatic
    And Terrestrial Plant Species, 201
    Animals, 194, 195
    Biodiversity, 108
    Fauna, 112, 193
    Wild Animals Species, 209, 253
Arjun—Kosa Kanda, 243
Atal Banda, 199

B

Badas, (Homestead Gardens), 42, 43, 48, 132, 302, 331
    Biodiversity in-, 113
    Homestead Gardens, 112
    Ownership Patterns of-, 302
    Pomegranate Cultivation, 114
    Variation, 112
Bali
Banda Tank, 163, 311
    Parab, 62
Bameni Bunda Tank, 196
Banana—Tapioca, 302
Begonia, 151
Bhitorkota Village of Koraput District, 36
Bihu Puja, 60, 61, 325
Biodiversity, 102, 257-270
    And its Management, 33
    Bearing Areas (BBA), 109
    Description of-, 111
    Identification, 109
    Bearing Areas, 336
    In Kondhpungar Village, 109-207
    Conservation, 328
    Domesticated and Wild, 33
    Management Committee, (BMC), 101
Biological
    Diversity Act, 2002, 101-103
    Researches, 103
Biomass, 302
Bodu Hontal, 37
Boko Sakadi Stream, 203, 206, 207
Bride Price, 41

C

Cashew
    Nut Plantation, 174, 309, 339
    Plantation, 74
    Trees, 174
Chaitra Parab, 62, 325, 335
Check Dam, 72, 74, 199, 203, 312, 340
Chilly Cultivation, 156
Chronic Diseases, 154
    Indigestion—White Discharge, 154
Clans, 36
    Hontal and Khora, 36
Community Forestry, 69
Conservation of Land Races, 101

Convention of Biological Diversity, 1992, 103
Cropping Seasons, 301
Cross-Cousin Marriage, 41
Cultivated
Crops, 258
Plants, 113, 219, 266

D

Dadiya Khora, 132
Dam for Irrigation, 72
Dasu Khora, 37
Degraded Forest Land, 173
Degraded/Restoration of Forest, 301
Dental Care, 282
Diki Banda, 196
Dishari (Head Priest), 61
District Koraput Orissa, 33, 34, 36
Diversity of Usages, 267
Divorce, 41
Dobona, 151
Domesticated
And Wild Biodiversity, 301
Animals, 114, 312, 313
Biodiversity, 103
Plants Species, 157
Alami—Ranja Benisi, 157
Trees, 114
Vegetables, 114
Wild Animals, 114
Dravidian Family of Languages, 40
Drinking Water Facilities, 73

E

Eastern Ghats Region, 34
Edible Wild Mushrooms, 292
Education, 41
Guarantee Scheme, 41
Education—Fisheries, 69
Energy Security, 58, 283, 291
Entrepreneurship Training, 70
Eucalyptus, 177, 339
And Silver Oak Plantations, 210
Plantation, 309

F

Family Forestry, 74
Farm Land, 303, 312, 338
Fauna And Flora, 301
Fence Spaces, 112
Sidi—Lantana, 112
Fencing, 150
Financial Security, 284
Fodder
Security, 58, 283
Yielding Plants, 284
Food,
Health and Energy Security, 289
Security, 58, 278, 290
Forest
And Wage Labour, 48
Protection and Management Committee (FPMC), 336, 340
Protection Committees, 73
Protection Mechanism, 70
Protection, 65
Fruit Bearing Trees, 303
Fuel Wood Yielding Plants, 291

G

Genealogies, 36
Ghantia—Apama rongo, 243
Ginger Cultivation, 59
Godsi Fish, 193
Grain
And Seed Banks, 66
Bank, 325, 335
Gram
Fund, 65
Panchayat of Semiliguda Block, 34
Vikas, 67
Green Manures, 156
Yielding Plants, 156
Gudia Kha (Farm Land), 44

H

Harvesting of Wood, 65

Head and Hair Care, 282
Health Care Security, 58, 280, 289, 291
Herbal
  Garden, 150, 153, 154, 302, 338
  Oil, 60
Hill Ranges, 166, 310
  Balipata, 166
  Balipata—Kudi Kanda, 310
  Bariamba, 166
  Kotrakari, 166
Home Gardens, 331
Homestead Gardens, 337
Hunting Implements, 108

I

Income
  From Agriculture, 48
  From Forest Products, 52, 55, 58
  From Wage Labour, 55, 56
  Generating Activities, 48, 59
  By SHG in Kondhpungar, 59
Indian Institute of Forest Management, Bhopal, 107, 324, 336, 338, 339
Inheritance and Succession, 41
Integrated
  Farming, 74
  Rural Development of Weaker Sections in India (IRDWSI), 33, 34, 36, 48, 64, 69, 70, 101, 105, 107-109, 150, 156, 170, 324, 325, 328, 336, 339
    Activities, 70
  Tribal Development Agency, 197, 198
Inter-Wild Animal Species, 252
Irrigation
  Facilities, 303
  Tanks, 156

J

Jakhar (Sacred Grove), 60, 61
Jakhar Devbta, 61
Jakhari Debta, 325
Jelinga, 302
Jhota, 302
Jute Bag Making, 59

K

Keu Kanda, 330
Khondhs Ethnographic Accounts, 40
Kalahandi District Odisha, 40
  Phulbami, 40
  Vishakhapatnam, Vizianagaram, Srikakulum (AP), 40
  Raigarh District of Madhya Pradesh, 40
Khonds, Hill People, 40
Koi Hirsa—Puruda, 243
Kond, 40
Kondh Lanugage, 40
Kondha, 40
Kondhpungar Village (KPR), 33-100
  Biodiversity of-, 33
  Geographical Area, 34
  Of Odisha, 40
  Speak Kuvi, 41
Kondhs, 35, 37, 40, 41
Kondhs-Sub-Tribes, (KST), 39
  Desi, 39
Kondh, 39
Kutia, 39
Kuvi, 39
  Penga, 39
  Songria, 39
  Kotra am Jhola Stream, 203
Kudi Kanda Jhoti Stream, 203, 204
Kuvi
  Kond, 40, 41
    Exogamous Clans, 40
  Language, 40
  Mother Tongue of Kondhpungar, 109

L

Lac Bangles, 41
Land
  And Water Bodies, 211

And Waterscape Elements, 225, 241-244, 251, 257, 302
Holding Patterns, 42
Landscape Biodiversity, 112

M

Main Festivals, (Annual Calendar), 60, 63
Major Festivals, 41
Dussehra—Mandia Rani, 41
Malti Khora, 36, 37
Management
Of Biodiversity, 108
Bearing Areas, 337
Plan, 33
Medicinal
Herbs, 243
Plants, 154
Microorganism, 101
Mixed Cropping Practices, 73
Monogamy, 41
Most Sighted Animals, 252
Bungo—Salim, 252
Mulberry Plantation, 84, 85
Mushrooms, 225
Musical Instruments, 108

N

Names of
Plant Species, 170, 171
Plants in Oriya and English, 222
Nanguli Kandha, 40
National Rural Employment Guarantee Act, (NREGA), 338
Natural
Dense Forests, 184
Resources, 34
Nayak, Headman, 64
Nilgundi, 151
Non-Governmental Organization (NGOs), 33, 64
Non-Timber Forest Product (NTFP), 311, 336

O

Oriya
And Kuvi Names of Vegetables, 139
Language, 109
Ownership Patterns of Badas, 302

P

Paddy Varieties, 305, 306
Papaya Plantation in Home Gardens, 139
Pasiamba Hills, 171
People of Kondhpungar and IRDWSI, 69
People's Organization, 64, 73, 181, 311, 335, 336
Details, 65
Photo Documentation, 108
Pitmara Tree Used as Toothbrush, 282
Planning for Planting Low Cost Houses, 70
Plant
Products, 288, 290
Species, 209, 210, 220, 266
Plantation Program, 170
Planting of Trees, 65
Plants
Consumed as Food, 278
Planted in Protected Forests, (PPP), 181
Ambo—Guginimal, 182
Ambo—Tentuli, 181
Used as Medicines, 280
Polygamy, 41
Praska—Melaka, 41
Preferred Domesticated Animals, 149
Fowl—Cat, 149
Protected Forest, 181, 182, 310, 339
Area, 245
Balipala, 181
Kudi Kanda, 181

Puligunta, 181
Wild Animals in-, 186
Protection
And Management of Plantation, 170
Measures, 310
Mechanism, 302
Pukali Village, 36
Pungar, Revenue Village, 34

R

Ragi Varieties, 306
Sonadei—Majhia Bodeb, 306
Rainfed Land, 45, 163, 305, 338
Crops And Trees Grown in-, 164
Wild Plant Species, 164
Rakhyas Puja, 60
Rituals, 60
Rituals-Birth to Death, 41
Road Side Plantation, 189, 313
Ambo—Usku Buta, 189
Ruhini Khora, 114, 132
Rules and Regulations, (Formulated by the Committee), 65
Rural Health in Environmental Program, (RHEP), 67, 68
Committee, 67

S

Sacred Grove (Jakari), 186, 311, 340
Select 8 Plants Species, 187
Wild Plants Species in-, 186, 187
Sadar Debta, 326
Sapura Hontal, 150
Scheduled Tribes, 40
Secured Sustainable Livelihood (SSL), 48, 74
Select Cultivated Crops, 221
Self-Help Groups (SHGs), 46, 48, 64, 66, 67, 73, 284, 285, 309, 311, 336, 339, 340
Formation and Training, 70
Semiliguda
Block, 33
Town, 34, 69
Sericulture, 73
Shifting Cultivation, 73, 74, 165, 166, 174, 308, 339
Area, 302
Crops Grown, 166
Alsian—Oil Seeds, 166
Fields, 166
In Bariamba Hills, 184
Jona (Maize)—Joda, 308
Kupa Khal, 168
Land, 45, 46
Wild Plants in-, 168
Silver Oak Plantation, 179, 310, 339
Sitha Kandha, 40
Social
Bondage, 58, 285
Forestry Plantation, 70, 170, 174, 309
Forestry Program, 73
Forestry Wild Animals in-, 172
Soil
And Water Conservation, 170, 171
Fertility, 301
Somba Hontal, 37
Sonidei Mahila Mandal, 66
Sources of Livelihood, 46, 328
Species And Ecosystem, 102
Species—Ada Gundicha—Sungo Poko, 245
Spiritual
Security, 285
Seeds, 58
Spiritually Empowered Seeds, 60, 325
State Biodiversity Board (SBB), 101
Strategies for-, 66
Agricultural Development, 66
Child Education, 66
Forest Protection, 66

Health and Sanitation, 66
Suan Varieties, 308
Subsistence Crops, 303
Ragi—Cucumber, 303
Sustainable
Livelihood (SL), 33, 102
Use of Biodiversity, 102

T

Tamarind Processing, 74
Tank Bund, 194, 195
Tanks, 340
Timber, 58, 284
Total
Annual Income, 56
Land Holdings, 46
Traditional
Council, 41
Head—Majhi, Nayak, and Jani, 41
Governance Structure, 329
Governance system Structure, 64
Governance System, 64
Healers, 154
Ragi Varieties, 307
Varieties of Crops, 302
Training of Self-Help Groups, 70
Trees
Ambo—Tentuli, 138
Grown in Badas, 132
Species in Badas, 137
Tribes of Orissa, 39

U

UN Development Program, 150, 194
Women in Agriculture Program, 326

V

Varieties of Fishes, 193
Vakur—Rohu, Mirkali, 193, 197
Vegetable Crops, 303
Tomato—Yam, 303
Vegetables Cultivation, 59
Vermi Composting, 74
Village and Regional Deities, 41

W

Wage Labour, 55, 56, 57
Water
Storage Tanks for Irrigation, 74
Tanks, 156
Waterscape Biodiversity, 110
Wet Lands, 45, 74, 162, 304, 338
Crops Grown in—, 162
Wild Animals, 162, 163
Wild Animal, 58, 155, 176, 312-314, 317, 323, 328
And their Usages, 292
In Badas, 141, 145
Baba Bilei—Tekor, 145
In Farm Lands, 159
Ada Gundiche—Sungo Poko, 159
In Herbal Gardens, 155
Species, 165, 209, 245, 251, 252, 302
Bonbilei—Thakua, 165
Wild
Biodiversity, 109, 110
Fauna and Flora, 327
Mango, 324, 225
Mushroom, 244
Plant Diversity, 312
Plant Species, 154, 174, 178, 225, 241, 242, 276
Plants, 174
Plants and Usages, 267
Plants in Badas, 141
Plants Provides, 330
Food Security—Social Bondage, 330
Plants Species, 182
Women Self-help Groups, 48
Women's Organization, 73